Yours truly
N. Lyon

LIFE

OF

GENERAL NATHANIEL LYON.

BY

ASHBEL WOODWARD, M. D.

HARTFORD:
PUBLISHED BY CASE, LOCKWOOD & CO.,
1862.

TO

Captain Miner Knowlton, U. S. A.

THIS WORK

IS SINCERELY INSCRIBED,

AS A TRIBUTE

TO PATRIOTISM, INTEGRITY, AND DISTINGUISHED ATTAINMENTS,

AND

A MEMORIAL

OF OLD AND UNINTERRUPTED FRIENDSHIP.

PREFACE.

SHORTLY after the fall of General Lyon at the battle of Wilson's Creek, the writer was requested by the relatives of the deceased to prepare an account of his life and services for publication. For this purpose journals, letters, and numerous other papers written by Gen. Lyon, were placed at his disposal.

The present work, however imperfectly executed, has been in all respects a labor of love. Gen. Lyon's purity of character, his honesty of purpose, and unfaltering devotion to the honor and welfare of his country, will render his name and memory ever precious to his countrymen. No one can become familiar with the life of Nathaniel Lyon, without feeling that in his death the Nation lost one of her noblest as well as bravest sons.

Lyon began his military career by taking an active part in the most vigorous and toilsome campaign of the Seminole war. We have described the difficulties and incidents of the struggle in general terms, as best showing what he and his comrades were called to endure while hunting the savages through those pathless wilds.

Gen. Lyon left a large amount of manuscripts relating to the Mexican war, upon which we have drawn freely. Numerous extracts have been made from his notes, and much use has been made of his descriptions of the battles, the people, and the country.

The writer would here tender his thanks to the brothers and sisters of Gen. Lyon, for the promptitude with which they have furnished valuable papers and information.

Thanks are especially due to Capt. Miner Knowlton, U. S. A., and Danford Knowlton, Esq., cousins of Gen. Lyon, for their zealous and active co-operation.

Dr. G. G. Lyon, now surgeon of the "Lyon Regiment," 3d Missouri Volunteers, kindly forwarded to the writer numerous printed documents relating to the campaign in Missouri during the summer of 1861.

Many others also have furnished valuable assistance, to whom the writer would here express his obligations.

FRANKLIN, CONN., March 26th, 1862.

TABLE OF CONTENTS.

CHAPTER I.

CHAPTER II.

CHAPTER V.

CHAPTER VI.

CHAPTER VII.

CHAPTER VIII.

CHAPTER IX.

CHAPTER XIII.

APPENDIX.

CHAPTER I.

On the 14th of August, 1861, millions of hearts were saddened as the telegraph announced far and wide, that Gen. Nathaniel Lyon had fallen in battle, four days before, while cheering on the soldiers of the Union. The nation was looking hopefully to him as one of her stoutest defenders against the power and purposes of rebellious citizens. From the inception of hostilities, extraordinary success had uniformly attended his bold, vigorous, and decisive measures. With a bare handful of men, he guarded the public property at the St. Louis Arsenal, though menanced for weeks by strong bands of open and secret enemies. During the period the spirit of secession held high carnival in the city, vaunting itself with the utmost insolence and self-assurance. But Lyon was not idle. While others slept, his wakeful brain was devising means to save the state from the calamities into which the machinations of the disaffected were rapidly hurrying her. Around the little nucleus at the arsenal, a strong force of volunteers was almost noiselessly gathered. When at length the time for action came, the brilliant exploit at "Camp Jackson" fell with crushing weight upon the astonished plotters of treason. Thenceforth the city of St. Louis was freed from the outward exhibitions of disloyalty. Enemies of the country no longer flauntingly displayed the insignia of rebellion in conspicuous places, but slunk away into secret corners whence the mutterings of discontent might not be heard.

The area of active operations now widened. Throughout Missouri, thousands were in sympathy with the disruptionists of the South. Gov. Jackson secretly aided their schemes, endeavoring at the same time, by craft and fair professions, to circumvent the Federal officers, and thus commit the state, without molestation, to the fortunes of rebellion. Men of assured and uncompromising loyalty seemed to be in a hopeless minority. Surrounded by defection and perfidy, the defenders of the Union labored under the gravest embarrassment that can befall the conductors of a military campaign.

In the face of innumerable difficulties, Gen. Lyon succeeded in organizing a small but effective army.

With this he moved rapidly into the heart of the State, crushing the growth of treason and raising the symbol of American Liberty over the homes of faithful citizens. On the twelfth of June, Gov. Jackson published an insurrectionary proclamation from the capital of Missouri. Ere the close of the week, he was driven forth a fugitive. Without allowing the enemy time to rally, Gen. Lyon swept over the country with wind-like velocity, making long marches in the hottest months of the year, and destroying the germs of rebellion at points widely distant, almost simultaneously. No where were the adversaries of the Union suffered to organize or gather strength. In places of supposed security, they were taken by surprise. So swift were the movements of this little army, and so uniform its success, that the country begun to regard it as ubiquitous and invincible.

Hurrying forward with incredible rapidity, he reached Springfield, a town of importance in the south-western corner of the state, one hundred and twenty miles beyond the terminus of the nearest railroad. In this vicinity the routed secessionists of Missouri were joined by large reinforcements from Arkansas, Louisiana and Texas. Emboldened by great superiority in numbers, and anxious to wipe out the stain of numerous defeats, they prepared for battle. Gen. Lyon's small force seemed entirely inadequate to defend the city against such overwhelming hordes. But he could not endure the apparent humiliation of turning back from an enemy, nor could he abandon the unionists dependent on him for protection, to be insulted, pillaged and murdered by lawless gangs of banditti. He determined to hold the position until relieved by reinforcements. Earnest and reiterated appeals for aid were sent to St. Louis and to Washington. The country listened with intense anxiety to the voice from that remote but important quarter. Yet the calls brought no response in men. Gen. Lyon, left to cope with a force quadrupling his own, was induced, by the desperate posture of affairs, to plan a night attack upon the enemy. The little army, full of faith in its leader, went boldly and even gaily forth to the banquet of Death. On the bloody battle-field of Wilson's Creek, that leader fell, while achieving the most brilliant but costly triumph ever won by American arms.

The interval since the death of Gen. Lyon is so brief that the sorrow of the nation is still fresh, nor has the magnitude of the loss diminished in popular estimation. Devoted patriotism, far-reaching foresight, judicious boldness, and uniform success, superadded to many noble qualities of heart, made him the idol of his soldiers and a favorite with the people.

Our victories in Missouri, aside from local importance, were of great moral value in relieving the depression consequent on the unfortunate issue of our efforts elsewhere. In many places a succession of reverses seemed to attend the Union cause. A valuable part of our navy had been sacrificed to the foul hand of treason in the navy yard at Norfolk. Privateers were preying upon our commerce with impunity. The magnificent army of the Potomac, which millions confidently expected was about to trample the last breath of vitality from the prostrate trunk of rebellion, had fled in disorder without accomplishing forty miles of the "road to Richmond." But in Missouri, as in Western Virginia, brilliant successes crowned our arms in every encounter, raising the despondent spirits of the loyal, and despite our disasters, causing the heart of the nation to beat high with hope.

It is fitting that we remember the heroes who have placed their lives as voluntary offerings upon the altar of our country. While we raise the granite shaft to mark the burial spot consecrated by their dust, we should also strive to embalm the precious words and glorious deeds which have made their names immortal.

Gen. Lyon* sprang from a worthy, brave and patriotic ancestry. Ephraim Lyon, his grandfather, served for twelve months in the war of Independence, and afterwards became a successful farmer and lawyer in the town of Ashford, Conn. The community reposed great confidence in his legal acumen, which was called into requisition in many knotty cases. From the anecdotes handed down traditionally among the people of the neighborhood, we select the following to illustrate the shrewdness and sagacity of "Lawyer Lyon," as he was generally called.

A bag of grain had been stolen from a mill, and the owner, thinking that the sack might be returned in the course of time with another grist, directed the miller to keep a look-out for the thief. After a while a quantity of grain was brought to the mill, inclosed in a sack exactly corresponding in appearance with the one purloined several months before. The unfortunate possessor was speedily confronted by an officer, armed with a warrant for his arrest. Being a quiet, inoffensive, and excessively timid old man, he was so overcome and confused by the charge that his perturbation was accepted as a sure evidence of guilt. Public opinion, at least, was convinced. As the day of trial drew near, the accused

* *Vide* Appendix A.

became deeply dejected, so that he was in no situation to lend personal aid to the refutation of the charge. But a friend, who believed him innocent notwithstanding the unpromising aspect of the case, sent for "Lawyer Lyon," confident that in his hands the mystery would be unraveled, if such a thing were possible.

In those days, all the coarse cloth in use was of domestic manufacture. The accuser produced several sacks in court and testified that they were all woven in the same web with the one which had been stolen. When the bag in dispute was compared with the others, it was found to correspond exactly in width, color, and general aspect. Lyon now requested the court to adjourn for an hour, and although the judge objected on the ground that the guilt of the party was indubitable, the favor was reluctantly conceded. He immediately employed three experienced women to rip the sacks in pieces and count the threads in the warp of each. Those produced in evidence were found to contain the same number, but the one alleged to have been stolen contained thirteen threads more. The women accordingly testified that this could not have been woven in the same web with the others, and the innocence of the man became so clear that the jury returned a verdict of "Not Guilty" without leaving their seats.

Amasa Lyon, father of the General, was also a substantial farmer of Ashford. In early manhood he took great interest in politics, entering zealously into the ardent contest which resulted in the elevation of Thomas Jefferson to the presidency. While that memorable election was pending, and both parties were making prodigious efforts to muster every voter, a young man wished to be admitted to the privileges of an elector in Ashford, but was fearful of rejection by the board of judges on the ground that he did not have the property qualification required by the laws of Connecticut at the time. The town was then controlled by a large Federal majority, which materially damaged the prospects of the candidate, as he was suspected of sympathizing with the opposite side. In this dilemma, Lyon advised him to go without reserve to the leader of the Federalists and solicit his aid, agreeing to coöperate himself by strenuously opposing his admittance. The ruse was entirely successful. Objections from a partisan so well acquainted with the political proclivities of the different members of the community, seemed to be sufficient proof of the orthodoxy of the applicant. His claims were acknowledged without further questioning, and he had the satisfaction of voting for Mr. Jefferson.

In the maternal line, the family of Gen. Lyon acted a conspicuous and highly honorable part in the Revolutionary War.

Col. Thomas Knowlton, a brilliant officer and devoted patriot, was uncle to Gen. Lyon's mother. While yet a boy he became distinguished for sagacity and valor in the struggles of the colonies against the French. Years later, when the battle-notes of Lexington aroused the American people to resist the aggressions of the British crown, he led a company of stalwart men from Ashford to Boston. This was the first organized body of troops that went from a sister colony to the aid of Massachusetts.

At the battle of Bunker's Hill, Col. Knowlton commanded the left wing of the provincial army, stationed on a strip of hard upland between the eminence and Mystic river—the key to the American works on the peninsula. He extemporized a novel kind of breastwork, by planting two rows of rail-fence parallel to each other, and packing the interval with freshly mown hay. Older officers ridiculed the contrivance as worthless; but subsequent developments showed the superior judgment of the projector. Gen. Howe twice led the flower of the British army against this position, and twice the British were repulsed with terrible slaughter. An impassable slough in front protected the breastwork from the approach of cannon, and to musketry it proved wholly impervious. The casualties behind the fence, from both attacks, were trifling. No further demonstration was made against the American left. In the third attempt to dislodge the Provincials, Gen. Clinton threw his force upon the front and right. Failure of ammunition now compelled the main body on the hill to retire. As it passed the position of Col. Knowlton, he joined in with the four companies under his command, covering the retreat. Fortunately, they had brought into action a much larger number of cartridges than the other troops, and still had a supply left. Retiring with deliberation, and obstinately contesting every foot of ground, they prevented the enemy from overwhelming the other divisions, now almost defenceless, on the retreat.

Col. Knowlton was killed in battle at Harlem Heights, Sept. 16th, 1776. Gen. Washington, in the general orders of the next day, says: "The gallant and brave Col. Knowlton, who would have been *an honor to any country*, having fallen yesterday while gloriously fighting, Capt. Brown is to take command of the party lately led by Col. Knowlton."

Thus fell, in the prime of early manhood, one of the most brilliant and promising of our Revolutionary officers.

Lieut. Daniel Knowlton, an elder brother of Col. Thomas, was the maternal grandfather of Gen. Lyon. Coolness, resolution, and bravery, were characteristic of the family. Lieut. Daniel served through the French and Indian wars, participating in many desperate enterprises. He was often sent in command of small parties, to scout in the forests,—a kind of service for which his courage and sagacity eminently fitted him. No duty connected with the long and bloody wars on the frontier, required more tact or skill than that of reconnoitering among the native wilds of the red man, where the slightest indiscretion might betray the venturesome explorer to the cruelty of the pitiless savage. From long practice some of the provincials acquired a marvelous degree of skill in tracking and eluding the enemy, almost rivaling the Indian himself in interpreting the signs which to the ordinary eye are either invisible or meaningless.

On one of these perilous scouting expeditions, Lieut. Knowlton captured three men belonging to a gang of blood-thirsty desperadoes, whose numerous atrocities had made them extremely odious as well as terrible. With a small force on hostile territory, it was unsafe either to retain or dismiss the prisoners. Duly impressed with the claims of self-preservation, the captors decided that the crimes of the miscreants entitled them to halters, and that the pressing exigences of the case justified no delay. Halters were accordingly made from the bark of hickory saplings, from which the culprits were soon dangling between heaven and earth.

Gen. Putnam, the companion of Lieut. Knowlton during several of the French and Indian campaigns, said of him, "Such is his courage and want of fear, I could order him into the mouth of a loaded cannon."

When Col. Thomas Knowlton led the Ashford company to the American Head Quarters near Boston, shortly after the battle of Lexington, Gen. Putnam asked the Colonel where his brother Daniel was. Being informed that he had gone in another direction, the General remarked, "I am very sorry you did not bring him with you; he alone is worth half a company."

Daniel Knowlton served from the opening to the close of the Revolutionary war. For about two years he was a prisoner in the hands of the enemy, being confined a part of the time on a ship in New York harbor. On one occasion, when pacing back and forth, with eyes bent on the deck, a British

J. J. SAWYER.

Birth-Place of Gen. Lyon.

officer impertinently and pompously inquired why he did not hold up his head, like a man and a soldier. Knowlton quietly replied, "In passing through fields of grain, I have noticed that the valuable heads bow toward the earth; only the empty and worthless stand erect." The questioner thereupon showed a proper appreciation of the answer, by bowing his own head and leaving the prisoner to pursue his meditations undisturbed.

Gen. Nathaniel Lyon was born in Ashford,* Conn., July 14th, 1818, the seventh child and fourth son of Amasa and Kezia (Knowlton) Lyon.

Several teachers who instructed Lyon in boyhood still survive, retaining vivid and pleasant recollections of the amiable and generous qualities, which even then made him a common favorite. They all testify that the early proficiency of *the youth* gave abundant promise of success and honor for *the man.* When very young he formed the plan of going to West Point, and from that time worked with a steady and unfaltering purpose. An intellect naturally vigorous, was improved by industrious application. Often while companions of equal years were at play or asleep, he was bending diligently over books, lay-

*Ashford was divided in the year 1847, the eastern portion, embracing the homestead of the Lyon family, being constituted a new town and called Eastford.

ing the foundations for the varied and extensive information of later life. The study of mathematics was prosecuted with zeal, partly from intense fondness for the pursuit, and partly from the conviction that the science of quantity afforded the most efficient means for disciplining the mind. In numerous ways, the qualities which suddenly blazed forth thirty years later, attracting the admiration and love of millions, were foreshadowed then. Stories of the Revolution—of the privations and sufferings patiently endured to achieve national independence—listened to over and over again from a mother's lips, produced a profound impression of the value of our blood-bought liberties. Lessons of patriotism were daily instilled at the parental fire-side. In such an atmosphere and under such training, love of country grew with his growth and strengthened with his strength, till it became a far stronger passion than love of life.

Says a teacher, Lyon showed his predilections when a school-boy, by always selecting for declamation, pieces of a patriotic and martial character, which he delivered with a degree of heartiness and effect that attracted universal commendation.

His affections as a son and brother were warm, rich, and active, and lent a bright coloring to the whole of his after life.

Lyon *graduated* at the old brown school-house in his native district a few months before entering West Point, and during a part of the interim that ensued, attended the academy at Brooklyn, Conn.

Always kind and considerate, he spurned whatever bore the appearance of imposition or cruelty, and was strongly averse to quarreling, or participating in rude demonstrations of any kind.

Retiring and studious habits do not form the surest passport to the favor of boisterous youth. School boys are sometimes disposed "to make game" of companions of gentler manners, and occasionally commit grave blunders in the estimate of consequences. When Lyon first went to the Brooklyn Academy, several old hands at the sport undertook to play upon him the usual practical jokes supposed to be essential to initiate new comers into the mysteries of such institutions. For a day or two the annoyance was borne without apparent notice. Inferring tameness as well as greenness, from the quietude of the "victim," they ventured beyond the point where forbearance ceases to be a virtue. As the first intimation of a change of tactics, two or three found themselves suddenly prostrate, with a pair of fists vigorously at work in uncomfortable and dangerous proximity to their persons. It is needless to remark that further efforts to expedite the cure of "verdancy" were dispensed with. Invariably courteous toward others, his nature rigorously demanded like treatment in return.

A story has been extensively circulated in the newspapers, with a view to illustrate Gen. Lyon's opposition to the dueling code, that he once tamely submitted to the indignity of a blow on the face, given for the purpose of either calling forth a challenge or convicting him of cowardice. It is manifestly impossible to disprove a statement, coming like this one in utter nakedness, with no allusion to time, place, or concomitants. But if a fact, it is nevertheless inconsistent with the general character of the man. It is true that he regarded the *duel* as a relic of barbarism, not less absurd than wicked. A determination, however, never to meet a brother mortal in single combat, by no means necessitates the patient endurance of a grievous insult. Nor does the training of the soldier inculcate a sentimental regard for the precept requiring us to turn the other cheek to him who smites us on the one. Gen. Lyon possessed great physical strength and agility, which no scruples of conscience could have deterred him from using at the cost of the individual who might venture upon such temerity.

Gen. Holt, then member of Congress from the

third district of Conn., procured for young Lyon the appointment as cadet at West Point, to fill a vacancy opportunely occurring in the western part of the state, there being none at the time in his native district.

He entered the Military Academy in the autumn of 1837, distrustful of his own abilities, but with full determination to employ his opportunities and talents to the utmost. From the first, devoted love of country was a controlling motive. Whether a student in academic halls, or a soldier on the field of battle, it was a cardinal purpose to be ever faithful to her interests.

We give a few extracts, taken almost at random, from his correspondence during this period.

Writing in August, 1838, he is induced by circumstances of a personal nature, to speak of the advantages enjoyed by the members of a family who spend the days of childhood and youth beneath the parental roof.

"At home one finds an experienced and affectionate father to guide; a loving mother to cheer; and brothers and sisters to share in the bounteous gifts of nature. Where it does not conflict too much with interest, a young man should delight to remain with his parents, conferring and receiving happiness from the interchange of kindly offices."

In March, 1839, he expatiates on the mysteries of the *Calculus*, having, like many others, found that branch of study to be a grievous stumbling block in the way of knowledge.

"The inventors of the Differential and Integral Calculus, have claimed that this branch of so called science, belongs to the department of mathematics; and laboring under that delusion have introduced it into the course of academical instruction for the torture of students. Such classification is obviously incorrect, because the principles of mathematics fall within the scope of the reasoning faculty. The Calculus, on the contrary, lies without the boundaries of reason, having originated in the vagaries of some remarkable but erratic genius, who must have discovered its outlines in the flights of a wild and disordered imagination. Enthusiasts afterwards collected the fragmentary materials thus furnished, and by an ingenious arrangement, sought to dignify them with a place in the temple of science. The imposture being too complicated for easy exposure, has at length succeeded in establishing its claims, much to the sorrow of the unfortunate students thereby made to suffer."

In previous letters to a sister, Lyon had complained of lack of interest and capacity in the art of *Drawing*. For the purpose of stimulating him to make more earnest exertions to overcome the difficulties in the way of success, she urges him to bring home specimens of his handicraft. In reply, he humorously expresses the fear that compliance will be impossible; because the finest specimens are retained as models by the teacher, while the visitors at the June examination are allowed to take away such as particularly please them. His collection being exposed to diminution from both causes, to an unusual degree on account of its rare merits, will in all probability be entirely carried away, to adorn portfolios and drawing rooms in different parts of the country.

While a cadet, Lyon engaged as heartily in the various diversions of student life, as in application to books, or the acquirement of skill in martial exercises. The holiday gayeties of senior year are thus described:

"On Christmas' and New Year's eve we had a fancy ball, in which cadets alone took part, appearing in such characters as suited their taste, and acting their respective parts with success. Our company was graced by the presence of the prince, the military chieftain, the sage, the scholar, the peasant, the quaker, the waiter, the beggar, and even the fool. Every thing passed off in excellent order, each making such remarks, and acting in such manner as the assumed character required. Had Old Pluto himself been present, it is doubtful whether he would have diverted the company more than did the distinguished personage who represented him."

Lyon graduated at West Point June 30th, 1841, ranking *eleventh* in a class which numbered fifty-two at the time of graduation, and over one hundred at the time of entry in 1837.

He was promoted Second Lieutenant, in the Second Regiment of Infantry, July 1st, 1841.

CHAPTER II.

In the month of November, 1841, Lieutenant Lyon left home to join the Second Regiment of Infantry, which was then engaged in the prosecution of the war against the Seminole Indians in Florida.

That contest is one of the most remarkable in the annals of modern history. A small tribe of barbarians, comprising but a few hundred adult males, successfully resisted, for a series of years, the strength of a large, civilized, and powerful nation. Many whites on the border had labored assiduously to provoke hostilities, believing that the conquest of the natives would be an easy task. But the days of revenge came quickly; and bloody and sorrowful days were they for the inhabitants of Florida. During the war scores of homes were laid desolate, and hundreds of victims butchered by the remorseless savage.

In carrying out the projects of the United States Government, for the removal of the savages, and the punishment of outrages, exceeding in brutality any that in the previous settlement of the country had stained the line of demarkation between the white and Indian races, our soldiers suffered hardships of unparalleled severity. Nor did the nature of the warfare afford the relief and excitement incident to fighting in the open field. Few opportunities were presented for the brilliant exploits or strategy which in a single day may make the reputation of a soldier. Toilsome marches over burning sands, and through dense swamps, in an atmosphere charged with subtle poisons, and in regions infested with countless hosts of annoying insects and venomous reptiles, were often wholly fruitless. Plans skillfully laid and vigorously executed were baffled by the cunning of the foe. The heroism of our troops was the heroism of unconquerable perseverance in contending long against obstacles of the most dispiriting character.

In such a warfare, the history of the individuals employed, whether in the capacity of officers or privates, is best given by describing the general features and difficulties of the contest. All underwent in the main the same experience, and to an unusual degree the story of one is the story of all.

The war itself was so unpopular at the north, on account of its apparant injustice, that few only were interested either in its success or incidents. But the brave men who fought on the soil of Florida—many never to return—deserve remembrance and gratitude from the whole American people. Our army was in no way responsible for the wrongs practiced upon the Indian by lawless renegades of the frontier, nor for the unconscientious measures adopted by the Government. Having gone thither in obedience to orders, it toiled long and faithfully to perform the labors imposed upon it, in the face of the most vexatious and trying embarrassments.

To understand the posture of affairs in Florida at the close of the year 1841, it will be necessary to revert briefly to the causes of hostilities and the previous progress of our arms.

The Seminole Indians were a branch of the Creeks. They originally lived on the banks of the Chattahoochee river, a few miles north and west of the present city of Columbus, Georgia. In the year 1750, Secoffee, a Creek chief, endowed, to a remarkable degree, with the characteristic bravery, cunning, and vindictiveness of the race, having had a continued and bitter quarrel with other head en of the tribe separated from the parent stock. With a large body of followers, he moved several hundred miles in a south-easterly direction, settling in the region called Alachua, the central and by far the most fertile part of the peninsula of Florida. In the year 1808, another band of Creeks broke away from their old homes, and descending the Chattahoochee, took possession of the country in the vicinity of Tallahassee. The Mickasukie tribe, the native owners of the soil, too weak to repel the hardy warriors from the north, gradually coalesced with the new comers.

On the 17th of July, 1821, Spain ceded the Floridas to the United States. A year later the total number of Indians occupying the territory was found to be three thousand nine hundred and ninety-nine, of whom one thousand five hundred and ninety-four were men. The belt of country lying between the Appalachicola and the St. Johns, as far south as Lake Monroe, was dotted with Indian villages and fields.

The Seminoles were a brave, resolute, and in many respects, honorable and chivalric people. Chiefs of marked ability had governed the tribes and clans ever since their establishment in Florida, and seem often to have striven earnestly to promote the good of the people. The English and Spanish while in possession of the peninsula, also treated the natives with consideration, thereby heightening their pride, and rendering them impatient of opposition or restraint. Haughty, patriotic, vindictive, and, withal, cultivated in no mean degree, they were far from being inoffensive creatures to be spurned with safety.

On the cession of Florida to the United States, the fertile fields of Alachua proved a strong temptation to lure emigrants from the exhausted plantations of the Carolinas and Georgia. Many families of wealth and refinement removed from the older districts in the hope of repairing decayed fortunes by the wealth of a virgin soil. Another class of people, of a widely different character, were there already. Desperadoes of various nations and complexions, fugitives, often from the hands of justice, had fled for shelter to the seclusion of these primeval forests. Men, exiled by crime from the communion of civilized society, now strike hands with the new comers, to dispossess the Indian of the land. Citizens and vagabonds, ignoring alike the claims of the native owner, clamor for the expulsion of the Seminoles from the most fruitful part of the territory. The Government is induced to interfere by the importunity of the petitioners. Commissioners are appointed to negotiate a treaty, with a view to open the central and northern portion of the peninsula exclusively to the whites, by the removal of the Indians. These, at first, meet the proposition of the Commissioners with mingled feelings of astonishment and indignation. Possessed of broad hunting grounds, that for three generations have securely descended from father to son, they keenly feel the hardship of subscribing to the conditions of a compulsory sale, and surrendering precious homes forever to the cupidity of strangers. But beset more and more by the innumerable difficulties contrived for their coercion by the ingenuity of a superior race, and influenced by the specious arguments of men professing to be friends, the majority of the nation at length reluctantly consent to meet the Commissioners at a suitable time and place. Fort Moultrie, a few miles south of St. Augustine, is selected for the interview. On the 18th of September, 1823, a portion of the headmen, in the absence of the most influential chiefs, signed a disadvantageous treaty in the vain hope of escaping further molestation. The coils of destiny are tightening around the doomed race, and no kindly hand is interposed to rescue it from the fatal embrace.

In consideration of certain moneys, gifts, annuities, and guaranties from the United States Government, the chiefs relinquished a large area of territory, and agreed that the tribes should be confined thereafter within metes and boundaries that forever excluded them from the northern and middle regions of the peninsula. They also stipulated to be active and vigilant in preventing absconding slaves or fugitives from justice from passing through or harboring in the district assigned them; and further, to use all necessary exertions to apprehend and deliver the same to the Government agent, who was to compensate them for the trouble and expense.

The Indians at once began to suffer the greatest injustice from the avarice and villainy of the whites. If a native was found straying among the old habitations and cherished haunts of the tribe, he was often treated with brutal indignity to prevent a repetition of the visit. Bad men, pandering to the unhappy thirst of the race, recklessly sold them spirituous drinks—the most prolific source of demoralization and crime. Often, while lying in a state of senseless intoxication, the victim was robbed of rifle, money, or whatever valuables the dealer could steal. On returning to consciousness and making search for the missing articles, he would be told that the gun or the horse had been sold for a drink. Notwithstanding the palpable falsity of the tale, recovery or redress were equally hopeless.

Such wrongs, being of daily occurrence, naturally prompted the Indian to retaliate. As the only feasible method of obtaining compensation for the stolen property, he learned to appropriate the cattle and utensils of the whites.

Another fruitful source of fraud arose from the clause of the treaty requiring the rendition of absconding negroes. Many slaves belonged to the tribes both by birth and purchase. But the owner was often despoiled of his property by force and perjury, because unfurnished with a written title and without rights in a court of law.

Numerous thefts and villainies were perpetrated on the border by miscreants from the States, all of which the heated animosity of citizens attributed to the hand of the red man. He bore the blame and the odium of all the crimes that cast their dark shadows over that dark land. Even where suspicion was rightly directed, not an offense was extenuated on the ground of grievous provocation, or the drunken insanity occasioned by the cupidity of the whites. Hundreds far inferior to the Seminole, in the noble and generous impulses that should belong to humanity, were appealing to the Government for protection against the outrages of the Indians! Those who had been instrumental in taking from the owners the fairest fields of Florida, were ready to provoke a war of extermination for the double purpose of grasping the residue of the territory, and holding the whole secure from intrusion. Mutual distrust and mutual injuries rapidly ripened into bitter hate.

For a long time the chiefs seemed disposed to act with integrity and honor. In some of their "talks" with the different United States agents, they dwelt eloquently upon the magnitude of their wrongs, as contrasted with the rectitude of their own actions. Humiliated at the deplorable condition of the people, they strove long to roll back the waves of intemperance and violence, and to preserve friendly relations with the whites. Now these efforts became more ineffective every day. Hostilities were imminent.

At this juncture, after much persuasion and delay, the chiefs were induced to meet James Gadsden, Esq., United States Commissioner, at Payne's Landing, where a second treaty was signed on the 9th of May, 1832. This instrument provided for the removal of the Seminoles, within three years from the date of its ratification, to the country of the Creeks, west of the Mississippi river. A delegation from the tribes was to be sent, under conduct of the United States agent, to ascertain from inspection the eligibility of the country proposed, and whether the Creeks were favorable to a reunion with the Seminoles as one people.

The chiefs selected for the mission appear to have been indifferently pleased with the appearance of the lands, and averse to the relinquishment of Florida. Yet, for reasons not well understood, they signed an additional Treaty at Fort Gibson, Arkansas, March 28th, 1833, in which they declare themselves well satisfied with the location provided by the Commissioners, and agree that their nation shall commence the removal to their new home as soon as the Government will make satisfactory arrangements for their emigration. Assuming that the Seminole delegates had authority to bind the rest of the tribe, the United States Senate ratified the treaty in April, 1834, thus making it a part of the "supreme law of the land." When the people at home heard of the proceedings at Fort Gibson, they were deeply incensed at the presumption of their agents. All insisted that the first duty of the delegation was to disclose to them the results of its examination, so that national action might be taken on a measure so vital to their future happiness, before removal to a remote and unknown region was irrevocably decided on. Under the leadership of the famous Oceola, the Indians rallied with fierce enthusiasm to oppose the fulfilment of the treaty. At the same time the United States Government was decided and peremptory in the adoption of measures for enforcing obedience to the terms of the agreement. A clash was inevitable.

The purposes of the anti-emigrating party were soon sealed with blood. Oceola, though of humble origin, by the magic of eloquence inspired the people to a wonderful degree with purposes of cruelty and daring. Hatred, long nurtured in secret, suddenly burst out in fiend-like and revengeful deeds. Charley E. Mathlar, a chief of importance and one of the delegation sent to the Mississippi, was murdered for favoring emigration. No one openly uttered a word of disapproval. On the 28th of December, 1835, Gen. Thompson, United States Indian agent for the Seminole tribes, and Lieut. Smith, while taking an afternoon stroll from Fort King, were literally riddled with balls. At the same time the savages, rushing from ambush, burned a sutler's shop within a mile of the fort, after shooting and scalping the inmates. On the 28th of the same month occurred the massacre of Maj. Dade's command, consisting of over a hundred men, two privates alone escaping, severely wounded, to tell the tale. The day ensuing, Gen. Clinch, with a strong detachment of regulars, was attacked, on the banks of the Withlacoochie, by

Oceola, at the head of two hundred and fifty-men. After a spirited fight of over an hour the enemy fled to the cover of a neighboring hammock.

Fiery passions, that had been gathering power for years, now found vent in acts of appalling atrocity. Florida became the scene of wide-spread desolation and ruin. In vain did the helplessness of women and children appeal to the vindictive heart of the savage. Almost the first intimation of war appeared in the flames of burning houses, and the death-shrieks of unpitied victims. Plantation homes—the favorite abodes of plenty, peace and tranquility—disappeared in volumes of smoke, leaving only blackened ruins and charred bones to mark the pathway of the destroyer. Fields, once cultivated, were left to waste. Citizens, stript of the means of support, fled for shelter to distant villages. Suffering and sorrow, in manifold forms, overspread the land.

Our government greatly underestimated the number, resources, and determination of the enemy. Having made a grievious mistake—to use no harsher term—in commencing the war, it erred again in the manner of its prosecution. Small detachments of the regular army were sent successively into the territory, under the delusive impression that the conquest of the natives would prove an easy task. A moderate volunteer force was also called into service. But year after year the war dragged on. Many of the savages perished in battle; many, despairing of success, voluntarily surrendered, and were moved to the region beyond the Mississippi. As they diminished in number they ceased to give battle in the open field, and confined themselves to operations of a cunning, stealthy, and disconnected character. Thorough knowledge of the country, and the difficulty of penetrating it, compensated for deficiency in men and munitions.

On entering the forests of southern Florida the United States troops plunged into a *terra incognita.* The face of the country is made up of pine barrens, hammocks, and swamps. The piney regions, though free from underbrush, are covered with a dense growth of low palmetto and saw-grass, whose sharp, serrated edges tear the clothing and lacerate the flesh of pedestrians. After heavy rains the surface is often inundated for miles on account of its uniform level, subjecting an army to extreme discomfort in marches even to the most accessible points. But the difficulties of traversing the pine barrens, though sufficient often to indicate the course of troops by numerous blood-stains, are mere trifles when compared with the obstructions to be encountered in the hammocks. Here the rich soil produces a dense and tangled mass of vegetation almost impervious to the foot of man. So thick is the growth that it is the work of hours to cut a path of a few feet in length, and after all the labor, the sides of the path form a perfect barrier against the vision as well as the step. Frequently intersecting the country in long spurs, the hammocks intercept the progress of civilized troops, and at the same time afford secure retreats whence the savage might sally forth, under cover of night, to perpetrate deeds of cowardly malice. Deep, sluggish creeks are numerous, and often bordered by impenetrable morasses. Many parts of Florida are also covered with cypress swamps which had to be crossed repeatedly in pursuit of the fugitives. The cypress has a broad funnel-like base, the main roots appearing to join the tree at a distance from the base, and throwing out their sharp edges on every side, so that little space is left on the surface between contiguous trees. The scanty intervals are thickly studded with "cypress knees," rising in sharp cones, and varying in height from two or three inches to as many feet. Festoons of moss hang in heavy arches overhead, obscuring the sun and almost shutting out the light of day. The swamps are generally covered with water, which conceals beneath its cloak countless inequalities, roots, holes, and spurs. Upon the surface floats a green scum, and when disturbed fills the air with noxious effluvia. The incautious soldier is liable, at any moment, to be submerged and buried in treading the precarious pathway. Through such places he is obliged to carry provisions and equipage upon his person.

It will be seen what rare facilities a country like this afforded for the concealment of the enemy. Relinquishing systematic operations, after the first year or two of the war, the Indians broke up into small gangs, and dispersed everywhere to act independently, as opportunity might offer, or impulse suggest. Often venturing into the immediate neighborhood of the whites, and stealthily watching for victims, they only left their coverts when sure of success. In this way the unguarded traveler mysteriously disappeared. Small detachments were overpowered and murdered. Sometimes an isolated family was aroused by the midnight yells of the savage, and allowed a momentary interval of awful consciousness between the sweet repose of life and the long sleep of death. By the time the flames—a sure attendant of the Indian's blow—raised the signal of alarm and brought avengers to the scene of woe, the assassins were far away. Broad sheets of water covered their footprints as they hurried to distant jungles. Our brave men, taking the fresh trail, would plunge into the trackless forests and hunt for days without discovering a trace of the invisible and intangible perpetrators of the crime.

People in the States, and even the Government, were at a loss to account for the ill-success of our arms. Congress became impatient; the country clamorous. One officer superseded another between the beginning of the year 1836 and the close of 1841, till Generals Clinch, Scott, Call, Jesup, Taylor, Armistead, and Col. Worth had successively commanded the army of Florida. Every new appointment brought a fresh flourish of trumpets, and a fresh revival of hope. Nothing more forcibly illustrates the impracticable nature of the war, than the ineffectual efforts of such an array of skillful officers to bring it to a speedier end.

In the autumn of 1841, extrinsic causes were potently at work to thwart the successful issue of military measures. A large class of civilians, in the capacity of clerks, traders, mechanics, and general laborers, were drawing the means of support from the presence of the army. The discontinuance of the contest would throw many out of lucrative employments. Patriotism, under the bias of gain, was too often sacrificed at the shrine of cupidity. Yielding to the suggestions of avarice, the vile sought occasions to give secret aid to the enemy.

But the most pestiferous mischief-makers were the negro interpreters and guides. Passing by night between the camp and hiding places of the Indians, they sold them ammunition and repeated the stories of designing whites.

Besides, a number of degraded Spaniards living on the gulf coast, industriously furnished the Seminoles with the means of continuing the war, and fomented the hatred of the savage by the circulation of shameless falsehoods. If any, disheartened by intolerable hardships, were about to surrender, these mongrels terrified them from the purpose by spreading the belief that the Federal officers were to show no further quarter.

From this hasty review can be seen what difficulties our commanding generals had to contend against—the impracticable nature of the country—the covert opposition of a large body of civilians who were feeding at the public crib—the treachery of friendly negroes—and the interference of foreign out-casts.

Early in January, 1842, the Company of Lieut. Lyon started with others to hunt the Indian chief Halleck-Tustenuggee. This eminent warrior towered high above the rest of the natives now left in Florida, both in physical and mental endowments. He was six feet two inches tall, well formed, erect, and sinewy. An intellect of deep native subtilty had been developed by the experience and vicissitudes of a remarkably eventful life. Savage, haughty, and self-reliant, he spurned the counsels of the whites, and asked not the advice of friends, trusting in lofty isolation to the resources of his own matchless craft. The dense hammocks and pathless swamps, whence he sallied forth as opportunity for mischief invited, were perfectly familiar to him. A band of thirty-five desperate followers, blindly devoted to his fortunes, and reposing implicit faith in the wisdom and certainty of his plans, were always ready without a question to do his bidding. The scene of their operations extended over a wide area, from Lake Monroe to the neighborhood of St. Augustine, and thence westward to the Oclawaha and Withlacoochee rivers.

For seven months practiced guides followed, unweariedly, the trails of this vindictive and dangerous gang. Large detachments, aided by the sagacity of friendly Indians, overcame almost insurmountable obstacles in exploring the country far and near. Efforts, conducted on a scale so extensive and thorough, at length baffled the ingenuity of the chief. It was ascertained that the band was hidden on the southern shores of Dunn's lake, and in the swamps bordering on Hawk creek. The spot was selected on account of its great seclusion and the ease of emerging upon the highways from St. Augustine to the south and west. The warriors were armed with rifles carefully selected from the spoils of murdered citizens and soldiers. Ammunition, and many necessaries of life, were procured in the same way.

With such skill and success were the forays of Halleck-Tustenuggee conducted, that the name became a word of terror throughout the settlements. Strong guards were stationed at Piccolata, on the St. John's, and even at St. Augustine, while a patrol kept continually crossing by the main road from the river to the Atlantic coast, in order to guard habitations from surprise, and save solitary travelers from an arm that never spared. Notwithstanding these precautions, the sudden and stealthy blow of the savage often fell upon remote points and left the evidences of his brutal work.

Elaborate preparations for capture were made on the discovery of the dread hiding-place. A body of sixty men, belonging to the second infantry, moved up and down the St. Johns to cut off retreat westward. Three companies of the same regiment, under command of Maj. Plympton, plunged into the forests with a determination to persevere in the hunt until every Indian was slain or captured. The party explored hammocks and swamps, penetrating where it was difficult for a snake to crawl. No hardships or perils deterred them from scrutinizing every place that could conceal an enemy. Abandoned huts and fields were occasionally found and destroyed. At length, having followed a solitary trail for several days, the troops overtook the savages posted in a hammock. They here made a stand, contrary to their usual custom, in order to cover the flight of the women and children who were a short distance in advance. For a few minutes the enemy fought resolutely, filling the air with terrific yells and whoops. After a volley the pursuers moved rapidly forward, when the Indians fled, leaving two wounded on the field. Of the regiment one was killed and two wounded.

From the scene of encounter a strong detachment followed the trail of the fugitives, as rapidly as was practicable to the river St. Johns, which was struck at the southern extremity of lake George. But the enemy had already crossed, the rafts and canoe employed for the purpose being in sight on the opposite bank. When the news reached Pilatka, Capt. Casey, also of the second infantry, and one hundred men proceeded in boats to the place of crossing, with orders to disembark there and follow the trail to its termination. Lieut. Wessels, second infantry, ascended the Ocklawaha with fifty men to intercept the enemy should he attempt to cross. While this force were lying in ambush at different fords on the stream, in hourly expectation of the Indians, Halleck-Tustenuggee, suspecting the trap, passed over the river ten miles south of any known ford into a swamp hitherto considered, by experienced guides, altogether impassable. Capt. Casey's party, who resumed the trail on the west banks of the St. John's, met with success very disproportionate to the severity of their labors. The course of the Indians brought them to a swamp several miles wide, and covered with water varying from one to three feet in depth. Through this officers and men laboriously struggled, carrying necessary provisions and equipage on their backs. After great hardship, upon reaching the opposite side, not a trace of the enemy was visible. Scattering in small parties to meet at some distant rendezvous, and putting the torch to the dry vegetation and other combustibles strewn upon the earth, they left no vestige to betray to the guides and trailers the direction of their flight. Thus the band of Halleck-Tustenuggee eluded the various detachments of pursuers that for two months exerted every energy to effect his capture. Though unsuccessful in the immediate object of the enterprise, the efforts of our patient and heroic troops were by no means fruitless. A powerful chief, who reveled in carnage and conflagration, was effectually dislodged from a stronghold extremely dangerous on account of its proximity to the settlements.

Associated with Halleck-Tustenuggee was an Indian named Powis Fixico or Short Grass. He had a small number of followers, and was noted for activity and cruelty. Some time before he acted as leader in the massacre of women and children at the village of Mandarine. Tommy, a son of Powis Fixico, having ventured to Fort Melon with petitions for food, was detained by Maj. Plympton. This officer, suspecting that Indians were secreted in a certain swamp, proceeded thither with a strong force, taking Tommy also. The boy disclosed the fact that Short Grass lived here, and gave assurances to the commanding officer that he could induce him to surrender if permitted to go on the mission. Accordingly, when advantageous positions had been taken about the swamp, Tommy was sent to his father with assurances of kind treatment if he yielded voluntarily, but of certain death if captured in arms. The youth soon came back accompanied by his father and four warriors.

As subsequently appeared, Lieut. Lyon, at one time, came very near taking Powis Fixico prisoner. A detachment of the second infantry was marching through a dense body of undergrowth where an Indian had been seen as they approached. On emerging into the comparatively open tract on the opposite side, not a trace of him could be found. Others thought that the Indian had hurried forward, but Lyon was convinced that he lay concealed somewhere in the thicket. So firm was this belief that he personally commenced a diligent search, only relinquishing it when compelled to move on by the command of the superior officer. After the Indian entered the camp he recognized Lyon as the "red faced" man who came close to his hiding place, and said that he had given up all hope of escape, when Lyon was called off just in time to save him.

On the 19th of April, Col. Worth surrounded Halleck-Tustenuggee, in the vicinity of Ahapopka lake, completely routing his forces. When the chief saw the superior number of the whites, and the folly of further resistance, he directed the warriors to disperse in squads of four or five. The women and children left the night before in the utmost haste, not even waiting to take needles, thread, or ornaments. The camp, bountifully supplied with meat, deer skins, implements of husbandry, and articles of clothing, fell into the hands of the assailants. Its position was remote and difficult of access. None but the trailer, whose sagacity in detecting signs of human presence had been sharpened by long experience in tracking the wily Indian, could have found the way to its deep seclusion.

Tracks leading from the hammock were followed by the guides till lost in the surrounding waters. One Indian alone was taken in the pursuit, and he proved to be the father-in-law of Halleck. This old man plead earnestly for the privilege of carrying a "talk" to his son, and that the troops might desist from further pursuit. As the warriors were dispersed, and the intervention of the prisoner seemed the only way of reaching them, he was sent to invite Tustenuggee to come to Col. Worth's quarters for a "talk." The crafty chief, stript of his possessions by the recent loss of the camp, concluded to accept the offer of a parley, hoping by false proffers of friendship to replenish his stores and escape. But the duplicity which had successfully deceived so often, in this instance failed.

On the 29th of April, to the great astonishment

of all, Halleck rode into the American camp accompanied by two wives and two children. Gracefully saluting the sentinels, and minutely observing every object, he proceeded with perfect self-assurance to the tent of the commander. Col. Worth, through an interpreter, held a long conversation with him. Before night the chief left, but returned the next morning with five warriors. For the next day or two the demands of the Indians for food and drink were exorbitant; yet unless immediately complied with, the language of the chief assumed a tone of overbearing insolence. The annoyance was endured with good grace, since the day of retribution was surely and rapidly approaching.

Col. Worth invited Halleck to visit Fort King. The chief readily complied, expecting to purchase a supply of ammunition at that point, while the rest of the tribe procured provisions at the camp. Thus furnished afresh with the sinews of war, they hoped to renew the contest with better success, in the meantime greatly amusing themselves, as was subsequently learned, in laughing at the credulity of the whites.

Lieut. Col. Garland, upon whom the command devolved during the absence of Col. Worth, was directed to devise measures for the capture of the entire band, and to send the prisoners securely bound to Tampa Bay. Several experienced officers visited the Indian encampment under pretext of showing attention to the aged, but for the real purpose of reconnoitering the position and ascertaining the feasibility of taking them forcibly by surprise. The location of the ground and the watchfulness of the savages were found to render the use of violence impracticable. Stratagem was accordingly resorted to. Our officers spent the first two days in zealous efforts to overcome the suspicions of the Indians—a work much easier from the absence of the chief. On the third a sumptuous feast was prepared in honor of Halleck-Tustenuggee, who was then to return, as they thought, and grace the banquet with his presence. Every member of the band assembled at an early hour, and all were highly delighted with the grand preparations for their entertainment. At an appointed time the guests were kindly informed that they were prisoners, and of the necessities which dictated the step. An express at once conveyed the news to Fort King. Col. Worth and Tustenuggee were seated together in front of the enclosure as the messenger galloped up on a foaming horse, and delivered the important package. When the haughty chief was informed that the band, which for many years had faithfully followed his fortunes through inconceivable hardships and tribulations, were now lying powerless in the grasp of a hated enemy, and that his own swift foot and strong arm were no longer free; his excitement and anguish were fearful to witness. The proud frame quivered; the eye blazed with impotent rage; and the breast heaved as if the heart within were about to break in agony.

To this intrepid chief the land of nativity was more precious than life. A Mickasukie by birth, he represented the ancient owners of the soil. Generous souls, remembering that the savage fought to repel the invader from a country which his ancestry had possessed for immemorial ages, will palliate the blood-thirstiness that was stimulated by wrong, and the treachery that weakness compelled him to employ in contending against the strong. The fact that this ill-starred warrior, after months of unwearied pursuit, was captured at length, not in the field, but by imposition and craft, heightens our estimate of his kingly qualities.

Henceforth the portion of Florida, north of lake Monroe, was freed from the permanent presence of the Indians. At the fatal banquet the net of the white man imprisoned in its folds the scourge and terror of the settlements. Not a man, woman, or child escaped to return to the former haunts of the tribe.

The company of Lieut. Lyon took an important part in the severe but patient efforts which resulted in the capture of Halleck-Tustenuggee. Lyon was ever at the post of duty; faithful, active and vigilant. Many returned home with constitutions hopelessly broken by the insalubrity of the climate and the hardships of the service, but he enjoyed vigorous health uninterruptedly.

Novelty of scenery and warfare rendered his first campaign a pleasant one despite its fatigues.

On the 27th of May, 1842, the second regiment of Infantry left Palatka, Florida, for Savannah, Georgia, to proceed thence to the Niagara frontier. During the period of its service in the Seminole war, since June, 1837, *one hundred and thirty-three* officers and privates had perished from disease and the hand of the Indian.

The long, expensive, and bloody contest with the natives of Florida, drew toward a close. The band of Halleck-Tustenuggee embarked on the 14th of July for New-Orleans; and thence proceeded to Arkansas.

Shortly after a general cessation of hostilities was agreed upon, a few Indians being allowed to plant their fields *temporarily* in the southern part of the peninsula.

CHAPTER III.

Lieut. Lyon was now stationed, for several years, at Sackets Harbor, on lake Ontario. Here was spent the easiest portion of his life. From the time he was ordered from this post to the close of his eventful career, he was called to endure, in the service of his country, an unusual share of deprivations and discomforts.

He enjoyed keenly his residence at Sackets Harbor, dividing the time between military duties, study, and the pleasures of general society. Of the place and people he writes,—"We are well situated here with many respectable and intelligent citizens around us. Of our officers and their families I can not speak in too high terms of praise. We have balls occasionally in town and parties in garrison." The gayeties of social life were tempered by regular attendance at the house of worship. "I always go to church twice on Sunday and sometimes at evening in the week."

During this interval many leisure hours were devoted to the study of law, and the legal knowledge and acumen thus acquired were often very serviceable to friends. We have before us an unpretending communication, written from Sackets Harbor to a relative, then engaged in the settlement of a complicated estate, which skillfully sifts the mass of evidence connected with the matter in dispute, and renders perfectly clear the naked point of obligation. Moral Philosophy, and the broad field of metaphysics claimed a share of his attention. He also took delight, as occasion offered, in investigating the phenomena of Mesmerism and kindred subjects which now and then obtrude themselves persistently upon the attention of the public. With a disposition to examine impartially different systems of belief, he was disinclined to accept of any unless established upon a basis of unanswerable reasoning. In political matters he was always deeply interested, and though in the heat of partizan excitement sometimes prone to extremes, no one ever doubted the honesty of his opinions.

To the annexation of Texas, a question then uppermost in the public mind, Lyon was earnestly opposed, believing the project to be impolitic and unjust, and often expressing the conviction that such an outrage upon the rights of a sister republic could not fail to bring its own bitter punishment in the end. He writes in May, 1844,—"*John Tyler* has virtually declared war with Mexico by sending troops to the Texan Frontier, and a naval force into the Gulf to oppose the operations of that State, in anticipation that our Senate will confirm his treaty. Such high-handed proceedings are not likely to affect us at present, but, in the final issue, will inevitably involve the United States in hostilities. It is to be hoped that the originator of these rash movements may receive a suitable reward for his madness and folly."

When the Mexican war opened, bringing the necessity of a large increase in the rank and file of the army for the purpose of filling up old regiments and creating new, Lieut. Lyon found constant occupation in recruiting and drilling fresh troops. At the outbreak of hostilities the second regiment of infantry was still stationed at different posts on the northern frontier and the Atlantic coast. During the summer of 1846, the companies were withdrawn from various garrisons and sent to Mexico. It was late in the season before they reached the Rio Grande. Already the victories of Palo Alto and Resaca de la Palma had been won. The strongly defended town of Monterey, after a bloody defense, had succumbed to the valor of our troops. But the gravest hardships were yet to be suffered, and the severest battles yet to be fought. In the coming drama the second infantry acted a conspicuous and honorable part. In numerous engagements it won the nation's praise for the intrepidity of its bearing, and the glory of its success.

On the 8th of December, 1846, Lieut. Lyon left Camargo, a town at the confluence of the San Juan and Rio Grande rivers, for the scene of active operations. The march was performed by companies E, G, H, and I, of the second infantry, under Capt. Waite, accompanied by the second regiment of Tennessee Volunteers, under Col. Haskell.

As it may interest some, brief notes are given of their progress, and of the appearance of the country as it presented itself to the eyes of Lyon.

Leaving Camargo early in the afternoon, on the 8th of December, the detachment proceeded eight miles and encamped for the night in a thick chaparral. The next day they marched fifteen miles through an undulating country. Various points on the road commanded landscape views of extraordinary beauty. The eye rests upon gracefully blended vallies and hills, that stretch away for many a league till lost to sight in the dusky distance. The region was evidently depopulated, as hardly a habitation was to be seen.

On the night of the 11th, the company encamped on the banks of a cool stream which afforded the first palatable water the men obtained after leaving New York.

The following day the command reached China, on the San Juan, sixty miles from Camargo—"a small town having a good church and other public buildings—all of stone. The houses are narrow and one story high."

They reached Mont Morelas the 17th, having passed for the last twenty miles "through a cultivated and populous country, abounding in luxuriant crops of corn and sugar cane. The inhabitants are industrious, and for that reason comfortable, well dressed, orderly, and courteous. Mont Morelas is a pretty Mexican town of two thousand people, with many fine dwellings built in the Spanish style of architecture. It contains a small church and large cathedral, which is still unfinished."

A report from Gen. Worth that Santa Anna was approaching Monterey with a large force, caused the reinforcements on the road to be hurried rapidly forward. Gen. Twigg's division, comprising the brigades of Colonels Harney and Smith, left Mont Morelas for Monterey the 18th of December, accompanied by Gen. Taylor. The 20th found them in the immediate vicinity of the city, when it was ascertained that the rumor was false.

Lieut. Lyon took the earliest opportunity to examine the celebrities of Monterey. After inspecting the singular architecture of the city, the construction of the Black Fort, and the splendid cathedral, he repaired to Arista's Garden—a favorite resort, on account of its extent and the elegance of its arrangements. Here the atmosphere was laden with fragrance, and the eye wandered with delight amid the rich profusion of tropical flowers.

The stay of the second infantry in this vicinity was destined to be short. A change in the plans of government caused a large body of troops to be detached from the force of Gen. Taylor and transferred to the Gulf Coast. Gen. Scott was to take immediate command of the army of invasion, and establish the principal base of military operations at Vera Cruz. In a communication to Gen. Taylor dated Washington, Oct. 22d, 1846, the Secretary of War apprises him of the project and directs him to have four thousand men, fifteen hundred or two thousand of the number to be *regulars*, in readiness to embark for Vera Cruz or such other destination as may be given, at the earliest practicable moment; provided his own plans are not materially interfered with, or his position too much weakened by the withdrawal of so large a force. Gen. Scott, in a letter to Gen. Taylor written at New York, November 25th, after deprecating the imperious necessity of the measure, says: "I shall be obliged to take from you most of the gallant officers and men, (regulars and volunteers,) which you have so long and so nobly commanded."

The administration agreed to raise and forward ten new regiments as soon as possible after the meeting of Congress; to provide at once the requisite number of transports and surf-boats; and to have a suitable train of siege ordnance ready for use against the defenses of Vera Cruz.

At the beginning of the year 1847, Gen. Taylor, with a force of eighteen thousand men, occupied the long line from the mouth of the Rio Grande to Camargo, and thence to Monterey and Saltillo. Gen. Scott was in the neighborhood of Brazos Santiago, working with tireless energy to perfect arrangements for a successful attack upon the commercial emporium of Mexico. Santa Anna held a force of more than twenty thousand men at San Louis Potosi, a strongly fortified city of sixty thousand inhabitants, situated among the mountains about half way between Monterey and the Mexican capital. From this central position the commanding general could either precipitate his legions upon the army of Gen. Taylor, should its weakness invite attack, or send large reinforcements to repel attempts upon the coast.

Nor was Santa Anna left in the dark respecting the designs of the Americans. Gen. Scott attempted to acquaint Gen. Taylor with the details of his plan. Lieut. Richie, the bearer of despatches, was assassinated on the road, and the important documents entrusted to his care apprised the enemy of the purposes of our commander.

The embarrassments of Gen. Scott were further complicated as it became evident that the administration was lukewarm in efforts to provide means for a vigorous prosecution of the war. Ambitious politicians had conceived the mad project of placing a partisan at the head of the army, with the rank of Lieutenant-General. The bill for raising ten additional regiments, which ought to have passed Congress at once, dragged along till near the end of the session. Yet the Commander-in-chief determined to commence operations according to the original plan with the resources at his disposal. In obedience to orders, Gen. Taylor forwarded a goodly part of his own troops to reinforce the army then concentrating for the capture of Vera Cruz.

On the morning of December 23d, after a rainy

night, Lyon's regiment with others began to retrace their steps over the same road along which they had so recently passed. Gen. Taylor accompanied the division for some distance. "He encamped at all times with the troops in unceremonious style; his habits, dress and manners being off-hand and informal. He does not repair to towns and cities to luxuriate, leaving the army at a distance, but as far as possible keeps with the men and in the country."

As the troops passed through Cardareta, Christmas bells were pealing merrily, as if no dark clouds of anarchy and war shut out the light of heaven from this afflicted land. The next day they left the Camargo road, reaching Linares on the 28th, where they encamped on the opposite banks of the stream that skirts the south side of the town. The place, like many others was deserted by the principal inhabitants, and presented an aspect of desolation. It is the custom of the people to plant *crosses* wherever a murder has been committed or a death occurred by violence. On this route they were erected thickly by the roadside—melancholy tokens of the depravity and lawlessness which corrupted the land.

Reaching Victoria the 4th of January, they remained till the 14th, when "in obedience to orders from Gen. Taylor, the division began to move in the direction of Tampico, where it arrived the 23d, and encamped near the town."

From Lyon's memoranda:

"The country adjacent to Tampico is low and profusely covered with vegetation. Lemons of good quality grow plentifully in the woods. The banana, the cocoa, the plantain, and other fruits of a tropical clime are found here. The inhabitants of the place are generally foreigners, civil, orderly, and more intelligent than we have met with elsewhere in Mexico. Nearly all of the houses are in the American style; while the principal streets are wide and well paved."

Gen. Scott arrived at Tampico the 19th of February, and ordered the immediate embarkation of all the troops for the rendezvous at Lobos island, a small body of land near the coast, about one hundred and twenty-five miles north of Vera Cruz. Lieut. Lyon reached the island on the 26th, where he found Gen. Scott with a fleet of fifty sail waiting for further reinforcements.

March 4th. "After a detention in the offing for thirty-six hours from head winds, a *Norther* sprang up at two o'clock this morning, taking us down opposite to Vera Cruz by sunset. We passed near enough to see the town and castle, and anchored under the lee of Verd Island, south-east of the city.

March 5th. "Late in getting under way. There being little wind, we moved slowly till the U. S. war steamer Princeton took us in tow and conducted us to the harbor of Anton Lizardo.

March 6th. "Harbor very quiet. Gen. Scott passes along the shore on board the Spit-Fire to examine the appearance of the enemy and discover a suitable place for landing the troops. On approaching the castle, he was fired upon. The third shot came near the boat, and the fourth, (a sixty-four pounder,) flew directly over it. News arrived to-day, through the Mexican papers, of a hard fought battle between Gen. Taylor and Santa Anna, south-east of Saltillo, in which the enemy retired.

March 9th. "Preparations are all made for disembarking. The steamers and war vessels take on board most of the men, and all move up under the island of Sacrificios. Gen. Worth's brigade disembarked about six P. M., without opposition from shore. The other brigades immediately follow and the landing of troops continues till midnight. Our regiment reached shore about ten P. M., stacked arms, and lay by them. About one o'clock in the morning a few men, in looking for water, fell upon the pickets of the enemy, who fired for some time, but without effect."

The landing was effected in sixty-seven surf

boats, each conducted by a naval officer, and rowed by sailors from the squadron. Two steamers and several vessels of light draft flanked the boats with a view to cover operations by their cross-fire. All expected to encounter vigorous opposition. But the Mexicans, supposing that the debarkation would be attempted at a distant point, were collected there to repel it, leaving other places comparatively defenceless. Three divisions, consisting in all of twelve thousand men, were transferred from the shipping to the shore without a casualty or accident. The scene and circumstances were admirably suited both to excite and exhilarate our troops. A small army, proudly conscious of infinite superiority in manhood, energy, and military skill, were knocking with hostile arms at the strongest gate of an empire that counts its people by millions. It seemed like the realization of the dreams and fables of ancient poetry, in the midst of the cool, well-balanced, statistical civilization of the present hour. Before this little band of hardy warriors, armies were to be scattered like chaff in the breeze. Neither temporary fortifications nor battlemented castles could obstruct their victorious march.

The landing was made on the south side of the city, and the line of investment occupied as rapidly as the difficulties to be overcome would permit.

On the 10th, Gen. Worth's brigade took position on the right of the line, and Gen. Patterson's in the center. Gen. Twiggs' brigade remained at the place of landing till the 11th, when it began to march for the position assigned it, on the north-west side of the city. Lieut. Lyon thus describes the events of the day. "The firing from town commenced early with eighteen and twenty-four pounders, just reaching our column. One shot came into Gen. Worth's line, but did no harm. Our advance encountered the enemy in the chaparral, and had something of a skirmish, in which a few were wounded. Balls continued coming from town, one of which passed through our ranks, killing Brevet Capt. Alburtis, and also shattering the foot of a private."

Several skirmishes occurred during the day, in which the enemy were invariably repulsed with loss. The brigade bivouacked at night, occupying the line in the direction of the Jalapa road as far as its strength would permit.

On the morning of the 13th the march was resumed. Making a detour to the left to avoid several ponds of water, the brigade, about twelve o'clock, reached the great National Road leading from Vera Cruz to the City of Mexico. A party of hostile cavalry drawn up at this point were

4

quickly dispersed without loss to the Americans. Several were taken prisoners and, what was not less acceptable to the soldiers, two hundred beef cattle and thirty casks of good wine fell into their hands. Shortly after noon the head of the column arrived at the village of Vergara, on the beach, two and a half miles north of the town, where Gen. Twiggs fixed his head-quarters. The line of investment was now complete.

The movements of the brigade from the place of landing were attended with severe toil and exposure. The guns of the enemy were admirably served, and kept up a well directed fire upon our troops whenever they ventured within range. At a safer distance from the city, beyond the reach of shot and shell, the country is studded with sand hills varying in height from twenty to two hundred and fifty feet. Dense and almost impassable forests of chaparral occupy the valleys and interspaces. During the period of investment, violent "northers" prevailed with few intermissions, filling the air with clouds of light, loose sand. The fervent rays of the sun not only rested upon the troops, but were reflected with dazzling brightness from the banks of sand beneath and around them. Water along the route was very scarce, so that the pangs of insupportable thirst were superadded to the other annoyances.

Of the means of land transportation expected from Tampico and the Brazos weeks before, only fifteen carts and one hundred draught horses had arrived. At the time there was but one depot for provisions and military stores, and this was located on the beach, several miles south of the town. Men were obliged to carry food, equipage, and munitions, for the distance of five miles over the sand and through the chaparral.

On the morning of the 14th, printed safeguards were sent to the Spanish, French, British and Prussian consuls connected with Vera Cruz, to protect as far as practicable the houses and property of foreign residents.

The operations of the siege were much delayed by the prevalence of northers and the lack of mortars and heavy ordnance. Gen. Scott, writing to the Secretary of War the 18th of March, complains that but two-tenths of the guns originally required had reached him.

Meanwhile an irregular fire was kept up from city and castle upon the lines of investment. Mexican *rancheros* made nightly attacks upon the American rear, but were always driven back with ease. Occasional skirmishes between reconnoitering parties took place within the works, and gave abundant evidence of the superiority of Saxon steel.

The north winds, which had aggravated the difficulties of the siege, on the other hand brought into the anchorages numerous transports laden with munitions and food. Reinforcements also arrived, and during the intermission of the gale, troops and material were rapidly transferred to the shore.

Several batteries of heavy armament were planted within twelve hundred yards of the city, magazines were arranged, and other preparations for the bombardment pushed with great rapidity. On the 22d of March, seven ten-inch mortars being in readiness to open fire, the Commander-in-chief summoned the Governor of Vera Cruz to surrender. The capitulation of the castle was not demanded, as Gen. Scott was in no condition to threaten it from want of heavy ordnance. Gen. Morales, who commanded city and castle both, promptly refused, assuring his excellency in reply to the demand, that he should defend both points at all cost and to the last extremity.

On the return of the flag with the response of the Governor, the bombardment was commenced. A litle later two steamers and five schooners belonging to the squadron, took position under Point Hornos, where they were partially protected from the guns of the castle, and with their heavy metal opened on the city. The enemy responded vigorously upon the fleet and the intrenchments. Their firing, though well directed, proved quite ineffective, for the shot grazed harmlessly over the sunken batteries, and the trenches offered too small a mark for the mortars. One of the shells, however, killed Capt. John R. Vinton, a brave and highly accomplished officer. A single private was killed and several were wounded.

During the next two days, heavy mortars and guns were added to the batteries. Large quantities of ammunition were sent from the beach in the night time, to the fortifications. Wagons loaded with powder moved to their destination within range of the enemy's guns, but no accident occurred. Meanwhile the firing was slackened, because a norther again sprung up, cutting off communication with the fleet, upon which the batteries depended for the supply of shells. On the 24th the wind abated and the lull was vigorously improved in landing ammunition of all kinds.

On the morning of the 25th, the heavy armament of the besiegers, now plentifully supplied with powder and missiles, opened a rapid and terrific fire. Shot and shells fell with frightful effect upon the habitations and defenses of the doomed city. Conflagrations broke out wherever the buildings were combustible and raged till every thing that would burn was consumed. Many hurried frantically through the streets seeking in vain for places of safety. Now the supply of food was almost exhausted and in many cases the pangs of hunger were added to the other horrors of the scene. Women and children emerged from the haunts of poverty, and with looks famished and terror-stricken, clamored for bread. Not a few of the unfortunate creatures perished in fruitless efforts to procure the means of life.

Meanwhile the guns of the enemy responded vigorously. The men continued bravely at their posts, fighting with a degree of obstinacy and resolution that excited the admiration of the besiegers. For hours the cannonade was incessant, neither side evincing the slightest disposition to yield.

But the foreign element at Vera Cruz, which embraced a large and influential share of the population, overcome by the hardships of the bombardment, through their consuls obtained permission to send a flag of truce to Gen. Scott. The accompanying petition prayed that hostilities might be suspended for a sufficient time to allow foreigners and Mexican women and children to leave the place.

The American commander, having previously sent safeguards to the consuls, and allowed every facility for the departure of foreigners to the neutral vessels of war under Sacrificios until the 22d, replied to the consuls that a truce could only be granted on application of the Governor of Vera Cruz, and that too accompanied by a distinct proposition of surrender.

On the return of the flag to the city, the bombardment was resumed and continued through the night, while the Mexican batteries remained silent. So great had become the distress in town, that the enemy was at length convinced of the futility of further resistance. Accordingly, early on the 26th, Gen. Landero, who took command on account of the feigned sickness of Gen. Morales, the Governor, made overtures of surrender. Articles of capitulation were signed and ratified the 27th. Two days later the Stars and Stripes were planted in triumph on the far famed castle of San Juan d'Ulloa.

By the agreement of the commissioners, the city and castle, with all the *materiél* of war and public property were relinquished to the United States. Officers and men were allowed to march out of the town with the honors of war, and retire on parole. Among the trophies of victory were four hundred pieces of ordnance, five thousand stands of arms, and a large quantity of military stores. Her chief commercial emporium was lost to Mexico, and became the base of successful operations against the national capital. All this was accomplished with small loss of life on the part of the Americans.

The regiment of Lieut. Lyon was stationed at the Jalapa road—a position which might readily have become the most perilous along the whole line of investment. Several times it was rumored that the Mexicans were advancing in force down this thoroughfare for the relief of the beleaguered city, and as often the second regiment of infantry was deputed to receive them. No one knew how formidable a force might be in the immediate neighborhood. But the enemy failed to make the attempt, so that the troops who guarded the main avenue of approach from the interior to Vera Cruz, had no opportunity to incur extraordinary danger, or win extraordinary praise.

The army delayed for several days to leave the coast, now insufferably hot and insalubrious, from want of the means of transportation. Cannon, ammunition, provisions, and equipage were to be conveyed for a long distance, while the principal part of the necessary wagons, horses, and mules had not yet arrived.

On the 8th of April, the advance division, under Gen. Twiggs, left Vera Cruz for the Mexican capital. The other divisions were to follow rapidly so as to be ready to lend speedy aid in case serious obstacles were encountered. As Lieut. Lyon belonged to the leading column, brief extracts are given from his memoranda.

April 8th. "We started for the interior at eight o'clock and marched twelve miles. For the first half of the distance the road was made by deep cuts through the sand hills, and its sides and bottom were intensely heated by the rays of the sun. Afterwards open, sandy plains succeed, where we encountered a slight but hot breeze. Officers and men suffered greatly from the heat, and more than half the number failed. Camp in a thicket to the left of the road, and just east of a fine stream and bridge.

April 9th. "March twelve miles to another fine bridge—day excessively hot, but not so severe as yesterday. The country along the road shows signs of cultivation at some former period, but is mostly neglected at present.

April 10th. "Marched only six miles, to the National bridge. At the left is a fortification built with the design to command the passage. It was expected that the Mexicans would here make a stand and contest our further advance. There were some evidences of such an intention, as the first bridge appeared as if mined recently, and obstructions were found in the road.

April 11*th*. "Advanced twelve miles to a fine bridge in a gorge of hills, and protected like the National bridge by an old military work on a high hill to the left. An outpost of about fifty Mexican lancers was found here, who fled and were pursued by the dragoons of Col. Harney. He afterwards reconnoitered and found the enemy intrenched in a strong position on the road some four miles in advance. He was fired upon by them. They are therefore expected to make a stand and give us a hard fight to-morrow.

April 12*th*. "Gen. Twiggs having called all his officers together yesterday, and announced his intention of attacking the enemy in advance at all hazards, we started at daylight with the full expectation of storming the heights. On approaching, reconnoitering parties were sent to the right and left of the road, when the outposts of the enemy fired upon our engineers and the guard. Capt. Johnston, of topographical corps, was badly wounded, as were several riflemen. Just before this a report came that fifteen hundred of the enemy were advancing upon the rear to attack the train. The dragoons and third infantry were sent back to meet them. Additional reports being received that a still greater number were threatening the rear, the second infantry was ordered back, and found everything quiet with no appearance of the enemy. Instead, however, of returning to join the advance, we kept our position. The head column returned to us and we all remained at the encampment of the previous night. Gen. Pillow arrived to-day in time to assist but was not called upon.

April 13*th*. "Did not start this morning, but a reconnoitering party was sent out to get information in regard to the enemy. Their report was favorable to an immediate attack. In consequence, however, of the fatigue of Gen. Pillow's command, and its need of rest, an order was issued by Gen. Twiggs delaying the forward movement till tomorrow, when we are to advance, the regulars taking the right of the road and the volunteers the left. Orders were also given to move in silence at midnight; but all this was countermanded by Gen. Patterson, who, having arrived the previous day, did not assume command till now in consequence of sickness.

April 14*th*. "Gen. Patterson, being in command, has ordered no movement. Gen. Scott arrived at evening.

April 15*th*. "The engineers, with Gen. Scott, went to-day to reconnoitre. I was in command of a camp of the escort. We proceeded to the rear of the enemy's left, but the reconnoissance was incomplete and unsatisfactory.

April 16*th*. "Remain in camp, and nothing important occurs. Serg't Day, a faithful soldier and Orderly Serg't of Company 'G,' having died last night, is buried. Received my promotion to-day as First Lieutenant, and assume command of Company 'D.'"

Lyon was promoted to the First Lieutenancy February 16th, 1847.*

The next day (April 17th) commenced the battle of Cerro Gordo. The American Camp rested on each side of the National road at *Plan Del Rio*, the termination of the *tierras calientes*, or the level country below. From this site the road winds circuitously among lofty hills whose commanding points had all been strongly fortified by the enemy. Along the whole length of the Mexican right, flowed the El Rio del Plan through a deep ravine, the precipitous sides of which afforded a perfect barrier to the approach of troops. The highway crosses this stream at the Plan del Rio, and after numerous windings passed to the right of the outermost batteries of the enemy. These were planted

* Register of the Officers and Graduates of West Point, by Capt. George W. Cullum, New York, 1850.

on the salients of three high and rocky ridges branching out from a common center in the rear. Seventeen guns were mounted here. A mile in the rear, at the point where the road approaches nearest to the river, a battery of six pieces swept almost the entire pass. A little further on, the cannon planted on the heights and tower of Cerro Gordo—the loftiest eminence of all—commanded the whole field. The main body of the Mexicans were encamped on the Jalapa road, west of Cerro Gordo, and protected by a battery of five pieces. Six hundred yards east of Cerro Gordo, and about the same distance north of the road, stands another hill that became the scene of important operations during the progress of the battle.

It was obvious that such a succession of strongly fortified heights could not be carried except at a frightful sacrifice. Gen. Scott, accordingly determined to cut a new road to the left of the Mexican defences, and partially out of reach of their guns, by which a force could debouch upon the national highway in the rear. Reconnoissances were daily pushed, and the road built, with great difficulty, over chasms and along precipitous hills, till the further prosecution of the work, without coming to an engagement, was interrupted by the proximity of Mexican batteries. The desired point of debouchure, though not reached, was believed to be quite accessible from the position already secured.

According to the plan of attack, Gen. Pillow was to assault the batteries in front, while Gen. Twiggs was to march by the new route and fall upon the enemy in the rear. On the morning of the 17th the division of Gen. Twiggs moved forward from Plan del Rio, and turning to the right, a short distance from the entrance of the pass, advanced for some time through the thick chaparral without molestation. As soon, however, as the movement was observed from the batteries, the guns opened a heavy fire upon the flank of the column. Owing to the distance, and the protection afforded by the inequalities of the ground, the troops suffered little injury.

A little in advance and on the left of the route was a ridge, which Lieut. Gardner, with a company of the 7th infantry, was directed to ascend, for the purpose of watching the movements of the enemy. In executing the order he encountered a large body of Mexicans, holding them in check till relieved by reinforcements. After a sharp struggle the enemy were repulsed and pursued to the hill east of Cerro Gordo, where they rallied. But the Americans carried the height by storm, notwithstanding a destructive fire upon their flank from the battery located where the National road approaches nearest to the river. Three successive charges were made to retake it, but without success.

Meanwhile, the rear of the division, embracing the company of Lyon, was ordered to hurry forward under cover of the advance, with the view of gaining the Jalapa road, and thus cutting off the retreat of the Mexicans. In attempting to execute the manœuvre, the column gained an advance position, when it was discovered by the enemy, who at once gave it their undivided attention, in order to prevent the consummation of a plan so fatal to their safety. Without responding to the musketry, it hastened onward till the tented field was in sight. There the enemy appeared in large numbers. An attack was too perilous to be ventured, and accordingly the detachment was ordered to retreat. It fell back "with alacrity, and as little confusion as could be expected, considering the shower of bullets," to a position covered by the Americans. The men slept on their arms during the night. Meanwhile, others were laboriously engaged in dragging cannon over the rugged way and up steep acclivities toward the summit of the height east of Cerro Gordo. Early the next morning two howitzers and a twenty-four pounder opened a brisk fire upon the enemy from this position. Col. Harney. who commanded here, organized a storming party to carry Cerro Gordo. Col. Riley's brigade, to which Lyon's regiment belonged, under the guidance of Capt. Lee, of the engineers, again started for the seizure of the National road at the site of the Mexican camp, in the rear of their other defences. As the regiments moved from behind the eminence, which had screened them during the darkness, it was necessary to cross a ravine swept by hostile batteries. From this time the column was also exposed to a heavy fire from infantry, who swarmed in increasing numbers upon the sides of the ridge to the left of the route. When the second infantry reached the foot of the hill, two companies, belonging to the regiment, A and I, were detached to drive in the skirmishers of the enemy. This force proving inadequate, two additional companies, B and H, were ordered to their support, and shortly after the residue of the regiment. Company D, commanded by Lyon, hurried up the slope, attaining the crest in time to share actively in the conflict. The fight was hot and spirited. Unable to withstand the steady valor of our troops, the Mexicans soon fled in hot haste and utter confusion, after suffering severely in killed and wounded. The advance of the second infantry thus gallantly stormed the reverse of Cerro Gordo, gaining the summit from behind, at the same time that Harney's brigade reached it from the front.

Another battery of five guns in the plain below, half a mile west of Cerro Gordo, had greatly annoyed the Americans, and was still playing vigorously. At the same place also a large body of lancers were stationed. This was a strong position in the rear of all the other fortifications here planted upon the National road, and was designed to cover the retreat of the Mexicans in case the defenses in front should be carried by storm. Col. Riley ordered the advance of the second infantry to move down and capture this battery, and the rest of the brigade to follow as soon as possible, for the purpose of occupying the Mexican camp. The companies of Capt. Canby and Lieut. Lyon hastened to execute the apparently perilous charge, and took the three guns on the right, the other two being taken by the volunteers of Gen. Shields. So panic-stricken were the enemy by the ill success of the day, that after two ineffective shots they abandoned this important post to the small but terrible handful of assailants. From the inability of the Americans to reach the Jalapa road at an earlier stage of the battle, many escaped, the cavalry taking the highway and the footmen fleeing into the woods. Here was found the carriage of Santa Anna, containing valuable documents and other curious articles. The unfortunate chieftain escaped on a mule, by fording the river and breaking through a narrow and difficult pass on the southern bank, whence he gained the road to Orizaba.

Lieut. Lyon pushed on, the same afternoon, in pursuit of the fugitives, as far as the village of Encerro, eight miles from the field of Cerro Gordo.

While these events were occurring in the rear, Gen. Pillow, according to the original plan, assaulted the eastern fortifications, but was repulsed with considerable loss. The works were defended by old troops of the line, and commanded by generals of unusual spirit and courage, considering their nationality. But after the capture of the batteries on the west, being completely hemmed in, they were forced to surrender.

The American force, in action and reserve, was not far from eight thousand five hundred; the Mexican about thirteen thousand. Our loss was sixty-three killed, and three hundred and sixty-eight wounded; that of the enemy much greater. Forty-three pieces of artillery, several thousand stands of arms, and many prisoners were captured.

CHAPTER IV.

THE day after the battle of Cerro Gordo, Lieut. Lyon, and indeed the main body of the army, elated by succèss, hurried on unconscious of fatigue, to Jalapa.

At this town the main body of the army remained for more than a month. During the interval, Lyon wrote an extended sketch of the physical appearance of the country, and of the institutions and character of the people. He notes the fact that in previous marches through the northern part of Mexico, our troops found no carriage roads. Different towns were connected by simple mule-paths, upon which no labor was expended to promote the convenience of travelers. But the highway from Vera Cruz to the city of Mexico is of the most excellent and substantial character. When new, it was paved with stone the whole distance. It was built by Spain at the cost of Government, while

Mexico was her province, as the great national thoroughfare from the seaboard to the interior. Whatever public structures in Mexico bear marks of good taste or great expense, are the fruits of Spanish enterprise. Since the revolution no new improvements have been undertaken, and the grand old works of the past have been suffered to fall into decay.

The experience of Lyon in Mexico leads him "to feel for the people, their customs, laws and religion, all the contempt and disgust that a heritage of puritan instructions naturally inspires for institutions and practices so much at variance with early teachings."

At Jalapa, charity prompts the candid observer to relent somewhat in the severity of his judgment, and to pity rather than loathe an unfortunate race. Elsewhere "the depravity of the people seemed the natural fruit of a corrupt priesthood and lordly aristocracy; but here many individuals of pure blood, education and refinement, are blindly devoted to their pagan worship."

Under a healthful state of religion, morals and government, Jalapa might become a prosperous and delightful city, for its natural advantages are of the rarest quality. Though lying within the tropics, its altitude is such that the climate is uniform and salubrious. Rains descend in due proportion, the verdure is rich, and the growth of vegetation luxuriant. At all seasons the fields are clothed in the beauties of spring. Here one avoids alike the raw blasts of winter and the heat of summer. Eastward the eye rests upon plains of arid sand, westward upon the heights of Arazala, white with an eternal crown of snow.

From the position of the town, between tropical plains and frost bound mountains, its market is plentifully supplied with the fruits and vegetables of every clime. Here, for the first time in Mexico, Lyon saw lots divided by *stone walls*, and *variety* in the cultivated products of the field, which continually reminded him of the choicest rural districts of New England.

"The town has a population of ten thousand, and many fine residences. The churches are massive edifices, elegantly finished within, and ornamented with pictures and statues, the most costly and beautiful. The Virgin-Mother is often presented in every attraction of female loveliness."

At Jalapa the privates were quartered in barracks and the officers found accommodations in the comfortable homes of the natives, the shelter of a roof being a luxury that Lyon had not enjoyed before since leaving New York the previous September.

Gen. Worth occupied the strong castle and town of Perote the 22d of April, without opposition. Col. Valasquez, the Mexican commissioner, turned over to the Americans the entire armament of the castle, consisting of fifty-four guns and mortars, besides a large amount of ammunition. None of the *materièl* of war had been removed by the enemy in the hurry of flight. The fortress itself contained ample accommodations for two thousand troops, with quarters for officers, store-houses, hospitals, and other appointments.

Lieut. Lyon remained at Jalapa with the main body of the army till the 22d of May. Gen. Worth had already pushed forward with the advance and taken possession of Puebla. The other divisions were delayed by the necessity of procuring supplies from Vera Cruz. On the 22d of May, the march towards the city of Mexico was resumed by the army, which was now furnished with an immense train.

From the memoranda of Lyon.

May 23d. "March to a pass called *La Hoya*, where extensive preparations had been made by the Mexicans to oppose us; but the pursuit from Cerro Gordo took them by surprise, and these important works were left, with seven guns spiked. The position was very strong and would have been difficult to be carried. The country along this road is thickly populated, and the scenery varied, grand and beautiful.

May 24th. "Marched ten miles to Las Vegas, an old dilapidated town of no importance. Road ascending and rough, with scarcity of water. Here first meet the Maguey plant.

May 25th. "Enter Perote and encamp on the north side of the famous castle, which is not a *castle* but a *fort*, with four bastions,—each front being about two hundred and eighty yards in length. The parapet is pierced with embrasures for one hundred guns. The ditch is very deep and wide; the masonry of good brick; and the whole work very strong. The fort is about half a mile from the town of Perote, a small, old and ruinous place."

During the next three days the army advanced fifty miles over an immense plain, unlimited in many directions by any salient boundaries. In other quarters, the broad level tract is skirted by distant hills, at the foot of which are seen villages of considerable size. The first half of the route is thinly inhabited, presenting no evidences of enterprise or thrift; but further west, the country becomes more populous and the fields show abundant indications of diligent and successful culture.

May 29th. "March twenty miles to Puebla, and

passing to the central part of the town, take up quarters in the San Augustine monastery. The great object of attraction here is the numerous churches—one hundred in number—all large and massive. To nearly every one is attached a convent. The cathedral on the Plaza is an immense structure of basaltic rock, with its interior richly finished and gorgeously decorated. Vast wealth is also piled up in every church in the form of pictures, images and other ornaments. The city contains about seventy thousand inhabitants. It is well laid out, with wide streets intersecting each other at right angles."

The city of Puebla is situated seventy miles southeast of the valley of Mexico, at an elevation of seven thousand feet above the level of the sea. In the coldest season the Fahrenheit thermometer ranges between 55° and 70°, and in summer the mercury seldom rises above 75°, in the shade. While the lands under high cultivation, yield grains of the choicest quality, and other productions in abundance, vegetation, owing to the rarity of the atmosphere, does not spring up so luxuriantly as upon a soil of less altitude.

At the time of Cortes' invasion, in the early part of the sixteenth century, the province of Puebla was perhaps the most populous, wealthy and highly civilized of the Mexican States. Here were found some of the most laborious monuments of human toil, reared either from sentiments of heathen veneration, or from the ambitious desire of the ancient race to bequeath to future ages enduring memorials of their grandeur and skill. Six miles from the city of Puebla stands the pyramid of Cholula, rivaling in magnitude the great pyramid on the Nile. Its base covers an area of forty acres, and it rises in terraces to the height of one hundred and seventy-seven feet. On the top once stood a magnificent temple dedicated to the worship of their principal God. At its base were the towers of hundreds of minor temples, and an immense city whose streets swarmed with throngs of devotees from every quarter of the empire. But the glory and the folly have departed forever. The pyramid rises *alone* amid the ruins of the past, for the deity once worshipped there with such lavish profusion of sacrifices and rites, failed to save from destruction the homes of his followers.

The long delay of the American army at Puebla gave the curious among our officers abundant time to make acquaintance with the wonders—natural and artificial—of this remarkable province.

This delay extended through the months of June and July till the 7th of August. Meanwhile the efforts of the administration to negotiate peace through its agent, Mr. Trist, had proved abortive, leaving no alternative but to carry the war to the gates of the capital.

On reaching Puebla, the number of effective men in the army of invasion did not exceed five thousand. Many causes aside from losses in battle had been active in thinning the ranks. Insalubrity of climate in the low regions near the Gulf proved a hundred fold more destructive than the arms of the enemy. The country was sprinkled with the graves of brave men who perished, not amid the roar of artillery, but from disease, in hospitals and by the road side. Others survived the malaria and pestilence to gain the mountainous districts with constitutions much shattered by exposure. The sallow complexions and cadaverous features of the Americans, on entering Puebla, showed that the subtle poisons of the air had battled fiercely with the strongest. The natives viewed them with wonder. They could not believe that these troops, so wan and way-worn, were the terrible men who had repeatedly routed their own proud armies, and charged resistlessly upon their forts and fastnesses.

It must be remembered that this small force was two hundred miles from the sea, in the heart of a hostile empire. All reinforcements and supplies from home must come this long distance, over a road that was commanded in many places by hills, and wound often through dangerous passes. Guerrilla bands ranged over the country, watching for opportunities of robbery or murder. Hence it was necessary to garrison cities and fortifications on the route, or leave them to be occupied by the enemy. These causes, it would seem, were sufficient to restrain our army from advancing further, till greatly strengthened by the accession of fresh troops.

The interval of delay was occupied in perfecting the drill and discipline of the men.

Reinforcements arrived at Puebla in various detachments, until on the 6th of August, 1847, the American army numbered fourteen thousand men. On the 5th of the same month, at a council of war, an immediate advance was determined upon.—Twiggs' division, preceded by Harney's cavalry brigade, again led the way, followed successively by the divisions of Quitman, Worth, and Pillow, on the three days subsequent.

Says Lieut. Lyon:

August 7th. "Having remained in Puebla since the 29th of May for the arrival of more troops, and also with the hope that some pacific arrangements might be made with Mexico, and the first object being obtained and the latter given up, it is decided to advance upon the capital. Gen. Twiggs' division starts to-day and marches over a slightly undulating country, for ten miles. The district is not much inhabited, though the lands are susceptible of high cultivation. In many places the fields contain fine crops of grain of various kinds.

August 8th. "March eleven miles to St. Martins through a level and well tilled country. The extensive valley of St. Martins is very beautiful, and mostly surrounded by mountains. The town contains two large churches and numbers about fifteen hundred inhabitants—chiefly robbers.

August 9th. "Advance thirteen miles to Les Melucos, a short distance up the highlands that separate the plain of St. Martins from the valley of Mexico.

August 10th. "Pass over the highlands to Cordova, leaving lofty mountain peaks to the left. This part of the road is elevated and cold. Pass the Rio Frio, where some preparations had been made by the Mexicans for defense; but they were abandoned. The only water on the road is the Rio Frio. Come in sight of the plain of Mexico, but not of the city."

In the march from Puebla to the crest of the mountain range, the army gained an elevation ten thousand feet above the surface of the sea. The beauty and grandeur of the scenery—the memory of recent victories—and the hope of fresh triumphs, produced a general feeling of exhilaration.

The route was full of interest to poet or scholar. Here were monuments of ancient civilization, carrying back the thoughts through many centuries of time, to the days when the arts and culture of the continent were confined to the homes of the Aztec. In the distance lofty mountain tops reposed in the region of perpetual snow, filling the air for miles around with the chill of their frozen mantle. The eye swept over a landscape of vast proportions, and from those towering heights seemed to penetrate further than ever before into the wonders of space.

Before the invaders lay the valley of Mexico, a deep basin of oval form, surrounded by a continuous ridge of mountains. On the south the Cordilleras separate into two chains, which, after circling to the right and left, again unite on the north, leaving an extensive and richly varied plain in the center. The length of the valley is sixty-three miles and its breadth forty-three.

The city of Mexico is admirably situated for defense. An environment of lakes and marshes presents insuperable obstacles to the approach of troops, except by the few causeways which diverge from the common center. One road only, the great national thoroughfare from Vera Cruz, enters the capital on the east. Descending into the plain it passes at first through a well improved district, sprinkled with occasional villages. Further on, at the distance of twelve miles from the city, it strikes an extensive and desolate waste, bare alike of vegetation and dwellings. In the midst of the flat, a solitary hill rises menacingly beside the causeway. This height, known as El Peñon, stands on the south side of the road, eight miles from the capital. On the opposite side, extending several miles east and west, are the marshy borders of Lake Tezcuco. Here the Mexicans had constructed elaborate fortifications. Battery rose above battery on the eastern and southern sides which were armed with twenty-six pieces of artillery.

El Peñon, defended by the valor of Americans, would have been impregnable. Careful reconnoissances convinced our generals that its capture, even from Mexicans, would involve a great and ruinous sacrifice of life. Days were spent in efforts to ascertain whether it were possible to reach the city without encountering the fire of its guns. To turn the position by the right, would require a detour of more than thirty miles around Lake Tezcuco, over a difficult route, and through strongly defended passes. On the left a road branched off from the main causeway a few miles east of El Peñon, and after passing through the village of Mexicalcingo, and across the canal from Lake Xochomilco, tapped the principal highway leading from Mexico southward. The country on both sides was covered by inundations, leaving only the narrow causeway for the advance of troops. The interspace, between Mexicalcingo and El Peñon, was traversed by ditches and buried under water. On the south was the barrier of Lakes Xochomilco and Chalco, which extended in a south-easterly direction to the spurs of the mountain range, that inclose the valley of Mexico. At the commanding positions about Mexicalcingo, was an almost impregnable system of defenses armed with more than thirty guns.

While reconnoisances, not less skillful than daring, were bringing these facts to light, parties were also engaged in exploring the southern borders of the lakes to ascertain the feasibility of a new route in that direction. Their reports were highly favorable. Gen. Scott, therefore, countermanded the orders he had previously given for the attack of Mexicalcingo, and directed the army to march at once around Lake Chalco.

On the 15th the march was commenced, Gen. Worth's division taking the lead. Twiggs' division having remained at Ayotla since the 11th, started from that place on the 16th in charge of the train. Owing to the retrogressive movement of the troops, the order of the columns was reversed, and Twiggs was left to bring up the rear. As he approached the vicinity of Buenavista, a force of six thousand Mexicans, a fourth of whom were cavalry, moved forward, in gaudy uniforms, with the obvious design of intercepting the train. The advantage of position and numbers would have inspired any but the basest of poltroons to make a vigorous attack. Taylor's battery was placed in position and a few shots sufficed to clear the field.

On the 19th the division reached San Augustine, having successfully conducted a cumbersome train over a route hitherto deemed impracticable by the enemy.

When Santa Anna discovered that Gen. Scott did not intend to attack El Peñon or Mexicalcingo, he withdrew the greater part of the artillery and troops from that quarter, and strove with all possible haste to establish strong lines of defense on the south and west. He threw up intrenchments and planted formidable batteries at the hacienda of San Antonio, on the Acapulco road, six miles south of the city. To guard against possible reverses, he also fortified the bridge and convent of Cherubusco, two miles further north, having determined to rely chiefly on these positions for the protection of the capital.

From the American head quarters, at San Augustine, Worth's division, with Harney's cavalry, were sent forward to reconnoitre, and, if practicable, to carry San Antonio. The position was found to be defended by a heavy armament and numerous garrison. It could only be approached in front on a narrow causeway flanked by deep ditches. On the right the ground was too wet and boggy to allow military movements, and on the left was the Pedregal, or field of lava, thought to be impassable for troops.

Gen. Worth was accordingly directed to threaten the place and keep the attention of the garrison occupied, while the engineers were active in exploring the Pedregal. The only way over it was a rugged mule-track winding westward from San Augustine, to the road from Magdalena to Mexico. On or near this road are several villages which will always be remembered from their connection with the events of the next few days. A little north of Magdalena was the factory of Contreras, and further on the hamlets of Ansalda and San Geronimo. Two miles north-east of San Geronimo was San Angel, a short distance beyond which this highway joined the network of roads south of the city. As will readily be seen the intervening space was occupied by the field of lava with its masses of broken rocks.

Capt. Lee, of the engineers, having gained the heights of Zacatepec, a commanding eminence in the midst of the field of lava, became convinced, from observation, that a way could be constructed over it, though with great difficulty. Gen. Scott accordingly directed the division of Gen. Pillow to undertake the task; and the forces of Gen. Twiggs to occupy the advance and keep the enemy in check during the progress of the work. On the morning of the 19th of August, Gen. Pillow marched west from San Augustine. Having accomplished the first two miles, which were comparatively easy, he sent forward working parties under the guidance of engineers to open the new route. In the afternoon the Americans came within range of the Mexican guns.

Gen. Valencia had planted a battery, mounting twenty-two pieces of artillery, on the slope of a hill west of the road from Magdalena, and opposite to its junction with the mule-path already mentioned. In front, between the position and the Pedregal, was a deep ravine, the bed of a mountain torrent. Half a mile north was the village of San Geronimo. No preparations had been made for the defense of the crest of the hill in the rear of the Mexican camp, for Valencia, relying upon the difficulties of the ground, had no thought that the position could be turned. Here was assembled a force of about six thousand men, which could be easily reinforced from the capital.

It was afternoon before Twiggs' division reached the Pedregal, from its encampment beyond San Augustine. The road was already completed as far as the hill of Zacatepec, where it emerged in sight of Valencia's battery. Twiggs' forces now moved forward to the front with the view of bringing on an engagement. Smith's brigade was ordered to advance along the mule-path directly towards the position of the enemy, and so soon as the conflict had commenced in that quarter, Riley's brigade was ordered to make a detour to the right, so as to fall upon San Geronimo and cut off the communication between Valencia and the city. The route taken by Riley's command was extremely difficult and toilsome. Rocks of every form were thrown together in every variety of confusion. Here were broad fissures to be crossed by leaping. A misstep might thrown the soldier down to the hard and dangerous bed below, imperiling limb and life. Here masses of stone were so arranged as to form an almost insuperable barrier. But over the rugged footing, up perpendicular walls, down steep descents, and across chasms, the men slowly and cautiously picked their way.

Having at length succeeded in traversing the field of lava, the brigade crossed two streams coursing through rugged ravines, and came upon the village of San Geronimo. The fourth regiment of artillery was left to search the place, while Col. Riley, with the second infantry, moved further on to gain a position from which he could study the country in the rear of the Mexican camp. Officers with small escorts were sent out to reconnoitre the grounds. These encountered squads of cavalry who at once communicated the alarm, and received strong reinforcements from head quarters by the narrow and difficult paths that wound westward among the gullies and hills. Augmented by constant arrivals of fresh troops, the Mexican lancers menaced the separate squads of the second infantry with destruction; but, notwithstanding the disparity in numbers, were kept at bay till the regiment was reformed and put in readiness to withstand any force that Valencia might send against it.

In speaking of the transactions of this part of the day, Lieut. Lyon says:

"We came in contact with large numbers of lancers who advanced and fired upon us, and in one case charged energetically, but were repulsed with loss, Gen. Frontera being killed. One of our men was killed and several wounded. At this time there appeared, in the rear toward the city, a force of about ten thousand men, in cavalry and infantry, accompanied by a small battery. This opened on us while the guns of the fort kept up a constant fire. We were now in danger of being cut off from our other forces, and fell back upon the village of San Geronimo, through which we had passed; and bivouacked in the lanes without cover, though exposed to a constant rain."

Santa Anna, in personal command of the large army which was seen approaching from the direction of the city, for the purpose obviously of forming a junction with Valencia, advanced to the high open ground north-west of San Geronimo, where he deployed his troops. Meanwhile Cadwalader's brigade having crossed the Pedregal and gained the road, formed in line of battle, and marching through the village took up an advantageous position on the borders of a ravine which separated the hostile armies.

Gen. Smith's brigade, which at first moved directly across the Pedregal to attack the intrenched camp in front, found that the project involved many and grave difficulties. The heavy guns of the battery commanded the way, and were admirably served by the artillerymen of the enemy. The depth and ruggedness of the gorge which it was necessary to cross in order to carry the position by storm, would expose the assailants to severe loss, even if the attempt proved successful. He accordingly withdrew the principal part of his forces, and moved northward over the field of lava, following the general course taken previously by Riley's brigade. Having reached the village of San Geronimo, he formed his forces on the right of Cadwalader, and assumed command of the whole. Gen. Shields reached the main road soon after dark, but did not advance to the village till midnight.

Santa Anna, foreseeing the inevitable destruction of Valencia's division, ordered him to spike the guns of the encampment, destroy the military stores, and draw off the troops under cover of darkness, by the circuitous paths in the rear. But that General, vain, arrogant and boastful, not only treated the command with contempt, but was so besotted with conceit as to imagine that he had already won a glorious victory. On the morrow he confidently expected to annihilate the "miserable remnant of North Americans," and to be acknowledged ere nightfall as the hero and deliverer of Mexico. The President, disgusted by the numerous and gross acts of insubordination on the part of Valencia, left him to his fate. Although his own army had been reinforced by masses of men till it numbered more than twelve thousand, Santa Anna showed no disposition to attack the American lines. Having stationed a corps of observation on the hill north of San Geronimo, he quietly retreated, soon after dark, with the main body of his forces, to San Angel.

Before daylight the next morning, the brigades of Riley, Cadwalader and Smith, were forming for the purpose of attacking the camp of Valencia in the rear. Gen. Shields remained at the village to guard against interruptions from Santa Anna who was supposed to be still hovering in the immediate vicinity. Reconnoissances commenced by officers of the second infantry in the afternoon, had been diligently prosecuted during the interim. With singular and inexplicable stupidity, the Mexican commander had taken no precautions to defend the approaches to his position from the west. At an early hour Riley's brigade marched by the flank in advance of the other troops, over the rocky, narrow and muddy way, without encountering either outpost or sentinel. The brigades of Cadwalader and Smith followed in succession. Riley gained the ravines at the foot of the hill on the opposite slope of which were the intrenchments to be stormed.

The men were formed in two columns and clambered as cautiously as possible up the ascent. The enemy did not discover them till they had nearly gained the summit. Here, while still screened by the crest of the hill, the lines, much disordered from the difficulties of the ground, were reformed for the assault. When everything was in readiness, the order for advance was given. The Mexicans, aroused at the last moment to an apprehension of the impending danger, prepared hastily for resistance. But their efforts were feeble, and they themselves were swept away like straws in a mountain torrent. The Americans, having discharged a single volley, rushed with terrific shouts into the intrenchments. The enemy opened a rapid and irregular fire of musketry which was delivered in the midst of too much confusion and alarm to be at all effective. For a brief interval, in the hand to hand encounter which followed, the clash of steel and the blows of gun-stocks mingled in sound with the cheers of the assailants. The struggle was very brief. Overwhelmed by the resistless charge, the Mexicans gave way to the frenzy of panic and despair. Seventeen minutes from the commencement of the fight, the stars and stripes, amid deafening shouts, were planted triumphantly on the parapet.

The enemy now sought to secure safety by a wild

and precipitate flight. Valencia mysteriously disappeared, no one knew where or how. For the mass now huddled together in inextricable disorder, escape was no easy matter, as the Americans, despite numerical inferiority, had encircled the position. In front among the rocks of Pedregal, were the volunteers of Col. Ransom; on the right the brigade of Gen. Cadwalader; on the left the brigade of Gen. Smith, while the forces of Col. Riley occupied the intrenchments. Small squads, indeed, stole hurriedly through the broad spaces between the American lines, and gained the mountains on the south. But the great body in a dense crowd—horsemen trampling on infantry, and the whole utterly demoralized by fear—plunged down the main road towards San Angel. Passing under a destructive fire from Smith's brigade, the remnant ran by the hacienda of Ansalda, and many who were fortunate enough to be in advance managed to escape; for Gen. Shields, left in charge of this part of the field, was occupied at the time with Santa Anna's corps of observation. When, however, this force saw the rout of the garrison at the camp, it retreated. Gen. Shields immediately moved his men so as to obstruct the passage of the road, compelling the fugitives, now hemmed in on every side, to surrender.

The whole number of Americans engaged in the battle did not much exceed four thousand men, of whom sixty were killed or wounded. The Mexican force, in and about the intrenched camp, was estimated at seven thousand, while Santa Anna, with twice as many more, was hovering within striking distance. Seven hundred of the enemy were killed and large numbers wounded. Over eight hundred prisoners were captured, including four generals. Among other trophies were twenty-two pieces of artillery, a large quantity of ammunition, and a valuable transportation train.

Thus was won the victory of Contreras—the first of the three brilliant achievements of our arms on that eventful day. One regiment of Riley's brigade, the fourth artillery, was left in charge of the captured camp and prisoners, while the rest of the troops pushed on in hot pursuit of the fugitives.

Santa Anna abandoned San Angel immediately after the overthrow of Valencia, and retreated to the works at Cherubusco. The advance of the Americans entered the town just as the rear of the enemy left. At this point Gen. Pillow assumed command, and ordered the troops to move forward to Coyacan, a village about a mile south-west of Cherubusco. Here, in obedience to orders from head quarters, a halt was made to await the arrival of the general-in-chief. As he rode past the men he was greeted with prolonged and hearty cheers; for the bright sun-shine and the flush of victory, succeeding a night of rain and gloom, inspired the army with tumultuous exultation. All were eager to continue the struggle so auspiciously begun, confident that, ere the close of the day, the last army of Mexico would be hopelessly broken.

Meanwhile, on the north of the Pedregal, Gen. Worth was making vigorous preparations to carry the position of San Antonio. Clarke's brigade and Col. C. F. Smith's light battalion were directed to march over the field of lava, south of the hacienda, and cut the line of retreat. Garland's brigade and Duncan's battery approached by the causeway in front, so as to strike in that quarter, when Clarke had gained the rear. But Gen. Bravo, the commander of the garrison, did not wait for the development of these plans. On learning the fate of Valencia, the main body retreated two and a half miles northward, to join the grand army then collected and collecting for the defense of Cherubusco. The rear guard fled from the fire of Clarke's brigade across the marshes and ditches, east of the causeway, in the direction of Mexicalcingo. Gen. Worth pushed forward through the abandoned works at the hacienda of San Antonio, and neglecting the fugitives in the fields, took the main road to Cherubusco. Although possessed of little information respecting the position or strength of the Mexican defenses he commenced the attack immediately.

Santa Anna's forces were drawn up a few hundred yards north of the village, on the opposite side of a stream that ran almost due east. Its banks were artificially raised to prevent overflow in time of freshets, and planted with rows of the maguey plant, affording an excellent shelter to screen the movements and guard the safety of troops.

At the bridge, on the highway from San Antonio to the capital, was the Tete de Pont, a fortification solidly and scientifically built. It was defended in part by one hundred deserters from the American army, who fought with the energy of despair. Near the western edge of the village stood a stone convent of massive proportions and great strength, now temporarily converted into a fort. It was surrounded by a field work, and its guns completely swept the whole field on the south and west. Here was stationed Gen. Rincon with three thousand men. The reserve, composed of troops continually arriving from the city, took position in the road north of the Tete de Pont, at right angles with the lines of Santa Anna.

The accompanying description of the battle is from the pen of Lieut. Lyon:

"The battle of Contreras having been gained on the morning of the 20th, Gen. Worth, who had not taken part in it, now hurried forward to bring on an engagement with his own division, and blundered upon the tete du pont, near the convent of Cherubusco. Here his division were drawn up and exposed to a murderous fire from the strong defences of the tete du pont, and to a flank fire from the works at the convent.

"The troops at Contreras having advanced toward the city, were sent to the assistance of Worth, and made an attack upon Cherubusco. These fortifications were surrounded by a dense growth of maguey, outside of which were large fields of corn. Our advance through the corn was necessarily blind and confused, so that, when within range of the enemy's guns, we were too much disordered to make a charge, and were compelled to stand exposed to a fire from men concealed among the maguey plants, behind breast works, and in the convent. Their volleys were very destructive to our ranks, which suffered many and severe casualties. Our own fire upon them was also effective.

"After retaining their position for more than an hour, the enemy were on the point of retreating, when the work (the convent) was stormed and carried. Here were secured about eleven hundred prisoners, among whom were over a hundred deserters from our army. The tete du pont was carried about the same time by Worth's division.

"A considerable force had been sent around to the rear of these works to cut off the retreat of the enemy. Before reaching the Augustine road leading to town, they were met at Portales by a large body of Mexicans, who engaged them warmly, and did not retire until the surrender at Cherubusco.

"This retreat was sharply followed by a small party of dragoons, who dashed boldly forward and entered the garita of San Antonio. Had our infantry and artillery now pushed forward, five lives would not have been lost in gaining entire possession of the city of Mexico.

"The attack upon Cherubusco, and consequent loss of life, was wholly unnecessary. Infantry could readily pass by the place to the right or left. Artillery, without going one iota out of the way, could have found an easy and practicable road by La Piedad. But Gen. Worth, having no share in the glory of Contreras, was determined to bring his division into action under whatever disadvantages. He, therefore battled against the works at Cherubusco, and having become engaged it was necessary to support him with additional force.

"Night now set in with rain and everything became quiet."

Never has the bravery of American soldiers, or the skill of American officers been more conspicuously displayed, than in the battle of Cherubusco. The enemy, on familiar ground and behind strong fortifications, outnumbered the assailants more than three to one. On the other hand, the Americans were obliged to advance over a field entirely unexplored, against defences of unknown character, in the face of a destructive fire from cannon and musketry. Different commands fought almost independently. Communication between the separate divisions was extremely difficult. The incessant roar of ordnance and crash of fire-arms, near and far, were the only messages of comrade to comrade. But the voice was mighty in inspiration. Every man acted the hero. The lines closed steadily and resistlessly upon the enemy, till the works were all carried, and the Mexican host annihilated as an army.

Dear, however, was the price of victory. One thousand of the Americans, of whom seventy-six were officers, were killed or wounded.

Capt. T. Morris, acting commander of the regiment, in his official report of the part taken by the second infantry in the events of the day, says, "Capt. Casey, among the first to enter the works, (at Contreras,) captured two pieces of the enemy's artillery, driving him from them, and then pushed forward with a detachment of the regiment, accompanied by Capt. Wessels and Lieut. Lyon, and pressed hotly upon the rear of the enemy, who soon raised a number of white flags, and their surrender was immediately accepted, when about two hundred prisoners, together with two pieces of artillery, were taken."

Lieut. Lyon aided in turning several guns upon the Mexicans, but, from want of proper materials, these could not be discharged.

Capt. Morris continues, "I here take the opportunity of recommending these two officers, (Captains Casey and Wessels,) together with Capt. J. R. Smith and First Lieut. Lyon, to the *special notice* of the Colonel commanding the brigade.

Lyon was promoted Brevet Captain August 20th, 1847, "for gallant and meritorious conduct in the battles of Contreras and Cherubusco, Mexico." He was made Captain in full, June 11th, 1851, by regular promotion.

CHAPTER V.

On the morning of August 21st, the army was distributed among the various villages in the vicinity of the capital, in a manner that indicated the suspension of hostilities. Gen. Scott was induced, by the representations of intelligent foreign and American residents in the city, to pause in the midst of victories in order to offer again the olive branch of peace. He no doubt acted from the humane desire of avoiding further bloodshed and of putting an honorable end to the war. But he under estimated the ridiculous vanity of the Mexican character, and the profound artifice and duplicity of the Mexican President. An armistice was agreed upon, and negotiations were commenced. The step was strongly condemned by many officers.

Lieut. Lyon thus expresses his views of the matter—"An armistice is determined upon to allow the

6

American minister, (Mr. Trist,) to propose terms of peace, without any security of success, or any compensation for consenting not to take the city when fairly within our grasp. From the attitude in which the parties stand, Mexico appears as conqueror, and as magnanimously consenting to listen to the humble terms of our minister. He proposes terms involving such a sacrifice of the advantages obtained by the arms and funds of the United States, that he feels sure Mexico will eagerly embrace the offer.

"Encouraged by the imbecility shown in the transaction, Mexico affects indignity at the idea of losing a small portion of the large conquests we have made, and taking advantage of time, perfects her fortifications, reorganizes her distracted forces, and prepares for a fierce encounter which she expects to sustain successfully, from the reduced condition of the American army, and from the belief that it is near starvation."

September 7th, 1847. "The negotiations having terminated, as also the armistice, our brigade, (Col. Riley's,) started from the village of Coyacan, where it had been quartered since the 20th of August, and moved towards the city, till we came upon the enemy's picket near La Piedad. Here remained during the night.

September 8th. "During the armistice, Gen. Worth's division was quartered in the village of Tacubaya, near Molino del Rey, which was supposed to be a foundery for ordnance. On the morning of the 8th, Gen. Worth was ordered to destroy the work. It might easily have been done by bombardment with heavy artillery, of which there was abundance. But he pushed forward his infantry against the stone walls of the position, and into the mouths of the cannon. The consequence was the loss, in killed and wounded, of nearly a thousand men, without any advantage, as the position was abandoned as soon as gained. A proper use of heavy artillery would have obtained all that was desired, without the loss of a single man.

September 12th. "The serious loss on the 8th dispirited the army very much, and made it incumbent to be cautious about unnecessary exposure of life. Consequently, demonstrations upon the city were suspended. After close reconnoissances, it was decided to open batteries upon the works at Chapultepec, and also from La Piedad, where Gen. Twiggs' division now lay. The bombardment of Chapultepec continued through the day.

September 13th. "The height of Chapultepec was stormed about eight o'clock in the morning and carried. This successful enterprise was rapidly followed by the advancement of our troops on the causeways leading thence to the city. Our heavy ordnance was brought forward with good effect, and the arches of the aqueduct afforded cover for the advance of our infantry, who, with the aid of the artillery, were soon in front of the gates of the city. There a severe and protracted struggle ensued, which, however, resulted favorably. Our troops entered the city at the gates Belin and San Cosme, just at night. Col. Riley's brigade having done little since the termination of the armistice, we were now moved forward to storm some of the positions inside of the city, still occupied by the enemy. We moved round to the north-west of the city, and having arrived at the gate, stopped for the night.

September 14th. "The city authorities having announced that Santa Anna and his army had left the place, we started forward, expecting a peaceful entrance. Soon after entering the town, we were fired upon in all directions from the tops of houses, windows, balconies and street corners. Our troops were sent to different parts of the city, and advanced from place to place over the tops of buildings. Many Mexicans were destroyed during the day. Our loss was not great, nor in proportion to that of the enemy."

During the street fight on the 14th, Lyon was

struck in the leg by a musket ball. Although the wound was slight, it became inflamed from his constant exertions, and disabled him for several days.

The dangers and hardships of the campaign were virtually ended by the triumphal entry of the American army into the Mexican capital. The series of brilliant victories which it achieved during the previous month, seem dream-like and marvelous. On the seventh of August, ten thousand five hundred men marched from Puebla to capture a city of one hundred and eighty thousand inhabitants, environed by a formidable array of defenses, and garrisoned by thirty-five thousand troops. How armies were routed and driven with excessive carnage from positions deemed impregnable by their defenders, before the little band of invincibles, will remain a wonder of history. On all occasions our officers of all grades displayed consummate skill and valor. The soldiery, under such guidance, learned to look upon victory as inevitable, and every where fought most obstinately till the victory was won.

On the first of November a large train was to start from the city of Mexico for Vera Cruz. The escort required to guard it calling for an officer from the second infantry, Lyon volunteered his services. Delaying one day (the fifth) in Puebla, the train reached its destination the 15th. Numerous bands of guerrillas were ranging through the country and hovering about the National Road, who subsisted by robbery and plunder. Want of men rendered it impossible for Gen. Scott to garrison isolated strongholds on the long line of march. A hostile country, exposed in many places to the incursions of large troops of banditti, lay between the army of invasion and the port which formed the only avenue of communication with countrymen at home. Mexicans, demoralized by overwhelming defeats in battle, sought revenge in punishing weak detachments.

The escort in this case, being very small for the length of the train, expected that the guerrillas would muster sufficient courage to seize upon some of the passes, and perhaps retard its progress. During the whole journey, however, not a gun was fired or hostile demonstration attempted, though Mexican cavalry were several times descried in the distance.

Lyon found Puebla sadly changed. Gen. Scott left there a large number of invalids under the care of Col. Childs. His effective force numbered about five hundred. Santa Anna, having gathered a few fragments of his broken army, appeared before the town on the 22d of September, and three days later summoned the commander to surrender. The invitation was politely declined. Col. Childs occupied of guerrillas were ranging through the country and hovering about the National Road, who subsisted by robbery and plunder. Want of men rendered it impossible for Gen. Scott to garrison isolated strongholds on the long line of march. A hostile country, exposed in many places to the incursions of large troops of banditti, lay between the army of invasion and the port which formed the only avenue of communication with countrymen at home. Mexicans, demoralized by overwhelming defeats in battle, sought revenge in punishing weak detachments.

The escort in this case, being very small for the length of the train, expected that the guerrillas would muster sufficient courage to seize upon some of the passes, and perhaps retard its progress. During the whole journey, however, not a gun was fired or hostile demonstration attempted, though Mexican cavalry were several times descried in the distance.

Lyon found Puebla sadly changed. Gen. Scott left there a large number of invalids under the care of Col. Childs. His effective force numbered about five hundred. Santa Anna, having gathered a few fragments of his broken army, appeared before the town on the 22d of September, and three days later summoned the commander to surrender. The invitation was politely declined. Col. Childs occupied the heights in the vicinity of the city. Santa Anna, from the town proper, began to bombard the American intrenchments. The fire was returned with spirit, and though the artillery on both sides did little harm, the enemy were held in check.

Meanwhile the Mexicans, sorely distressed for the means of subsistence, showed symptoms of insubordination. The general was forced to procure supplies at once, or desist from further efforts. It was now reported that a valuable train was approaching from Vera Cruz, and on the first of October, Santa Anna withdrew the troops from Puebla to intercept it. Before coming, however, to any general engagement, they nearly all deserted him, and this child of checkered fortune was again left a homeless and friendless wanderer.

Thus ingloriously and sadly ended the political career of Santa Anna in Mexico. Recalled from exile a few months before, and hailed as the deliverer of the nation, he applied all the powers of his remarkable genius to the task before him. Three large armies he raised and lost. At Buena Vista, Cerro Gordo, and in the valley of Mexico, were dissipated the legions with which he battled in vain to crush the invader. Amid discontents, treachery and revolutionary movements at home, he had long managed to retain ascendency by his wonderful skill in the arts of intrigue.

No one, either friend or foe, who took part in that eventful drama, at all approached the Mexican chief in far reaching and over reaching diplomacy. Seldom has genius of so rare a quality been so uniformly unfortunate. Raised at once from seclusion to the height of popularity and power, he sunk down in a few months, despite prodigious efforts to stem the current of fate, into the depths of disfavor and humiliation.

Had a general so thoroughly acquainted with the resources of the country, and so regally endowed with the essential attributes of a leader, commanded brave men, far different would have been the issue of the war. But Santa Anna stood alone. Domestic revolutions had debauched the nation. Subordinates of high rank, in the midst of public calamities, were engrossed with the intrigues of political factions. Thus his masterly efforts were frustrated by the poltroonery of the army, and the groveling ambition of party leaders.

Lyon makes interesting comments on the state of affairs along the National road.

"The siege of Puebla, by Santa Anna, after his services at the city of Mexico were dispensed with, though vexatious from its obstinacy, was much less damaging to our troops than is usually believed; for they held possession of a large portion of the city on the northern side, and did not suffer in the least from want of food or water. They would also have escaped injury from the enemy's fire, but for their own voluntary and reckless attacks. Our troops often showed their characteristic rashness and folly, by charging upon stone walls and other works defended by Mexicans.

"The affair of Capt. Walker at Huamantla, by which he lost his life, was also rash in the extreme, and like many other blunders in this war, would never be overlooked or excused, (even by a people as enthusiastic as ours,) were it not for the uniform and brilliant success of our arms. We could never hope for such results by fighting in like manner against any other than a Mexican foe.

"The inhabitants of Puebla are now returning home and manifest much chagrin and disappointment at the conduct of the troops under Gen. Lane. Being raw, reckless and undisciplined, their manners are highly offensive to one accustomed to the courteous bearing of regulars.

"In Vera Cruz a great change has taken place from the removal of natives and the establishment of Americans in their place. Some merchants and tradesmen still remain and drive a profitable business; but office-holders, drovers and nondescripts have been obliged to leave in large numbers. Americans are rapidly taking the vacant places, and Yankee signs of all sorts are stuck upon most of the windows and doors. Yankee enterprise is also rebuilding the portion of the city destroyed by the bombardment, and indeed the place begins to wear the appearance of a thorough going Yankee town.

"Gen. Lane has at Puebla between three and four thousand men; Gen. Patterson about the same number at Jalapa; the 15th infantry is at the National Bridge; a battalion of Georgia volunteers at San Juan; and a small detachment of Pennsylvania volunteers at the castle of Perote. Within a few days Gen. Butler has started for the interior with six thousand men and more are soon to follow. There are now over twenty thousand U. S. troops in the country, and others still arriving. Unless Uncle Sam levies upon Mexico, his pockets will be sorely drained to support the wild and wasteful boys whom he has sent here."

The train and escort under command of Col. Johnston of the voltigeurs, left Vera Cruz for Mexico, November 29th, and reached its destination the 20th of December, having stopped two days at Jalapa and one at Puebla, to allow the forces of Gen. Butler to get out of the way, as he persisted in keeping ahead.

Lyon gives a brief epitome of events at the capital since his departure nearly two months before.

"On arriving at the city of Mexico, I find many military changes have recently been made. Generals Worth and Pillow, and Bvt. Lt. Col. Duncan are in arrest; Gen. Twiggs has gone to Vera Cruz to take command of the post; Gen. Pierce has resigned; and Generals Quitman and Shields have left the country. In consequence Col. Riley, second infantry, has become third in command, and has been sent with a separate brigade to Tacubaya, a beautiful village about three miles south-west from the city.

"The Pittsburg Post having published a letter, purporting to be from the pen of an officer, which described the operations of Worth's column in the valley of Mexico, and noticed Worth, and other officers of his division, favorably, while it reflected upon Gen. Scott's armistice; the Commander-in-chief availed himself of an order from the President, directing officers not to write from the seat of war for publication, nor allow their letters to become public. Having reiterated the order, Gen. Scott characterized the letter as "scandalous," and said it required a good deal of charity not to believe that the persons most conspicuous in it were the authors of it, or at least procured it to be written.

This insulting imputation required Worth to inquire if he was pointed at by this order. Gen. Scott replied that it pointed at the authors of the letter. Gen. Worth responded that his question was not answered, and Gen. Scott again replied it was all the answer he should give. Hereupon Gen. Worth perferred charges against Gen. Scott, for ungentlemanly and unofficer-like conduct. These, together with the accompanying letter addressed to the Secretary of War, Gen. Scott considered disrespectful to himself, and Worth was accordingly arrested. In the meantime Col. Duncan acknowledged himself to be the author of the "scandalous" letter, and was arrested for violation of the President's order. Gen. Pillow was arrested for some disrespectful communication addressed to Gen. Scott.

"Generals Butler, Patterson and Lane are in the city. Gen. Cushing has a separate brigade and is stationed at San Angel, six miles south."

The fighting in Mexico was over and Peace at hand. Peña y Peña, President of the Supreme Court of Justice, assumed the reins of government after the compulsory resignation of Santa Anna. He addressed eloquent appeals to the different states, urging them to send deputies to Queretaro, with a view to put an end to the war by negotiation. The old congress was dissolved on the

1st of January, and the next congress, composed of recently elected members, organized on the 8th.

Meanwhile, the powers of Mr. Trist, the American commissioner, had been withdrawn by President Polk. This man, however, did not permit either the total want of authority, or the suggestions of modesty, to restrain him from volunteering his services as agent of the United States. Since his advent in the country he had been conspicuous in numerous intrigues, and having acquired a taste for Mexican negotiations, found it impossible to tear himself away from the delightful field. He strove to justify his assumption of power, on the ground that the necessities of the case were imperative. The treaty that grew out of this unauthorized mediation, was signed February 2d, 1848, at Guadalupe Hidalgo, by Nicholas P. Trist, on the part of the United States, and three commissioners on the part of Mexico. It was formally submitted, by President Polk to the American Senate, notwithstanding its spurious birth, and after some discussion, and several important amendments, was ratified by that body the 10th of March.

The President appointed Nathan Clifford, Attorney-General, and Ambrose Sevier, United States Senator, to carry the treaty, as modified, to Mexico. The congress of that country met, after some delay, and, by a large majority, ratified the instrument.

The two nations were now at peace, and the victorious army was at liberty to return home.

On the 30th of May, the advance, under Gen. Patterson, left Mexico for Vera Cruz. Other divisions followed at short intervals. The second division of regulars, to which Lyon belonged, now under the command of Gen. Kearney, started, on the 6th of June, and reached Perote, one hundred and sixty miles distant, on the 14th. Having remained there five days they moved on to Jalapa.

Gen. Worth commanded the rear. He left the city of Mexico on the 12th of June, when all authority was transferred to the Mexicans. On the 24th of the same month the last of his forces reached Jalapa.

Writing from Jalapa, while his division was waiting there, Lyon says:

"On leaving the large city of Mexico, where our army has remained for nearly nine months, scarce an American feels the slightest regret, or can call to mind a single attraction for which he would wish to stay longer. On the entrance of the American Army into the city, the whole Mexican population were not only cold and repulsive in their conduct, but either felt, or affected, a haughty superiority and frowning contempt. This arose, in part, no doubt, from a preconceived notion, natural to all Spaniards and their descendants, and now artfully encouraged by designing men, that they are superior to every people, and particularly to the Americans. These were represented as a horde of Vandals, descending in savage ferocity upon their innocent and unoffending neighbors, to desecrate their holy temples, destroy their pure religion, and to degrade and enslave their people.

"A short experience, however, served to dissipate, in part, these various illusions. Many of them, particularly the ladies, evinced a strong desire to become acquainted with American Officers. From this they were long dissuaded by priests and others, who threatened persecution, both from neighbors and the government, against such as showed favor or countenance to the invader. But threats did not entirely avail, for, on observing the friendly disposition of the Mexican ladies, our officers evinced their appreciation of the compliment by endeavoring to render themselves agreeable in turn. This led, in some cases, to a very favorable understanding, and nothing but the dread of persecution, on the withdrawal of our troops, prevented an extensive and pleasant acquaintance.

"Among the women of the upper classes in Mexico

there seemed to be many of excellent character and disposition. They are beautiful in form and features, transcendently graceful, and appear every way worthy of a better race than the one around them.

"But you will conclude from these remarks that I am justifying your apprehension that I might fall in love with some Mexican Siñolita. Even had I been so indiscreet, you must remember that I am now returning to our own good country, there to behold the fair faces of American ladies, so pure and bright, so beautiful and lovely, that if I do not lose my senses altogether, I shall certainly lose all recollection of the ladies of Mexico."

Speaking of the desires and prospects of the officers, he continues, "Most of us would like to go back to the north, where we came from, but all depends on the pleasure of our excellent president, and his pleasure, I fear, will conduce very little to our own."

Lyon's regiment reached Vera Cruz the 2d of July. Finding no transports in readiness it encamped on the beach near the city, where all suffered greatly from the intense heat. There were numerous cases of sickness, caused, partly by the insalubrity of the place, and partly by the excessive fatigue of recent marches, which, by order of Gen. Kearney, had been long and rapid.

CHAPTER VI.

Six companies of the second infantry, including Lyon's, embarked for New Orleans the 8th of July, '48, on board the ship Robert Parker. Having arrived at that city the 17th of the same month, the regiment left the next day for Pascagoula, a fashionable summer resort on the Gulf, in Jackson County, Mississippi. Here they landed and encamped, on the 20th, expecting to remain several months to discharge war men, recruit and reorganize. But orders soon came to repair with haste to St. Louis, Missouri. Accordingly, the wearied troops broke up the encampment, on the 25th, and the next night were again in New Orleans. The evening of the 28th, the entire regiment left on the steamer Sultana, for St. Louis, and reached its destination the 3d of August, when the men were transferred to Jefferson Barracks.

Lyon says of the passage:

"Good company and fine accommodations contributed to render our trip up the Mississippi pleasant. But in passing along this great outlet of the glorious and thriving West, I was disappointed to find so few settlements on the banks of the river, and the towns all small. The whole margin of the stream, for a great distance from the banks, is a rich alluvial bottom, with the immense vegetable growth of many past ages still undisturbed."

But the regiment was not destined to enjoy a lengthy period of repose, or remain long amid the comforts and refinements of the older states. Some time before, California had been designated as the next theatre of its operations. Gen. Kearney, commander at Jefferson Barracks, was vested with wide discretionary powers as to the time and manner of forwarding the troops to that territory, since his ample knowledge of the country, derived from personal experience, well fitted him for the direction of the matter. As the officers were desirous of going by sea, he recommended that course to the Secretary of War.

During the month of August, Capt. Lyon was busily engaged in drilling recruits, with which the regiment, greatly reduced by fighting and disease, was filling up to the required standard, preparatory to its departure. Having obtained leave of abse he started the last day of the month to revisit the East and the home of childhood.

Being a close observer of society, and of the effects of different social systems upon the prosperity and general development of communities, he compared, as carefully as opportunities would allow, the cities and villages on the route with those which he had recently seen in the passage from New Orleans to St. Louis. His mind had been early impressed with the conviction that servile labor afforded an inadequate basis for genuine and permanent growth. Economists, reared amid northern institutions, assume, as an axiomatic truth, that free competition, under a liberal form of government, presents the prime requisite of a prosperity at once self-sustained, self-reproducing, and, therefore, perpetual. With regard to questions of this character, opinions generally come as an inheritance, and are cherished through life as precious heir-looms. But, in this case, the contrast between the stagnant towns, ruinous habitations and neglected acres on the banks of the Mississippi, and the exuberance of thrift and culture, so common at the north, were certainly suggestive of radical differences in the organization of the two sections.

Lyon, on the way home, turned aside to spend a few days at Sackets Harbor, where he was stationed for four years previous to the campaign in Mexico. The visit was extremely satisfactory. He lingered with delight amid scenes that brought to mind the social enjoyments, the communings of friendship, the tranquil hours of study and thought, which were then unbroken by the din of war. But the most eloquent appeals to his warm heart, were the greetings of the friends of by-gone days.

He arrived home the 15th of September, finding his "good mother in tolerable health, and not suffering from the weight of years as much as, in her advanced age, might be expected."

After a pleasant visit among relatives and friends, he rejoined his regiment at Fort Hamilton, in New York harbor. It had been sent forward from St. Louis with the view of going to California by sea.

Companies C, G, and I, with Bvt. Brig. Gen. Riley, sailed on the "Iowa;" companies A and F, on the "Mary and Adeline;" companies D and H, on the "Rome." The three remaining companies were left behind to procure additional transports. The embarkation took place on the 5th of November, and a few days after the ships started on the voyage.

After a somewhat tempestuous passage, the two hills on Cape Frio appear in sight on the morning tioned for four years previous to the campaign in Mexico. The visit was extremely satisfactory. He lingered with delight amid scenes that brought to mind the social enjoyments, the communings of friendship, the tranquil hours of study and thought, which were then unbroken by the din of war. But the most eloquent appeals to his warm heart, were the greetings of the friends of by-gone days.

He arrived home the 15th of September, finding his "good mother in tolerable health, and not suffering from the weight of years as much as, in her advanced age, might be expected."

After a pleasant visit among relatives and friends, he rejoined his regiment at Fort Hamilton, in New York harbor. It had been sent forward from St. Louis with the view of going to California by sea.

Companies C, G, and I, with Bvt. Brig. Gen. Riley, sailed on the "Iowa;" companies A and F, on the "Mary and Adeline;" companies D and H, on the "Rome." The three remaining companies were left behind to procure additional transports. The embarkation took place on the 5th of November, and a few days after the ships started on the voyage.

After a somewhat tempestuous passage, the two hills on Cape Frio appear in sight on the morning of December 23d, and by nightfall the light at the entrance to the harbor of Rio Janeiro glimmers in the distance. The next morning the ship was standing in toward the mountain chain that here skirts the coast of Brazil. Passing through a narrow inlet between two lofty cones, the ship was anchored in the majestic bay of Rio Janeiro, to await the inspection of the custom house and quarantine officers. Many gentlemen of the U. S. navy came on board during the day to welcome their fellow countrymen, and discuss the news from home. They were mostly connected with the Brandywine and Brig Perry, which were then in port, having been stationed on the coast of Brazil for the suppression of the slave-trade. The traffic was carried on boldly by direct importations from Africa, and notwithstanding the vigilance of the cruisers, many of the piratical miscreants eluded capture. A little before two slavers had been taken while sailing under the American flag, and the crews sent to the States for trial.

On the 25th, the "Rome" floated up the bay and came to anchor near the city. In the afternoon the "Iowa" entered the harbor.

The stay at Rio Janeiro was delightfully occupied by the officers of the regiment in visiting the celebrities of the place and enjoying the hospitalities which were profusely extended to them by their countrymen. Members of the navy, numbers of whom were comparatively at home in the city, were unwearied in efforts to make the time pass agreeably. Several elegant entertainments were provided where the songs of the Union carried home the thoughts of soldier and sailor, making them doubly proud of their own sweet land of liberty. When the day of departure came, those who had met as strangers a few days before, separated with the mutual feelings which are usually reserved for the tried friendships of years.

Capt. Lyon explored the town quite thoroughly, and made a record of his observations.

"The harbor of Rio is very capacious, being twenty miles in length and three in width. The city, which is on the south side of the bay, is built on islands, hills and valleys, into which the shore is everywhere broken. It is much scattered and can not be well seen from the harbor. The Spanish style of architecture prevails, the buildings being of stone. Granite is abundant and much used. It is this rock which composes the mountains around the harbor, that rise in succession as they recede, making an amphitheatre at once beautiful and majestic."

A fresh breeze from the land carried the "Rome" gaily out of the harbor of Rio Janeiro the 2d of

January, 1849, and in a few hours the lofty mountain tops were lost to view. Favoring breezes wafted her swiftly onward into the boisterous seas that beat upon the southern shores of the continent. Here they found a disagreeable climate, and were much delayed by adverse winds. But strange sights and experiences afforded ample compensation for the annoyance of cold and tempest. At morning and night the sun skirted along the horizon, as if afraid to venture far toward the zenith, or to plunge beneath the waves. The twilight continued through the night. The heavens were studded with new constellations and glowed with unfamiliar lights. Cape Horn was at length doubled and the ship was pointed toward a more genial clime.

As the heavy fog rose from the sea at midday on the ninth of February, the entrance to the bay of Valparaiso was seen twelve miles ahead. The Rome came to her anchorage about four o'clock in the afternoon, and found the Iowa two days before her.

Lyon, in describing the appearance of the city, writes: "The harbor of Valparaiso is an indentation into the mountain ridge, which here rises like a steep wall along the coast. The city is built on the southern extremity of the bay, and consists of one, and in some places of two streets extending for a great distance from east to west, near the water's edge. Here the principal part of the business is transacted, and here, also, are many fine residences. The streets, though narrow, are clean and well paved. Above and behind them rise almost perpendicular hills, on which the dwellings of the lower classes are built. The town contains fifty thousand inhabitants, who seem well behaved and polite to strangers, and compare favorably with other descendants of the Spaniards in America.

"During our stay in Valparaiso, the American residents were exceedingly attentive to us, entertaining us with rides, dinners, and parties—courtesies peculiarly grateful to one in a strange and distant land."

The Rome left Valparaiso the 16th of February. Entertainments were given on board, the evenings of both the 3d and 4th of March, to celebrate the events of Mr. Polk's administration, and honor the advent of Gen. Taylor's. Capt. Lyon placed a much higher estimate upon the skill which the retiring President had shown in the management of state affairs, than upon his rectitude in the distribution of political favors. "Mr. Polk's administration has been engaged in many important enterprises, and has managed all with distinguished ability, firmness and perseverance· and has been eminently successful in every measure of national policy. But in that prerogative of the executive most liable to abuse—political patronage—Mr. Polk has been grossly selfish, short-sighted and corrupt; both degrading his office and doing mischief to his country.

"Gen. Taylor, from natural integrity of purpose, will honestly and perhaps firmly pursue the course which he believes to be for the national good. But defective education and the want of experience will render it dangerous for him to modify the policy of government in material matters, unless guided by advisers of marked ability."

The Rome arrived at Monterey, California, April 6th, 1849. On the 12th the Iowa entered the harbor, and the following day Gen. Riley entered upon his duties as Governor of the territory.

Less than three years before, the American flag was first raised at Monterey and San Francisco. In the course of a few months a small detachment of United States marines and soldiers succeeded in establishing the supremacy of their government over an immense area of country on the coast of the Pacific. At that time California was almost a *terra incognita*, and seemed likely to remain so for many years to come. But in the swift march of events, the eyes of the world were soon centered upon this long neglected region. Suddenly the tidings went forth over mountain and over sea, that treasures of untold value lay buried in her bosom. In the olden days empires shook with the trumpet-blasts that summoned the people to reclaim the Holy Sepulchre. The footsteps of high-born and lowly alike, throughout the broad domain of christendom, were turned reverently towards the Orient to deliver the sacred fields of Palestine from the rule of the infidel. If the modern crusades to the land of gold be less disinterested and less poetical, they will probably prove more important in their influence upon the progress of civilization.

Here, at last, a nation was born in a day. From four continents and from distant islands, men flocked to the new El Dorado by thousands. The rapid growth of the successive tiers of states that already occupied half the breadth of the North American territory, ceased to excite astonishment, now that another commonwealth, rich in all resources of empire, had attained the stature of manhood almost at the moment of birth. California, like Minerva, leaped forth in panoply from the brain of her sire.

The second regiment of infantry reached Monterey when the frenzy of the gold excitement was at its height. The tide of emigration was rapidly pouring upon the shores of the country the waves of population. Never before was such a heterogeneous mass of humanity thrown together in close and intimate contact. Men of all religions and no religion—of every grade of moral and social development, from the unkempt savage to the polished gentleman, were digging in the same pits and mingling freely in the intercourse of daily life. Among a population composed of elements so incongruous, it was reasonable to expect numerous delegations of villains and desperadoes. California offered a tempting field for the operations of cut-throats, gamesters, and scoundrels of every variety of attainments. Here was an asylum from the consequences of past crimes, and here were hosts of unsophisticated adventurers, seemingly ready victims for entanglement in the artfully contrived snares of cunning and duplicity.

Nor was an expectation so natural at all in fault. California became the rendezvous of felons, malefactors, convicts who had graduated in the prisons of other lands, drunkards, vagabonds, adepts in all elaborate systems of iniquity, pirates, land-sharks, and other classes innumerable and nameless, who plunged without scruple into schemes of fraud, robbery and plunder. Nearly every city of Europe and America, not to mention Asia and the islands of the sea, yielded its quota of abandoned wretches to swell the flood of emigration to the land of gold. Friends of religion, order and civilization, who anxiously watched the westward progress of the star of empire, as it followed the course of the sun around the earth, trembled for the new State on the shores of the Pacific. Thousands of good citizens, with hearts loyal to justice and right, had also, it is true, gone thither to seek homes and fortune. Elements so powerful and so radically at variance, could not long live side by side in peace. Another of the ever recurring battles between good and evil, justice and iniquity, was to be fought. Upon the issue hung the fate of a territory bounteously endowed with the richest gifts of nature ; and in that fate was involved the destiny of millions unborn.

Many circumstances seemed ominous. The unorganized condition of affairs threw together the well disposed and the vicious in promiscuous association. Evil communications corrupt good manners. Garments, hitherto unsoiled, might now be stained by the thick pollution which flourished everywhere. Emigrants were separated, too, from the most precious and potent influences that in years agone had served both to restrain and ennoble. Men herded together in large crowds with no mothers, wives, or sisters near to point them heavenward. Few churches if any, had been established at the mines, so as to embrace the neglected laborer within her kind and sheltering fold. While the most effective agencies for the preservation and diffusion of virtue were dormant, all the machinery of the Power of Darkness was driven to its utmost capacity. Disorder and riot, corruption and violence, bore sway as never before within the jurisdiction of the United States.

Yet, notwithstanding the complexity of evils which at first cast ominous shadows athwart the future pathway of California, she happily emerged soon from the gloom, and now, after the lapse of a decade, compares favorably with the best of her sisters in the qualities that give assurance of a noble and glorious destiny. Crime, once so open and insolent, has been crushed with iron hand. Vice has withdrawn from market-places and street corners, to skulk timidly in by-ways. Speedy retribution overwhelmed the cohorts of wickedness that vainly strove to make the future temple of civilization a den of thieves. Guilt, in many ways, stung itself to death. As the original crop of renegades disappeared, fresh hordes were intimidated by the vigorous administration of justice, from rushing in to fill their places.

Such progress, in the right direction, in the face of innumerable obstacles, should give us confidence in the inherent strength of our Government. A self-organized society sprung up amid the chaos of lawless, greedy and discordant elements, which, in a short period, without assistance from armies or navies, succeeded in asserting its supremacy over all. This was a severe but most satisfactory trial of the formative energy of free institutions. No campaign of martial conqueror ever equaled in magnitude the peaceful triumph of order and virtue, though left to fight the battle alone. If civil liberty, as understood by the founders of our constitution, be a vapory mist that can hang upon the hills only at the early dawn of national existence, without coherence to withstand the fiery trials of the meridian, we should never have witnessed the rapid and sure reforms effected under its banners in California. The wonderful record of that State ought to assure us that neither foreign power, nor domestic discontent, can avail to overthrow a fabric reared upon the foundations planted by the wisdom and consecrated by the blood of the patriots of the Revolution.

At the time when the second infantry landed at Monterey, the army officers were naturally apprehensive that their services might be called in requisition for the discharge of most unpleasant duties. Americans at the mines, profoundly impressed with the conviction that the "Manifest Destiny" of the race justified any claims, however extravagant, regarded the gold as their own exclusive property, and looked with evil eye upon the crowds of semi-barbarous interlopers who flocked thither to share the spoils. These feelings of dislike, finding expressions in acts of annoyance and derision, were, at first, heartily reciprocated. Frequent and bloody broils seemed imminent. Had the United States forces been sufficiently strong, large detachments would probably have been stationed in the mining districts as a precautionary measure. Fortunately, perhaps, the troops at Col. Riley's disposal were too few to permit the arrangement. Chinamen and Yankees, Sandwich-Islanders and Europeans were left to dig in company without interference or supervision from the soldiery of their affectionate Uncle at Washington. And, as the issue proved, the authority of the civil magistrate, aided by the good sense of the miners, was found adequate to the preservation of peace. Indeed the very prodigality of nature, after a while, served to reconcile dissimilar races, and inaugurate an era of mutual forbearance and good will. Perhaps the auspicious change was hastened by the fact that the incomparable and somewhat unscrupulous shrewdness of emigrants from the States had gradually devised many ingenious devices for transferring the dust of tawny skinned diggers into their own capacious sacks. Finding it easier to live by wits than by work, they made a great convenience of Sonorans and Asiatics, in carrying the idea into practical operation.

Military service in California was, under its best aspects, laborious and wearisome. A frontier, extending hundreds of miles, was to be protected against the incursions of the Indians. Some of the stations were buried in the depths of the wilderness, and almost entirely secluded from intercourse with the world. The comforts of life were scarce and costly. There were no daily newspapers or telegraphic dispatches, and very few altercations with the savages to break the heavy monotony.

Gen. Smith, commander of the Pacific Division, believed in the policy of keeping the troops as far as possible from the mines. The extravagant price of labor in the ordinary departments of industry, when compared with the pay of the soldier or sailor, caused, among these classes, intense dissatisfaction with services which now appeared to the last degree contemptible. Tales of the wondrous wealth of the gold region produced a general mania, that seized irresistibly upon mariners the moment their feet touched the enchanted soil. Vessels, on coming to anchor in the bay of San Francisco, lost their entire crews. Captains and mates barely withstood the temptation to abandon ship and follow the impetuous throng. Many of the oldest and most reliable mariners, with non-commissioned officers, deserted in a body from British men-of-war, a thing before unknown in the royal navy. The few companies of United States troops in the territory were reduced to mere skeletons from the same cause. In the morning the commanding officer would find that the sentry, with a band of confederates, embracing perhaps a third or fourth of his force, had left the camp under cover of night. There was no difficulty in discovering their course. Whether going singly, or in groups, they took the nearest way to the mines. Sometimes, until experience taught another lesson, pursuit was made with strong detachments. But this plan of procedure was soon abandoned, for the malady was found to be, not only deep-seated, but contagious. Nine times in ten the pursuers would join the fugitives, when, with fresh courage, the whole band hurried on in company. The officer in command could do nothing better than smother his chagrin, and, while riding homeward, ponder upon the insecurity of human power. So universal was the demoralization, that Gen. Persifor F. Smith, the experienced head of the Pacific Military Division, writing to the war department at the beginning of

1849, expressed regrets that any troops were on the route to California. He was confident that the men would all desert at the first opportunity. It was his opinion that the peace of the territory could be safely entrusted to emigrants, from the United States, acting through the civil authorities. The experiment of establishing the troops at a distance from the mines, in order to prevent desertions, after a thorough trial, proved signally ineffectual. The further the men were removed from the center of all thoughts and longings, the more intense became the gold mania. Dragoons, stationed at the extreme southern border, with sublime audacity, appropriated, to private use, the horses, arms and outfit furnished by government, and then unceremoniously *seceded* from the service. Infantry took the long road on foot. As it was impossible to carry provisions, deserters subsisted by plundering the inhabitants along the route. All opposition to these extortions was silenced by brute force. The troops sent thither for the protection of the people against Indian outrage, became far more terrible than the savages themselves.

After a brief interval at Monterey, Captain Lyon's company having been filled up by recruits to the standard of sixty-four privates, embarked April 16th, 1849, for San Diego. Company H sailed for the same destination ten days later. Lyon's force was subsequently instructed to remain and garrison the town of San Diego, while the other company was detached to form a part of the escort for the commissioners appointed to run the boundary line between the United States and Mexico.

Gen. Riley, taking a view of the military necessities of the territory quite different from that adopted by Gen. Smith, wished to keep the troops concentrated, and was averse to the establishment of posts on the distant frontiers. After furnishing a suitable guard to escort the commissioners, he was in favor of retaining the government supplies at Monterey and San Francisco, and of stationing at the mines all the army not required for the protection of the depots. This policy would expose the people of southern California to the unrestrained incursions of the Indians. But it was thought that the inhabitants would suffer less from the depredations of the natives than from the lawless violence of the fugitives sure to desert from any force sent thither. Dissimilarity of language and customs among the tribes, rendered any general combination against the whites highly improbable. Subsequent developments, however, occasioned material changes in the original programme of the General commanding.

For the next few years Captain Lyon was subjected much of the time to extreme hardships and privations. Short periods of repose, at different military stations, were interrupted by campaigns against the Indians, and long journeys, often performed alone, over the dreary mountains and deserts of the country. The sweets of quietude were seldom tasted. A disposition fearless, adventurous, and uneasy, except amid the excitement of incessant activity, kept him continually on the wing. The same rapidity and decision characterized his movements then, which ten years later carried dismay and overthrow into the camps of traitors in Missouri. Whenever he guided the affairs of an expedition, the blow was struck at once and effectively. Before the insolent savage heard even the faint premonitory rumblings of the distant thunder, the fury of the storm was upon him. If Lyon started forth on an errand of vengeance, his little band swept like a hurricane over plain, marsh and mountain. If called to accomplish a given work, he adopted plans with the quick intuition of genius, and always carried them into immediate execution.

Our national career has been so peaceful that few of the present generation of military commanders have had the opportunity to prove the qualities of leadership on the field. A martial people like the

Americans must, in the nature of things, contain a fair proportion of men fitted to guard her liberties and defend her honor by leading armies both to battle and to victory. In the dark hours of our history, generals equal to every emergency have sooner or later invariably appeared. Often, indeed, the lesson of wisdom was taught by painful reverses. Men taken from the common pursuits of life could hardly be expected to cope, at first, with officers carefully instructed in the schools, and trained by long experience in the camp. In the early years of the Revolution, the enemy gained many advantages over our badly equipped and poorly fed armies. An insolent foe occupied our towns and wasted our fields. But

"Sweet are the uses of adversity."

Every encounter, rich in instruction, strengthened the arm and steadied the purpose of those who had staked all for liberty. Before the close of the war our self-taught generals were fully the peers of the most accomplished British officers. But for nearly forty years no worthy foeman has tempted the keen edge of American steel. The blades of American soldiery have been unsheathed only against imbecile Mexicans and unskillful savages.

Wherever Lyon held control of military affairs, (and a respectable share of experience certainly fell to his lot,) he was signally successful. Men are great, not absolutely, but relatively. We judge of their abilities by placing them side by side with others who have been eminent in the same callings. We can not compare Lyon with the distinguished warriors of the past, for he was stricken down at the threshold of a career, of which the brilliant opening is but the prophecy of what might have been. Yet it is safe to say that he everywhere exhibited the very qualities of generalship that have shone most conspicuously in the first of military chieftains.

Officers like Lyon, of vigilance, zeal and skill were soon needed on the frontiers of California. By the XI. article of the treaty of Guadalupe Hidalgo, the United States government pledged itself to restrain the Indians within its jurisdiction from hostile incursions into the territory of Mexico. Good faith required the establishment of competent garrisons along the border.

Gen. Riley's hope that friendly relations would be maintained between the settlers and the natives, proved ill-founded. The United States, through both civil and military authorities, have for the most part shown a laudable anxiety to preserve peace with the primitive owners of the soil. But from the first the kind intentions of government have been continually frustrated by the rascalities of a certain class of whites that have ever hovered, vulture-like, on the border line of the settlements. For fourscore years, as the natives have retired before a civilization they were powerless to oppose, the same dark blood-stains have marked every step of the way. Wrongs perpetrated by the "sovereigns" of unbought acres have stung to madness the vindictive spirit of the savage, and provoked retaliatory blows. The frenzy of bad passions once aroused, pauses not in the thirst for revenge with the punishment of the guilty. Too often the hand of the now cruel and pitiless destroyer has fallen heavily also upon the habitations of the innocent. The crime startles and appals the community, while the provocation is forgotten. Government, besieged by the clamors of the populace, is forced from its position of protector, and is compelled to hunt down the Indian as if an irreclaimable enemy of the race. In the contest thus commenced, he either perishes in fight, or is driven from his heritage to find temporary repose in the seclusion of still more distant wilds. But like the traveler imprisoned between precipitous rocks and the rising tide, he finds no escape. Every moment the surging flood renders the foothold more precarious. With terrible and measured certainty the doom approaches, and no struggles can avert it. Sooner or later the waters close over him and he disappears forever from the haunts of men.

San Diego, where Capt. Lyon first found a resting spot on the western shores of the continent, and whither he more than once returned during his stay in California, is one of the garden spots of earth. Standing on the same parallel of latitude with Charleston, S. C., it enjoys a climate surpassing in salubrity and loveliness any to be found on the Atlantic coast. Further north, ocean-winds at certain seasons cover the coast with chill and disagreeable mists. Here, however, the air is pure and the sky brilliant. In summer the atmosphere is cooled by the sea-breeze, and tempered in winter by the warmth of ocean-currents. The order of the seasons is marked more by the varied succession of flowers, fruits and grain, than by abrupt changes in the temperature. Here, too, flourish the vine, the fig, and other lucious fruits of the tropics, in the same fields with the hardier growths of the North. To manifold advantages of climate and soil, is added a spacious and land-locked harbor. In the course of time, this new Eden on the Pacific will be the center of a peculiar civilization, blending the charms of repose with the grandeur and beauty, for which the materials are destined to float thither over the seas and descend in golden sands from the mountains.

Capt. Lyon's first experiences at San Diego were of the kind to be expected in a new country where all ordinary methods of procedure were swept away before the sudden irruption of thousands. Bricks were to be made without straw, and almost without food for the sustenance of the laborer. Supplies ordered for that post from San Francisco the previous winter, had failed to arrive. This was particularly unfortunate, as the stores for the escort detached to accompany the commissioners for running the line of division between California and Mexico were to be drawn from the depot at San Diego. Lyon was untiring in efforts to ascertain the wants of the service, and the best means of relieving them. The first part of the task was sufficiently easy, for deficiencies thrust themselves upon the sight at every turn. To the more laborious work of rendering his command comfortable and effective, he unweariedly devoted the powers of his fertile mind.

In accordance with suggestions from the southern department, the supplies at San Pedro and Los Angelos were transferred to San Diego. The post at San Louis Rey, forty miles farther north, was abandoned and the public property forwarded to the same place. All the means of transportation at the above-named stations, except such as were absolutely necessary for the conveyance of the troops returning to Monterey, were likewise consigned to the care of Capt. Lyon, then acting as assistant quarter-master.

But at that time Lyon did not long remain at San Diego to enjoy the improvements introduced by his energy. He was soon ordered to Benicia, where he was detained on duty till the middle of September, from the fact that several officers had been detached from the post for reconnoitering service among the mountains. So soon as others arrived to assume the responsibilities of command, he left for Major Miller's camp on the Stansilaus river, in the valley of the San Joaquin.

A military station had been established at this place for the purpose of preventing altercations between the Indians and whites, and for the maintenance of peace and order among the heterogeneous population then gathering in large numbers about the waters of the Stansilaus, Tualumne and Merced rivers. A large proportion being foreigners, the authorities were apprehensive that jealousies between them and the Americans might ripen into contentions and riots destructive to the best interests of the territory. But like other gloomy forebodings, apparently justified by the assemblage of such tumultuous elements in close contiguity, this fear happily proved groundless also. Chinese, East-Indiamen and Sandwich-Islanders, from wholesome feelings of awe for the Anglo-Saxons, behaved remarkably well and were highly prosperous. The good order voluntarily preserved among the miners, and the general prevalence of peace with the Indians, left little for the garrison to do.

On the approach of cold weather, Maj. Miller's command was ordered to Benicia, as there were no winter quarters at the post on the Stansilaus. Says Lyon, writing the last day of the following February:

"We have spent here a very pleasant winter. But you are not to suppose our pleasure consists in dashing sleigh rides, or blustering through the drifted snow. Snow is rarely seen on the distant hills, and our cold wet weather is much like the April storms at home, followed by the same beautifully bright and sunny days. Not a night is so cold as to interrupt the constant peeping of the frogs, or the growth of grass and other vegetation.

"We have at Benicia a fair proportion of ladies, both native and from our own country. Indeed, all things, considered, this is the most pleasant place for a residence in California. It is not, however, much of a business town, nor is it rapidly improving.

"I was in San Francisco the other day, and was surprised at the vast rapidity of its growth. Within one year, on the spot has arisen from nothing, a city twice as large as Hartford or New Haven."

CHAPTER VII.

During the summer of 1850, Capt. Lyon conducted a brilliant campaign against the Indians living in the neighborhood of Clear Lake, and among the fastnesses of Northern California. The outrages that provoked the expedition were singularly revolting and inexcusable—the punishment that overtook the guilty, unexpected and terrible.

Capt. Warner, of the topographical engineers, had been sent the previous season to the head waters of the Sacramento, to collect information relative to the resources of the country, to select the site for a military post, and to ascertain the practicability of a railroad route through the northern passes. While engaged in the duties of the mission, he was brutally murdered by the savages. In the autumn a number of tribes about Clear Lake having formed a kind of league, and still farther trusting for security to the inaccessible character of their retreats, killed several whites. Lieut. Davidson, with a company of dragoons then stationed at Sonoma, made prompt pursuit. The way was difficult, offering many impediments to the approach of troops. Having at length, after much difficulty, come in sight of the enemy, the detachment had the mortification of finding itself without the power to inflict any injury. The savages took refuge on the islands in the lake, whither it was impossible to pursue without boats, and emboldened by the safety of the position, amused themselves with taunting the whites. As there were no means at hand for reaching the islands, the force was obliged to return without accomplishing its mission.

Although the lateness of the season rendered further operations impracticable for the time, the determination to chastise the offenders was by no means relinquished. Preparations were made to invade the haunts of the savages with a strong force in the spring. Major Seawell was first selected for the command of the expedition. An order from the President for a court martial in Oregon, took him away from the theatre of operations, and it became necessary to appoint a substitute. "The lot," says Gen. Persifor F. Smith, "fell most happily on Brevet Captain Nathaniel Lyon, second infantry, and he marched immediately." Several months had been occupied in getting the equipments for the campaign in readiness, and on the arrival of Lyon the men were prepared to start. With customary promptitude he caused the troops to be put in motion at once.

Lyon was at Monterey when the order came appointing him to the position vacated by the departure of Maj. Seawell for Oregon. He hurried immediately to Benicia, where he arrived on the night of May 4th. The next morning he assumed command of the expedition. Having spent the day in perfecting arrangements for alleviating as far as possible the discomforts of the men on the march, and for securing the highest degree of efficiency, he started from Benicia on the sixth. The plan of the campaign was to rout the Indians on Clear Lake, and then proceeding northward to Pitt river, the principal continuation of the Sacramento, to punish the outrages committed in that quarter. There was no difficulty in ascertaining the guilty parties, for the offenders gloried in their acts and boldly defied the whites. Reposing implicit confidence in the security of their island-retreats, inclosed by mountain ranges impassable for carriages, they had become very insolent, giving way unreservedly to the impulses of brutal passion. The region which they occupied, so impenetrable and picturesque from the blending of mountain, lake and valley, has been called the "Switzerland of California."

Captain Lyon with habitual celerity pushed forward the column. Three boats capable of carrying a strong detachment of men, were taken from Benicia on wagons. When the troops reached the base of the alpine barrier, all the wagons except those expressly prepared for the conveyance of the boats over the height, were left behind. The entire strength of the teams was now employed to draw up the vehicles separately, while the men lent assistance at the wheels. In this manner the toilsome ascent was slowly gained. The column descended the difficult way on the opposite side, and without the knowledge of the Indians, concealed the boats in the marshes on the southern edge of the lake. The entire march from Benicia was accomplished in less than six days. From the position thus reached, the waters stretched away in a north-westerly direction for nearly thirty miles.

On the 12th, Lieut. Davidson, with a company of dragoons, was sent around the western shore to co-operate with the infantry who were to ascend in boats. When the Indians discovered the approach of the whites, they began to congregate on an island not far from the northern borders of the lake. As information respecting the invasion reached the different haunts of the natives, they sought with all dispatch the common rendezvous. Canoes and a kind of craft made of tulé, kept plying between the main and the strong hold, which with childish conceit they imagined impregnable. Once there,—all apprehensions vanished.

On the 14th, Lieut. Davidson and Lieut. Haynes with a mountain howitzer came upon a rancho, killing four warriors and capturing a chief. Dispositions for a final and decisive attack were arranged the same day, to be carried into effect the following morning.

A strong force was extended along the shores nearest to the position of the enemy, in order to intercept any fugitives who might attempt to escape. Three sides were thus closed by a cordon of troops. Yet the Indians looked upon these preparations with derision. Still ignorant that the invaders were provided with means of transportation across the water, they grew bold in the confidence that the island was inaccessible. Once already, dragoons, after riding over the same ground, and apparently threatening them in the same manner, had gone away without inflicting any injury. The sight of the soldiers and the manœuvering, afforded the savages infinite delight, for they fully expected that the whites would be obliged to return home, thwarted and chagrined as before. Some in broken Spanish taunted the men with the distance, and challenged them to wade into the water, at least, if they came for a fight. A variety of coarse expedients and coarse insults in familiar use among the Indians, were employed to indicate their enjoyment of the supposed mortification of the troops. All at once the train of self-gratulation was turned to dismay. Suddenly as the three boats hove in sight around a point, howls of rage and despair arose from all parts of the island. Yet the savages opened the battle manfully and with showers of arrows strove to dispute the landing. As the distance lessened, however, the well directed fire of the infantry made frightful havoc, destroying many before the men reached the shore. The ground was already thickly strewn with the bodies of the slain, when the Indians, disheartened by the comparative worthlessness of their weapons, and the futility of the defense, sought to avoid the fatal discharges of musketry by hiding among the tula in the neighboring waters. On the east and north the growth was very dense, extending from the island to the shore. But they were not destined to escape thus, for their punishment was not yet sufficiently severe. A less resolute commander than Lyon would have been satisfied to treat the fugitives to a few random volleys, and then leave them in their slimy concealments to reflect on their follies and misfortunes. But he wished to make thorough work, and teach the savages what kind of punishment to expect thereafter for the murder of whites. The men were directed to sling their ammunition around the neck, and follow into the tula. The order was eagerly obeyed. Notwithstanding the novelty of the warfare, and the embarrassments of fighting when entangled among rushes, and in water up to the arm-pits, the troops were highly successful. The pursuit was rapid and the search thorough. Nearly a hundred of the enemy perished, while not a single casualty occurred among the assailants to mar the pleasure of the triumph.

The rancheria extending about half way around the circumference of the island, was destroyed, together with a large amount of stores.

Having now satisfactorily chastised this band of savages, and made them realize that no spot, however remote or inaccessible, could afford shelter from the sure and fatal consequences of violence, Lyon turned his attention at once to other tribes upon whom rested the guilt of like offences. Not a moment was lost either in rejoicings over the victory, or even in resting from the fatigues of the laborious march over the mountains.

Believing that the Indians on Russian river had participated in the recent murders, Capt. Lyon hastened toward the sources of the stream in the expectation of finding there the warriors of the chief Chapo. But the wigwams were deserted. A careful and extensive search discovered no one. Scenting the danger from afar, the wretches had fled to the shelter of distant fastnesses. Lyon then descended the river twenty miles to pay his respects to the Yohaiyaks, who at the time were harboring Preesta and his followers—a gang particularly notorious in connection with the atrocities that provoked the war. Night and day the circuitous march from Clear Lake was vigorously pushed, and the enemy were again taken by surprise. Aware, however, that an expedition was in the neighborhood, and from the consciousness of guilt apprehensive of a visit, they had retired to a dense jungle and made some preparations for defense. This position on an island in the midst of a slough, formed by water from Russian river, was well selected and formidable. Thick undergrowth covered the surface to a great extent, while in the part where the savages mostly sought concealment, trees both dead and alive lay horizontally in all directions, with the interspaces blocked up by a net-work of vines. A small number of well armed and determined men, familiar with the locality, could have held the place against a greatly superior force.

On the morning of the 19th, the troops discovered the Indians. Arrangements were immediately made for the fight. The position being entirely surrounded by mud and water, the attack was much embarrassed. But the difficulty of reaching the enemy only rendered his destruction more sure and signal. There was no avenue for escape so that "the island soon became a perfect slaughter pen." Yet its defenders proved themselves no cravens for they fought bravely and obstinately till driven from the last thicket. Arrows flew thick, but the veteran infantry heeded them no more than if the harmless toys of children. The other weapons of the enemy were equally useless. And yet in the midst of the carnage which they saw it was impossible to avenge, they continued to fill the air with shouts of encouragement, giving up the conflict only when a hundred warriors lay dead and dying on the ground. None of the troops were killed. Two were wounded.

After the battle the dragoons were sent to Benicia by way of Sonoma, in order to have the horses shod. Lyon crossed the mountains between the valley of Russian river and the lake, reaching Anderson's Rancho at the end of a two day's march, on the 21st of May. Gen. P. F. Smith writes respecting the management of the campaign, that he has learned the facts "from the officers who have returned this day, (May 25th;) they all unite in awarding to Capt. Lyon the highest praise for his untiring energy, his zeal and skill, and attribute his success to the rapidity and secrecy of his marches, and skillful dispositions on the ground."

The veteran general can not let the mail leave without expressing his "highest praise of Capt. Lyon's conduct."

During the passage down Russian river, an Indian was taken prisoner, who made certain disclosures, interesting, because confirmatory of suspicions prevalent among the well informed. The captive asserted that Spaniards in the vicinity had industriously instigated the crimes for which the immediate perpetrators were then suffering terrible retribution. A variety of circumstances coming to the knowledge of the officers in different ways, pointed to the same conclusion. But the low intriguers cunningly covered the footprints of mischief so as to screen themselves from detection. The penalty was paid by the victims of their duplicity. While there may be many noble exceptions to the rule, the Spanish living on the American frontier have, too often for the credit of the blood, proved selfish, crafty and treacherous neighbors. In the Florida war they did infinite harm by inflaming the passions of the Seminoles through the circulation of shameless falsehoods, and by supplying the means for continuing hostilities. Members of all other civilized communities, at least in times of international peace, seem impelled by the voice of a common humanity to aid one another in guarding against surprise or injury from the brutal instincts of the savage.

The number of the Clear Lake Indians was variously estimated at from fifteen hundred to two thousand. One would think that tribes reared in a hardy climate and amid Alpine scenery, would possess the attributes of a noble manhood. On the mountain ranges, in the rich valleys, and along the borders of beautiful lakes, it would be natural to look for sagacity, honor, pride and modesty among the people. Such favorable preconceptions, however, were entirely untrue. A country abounding in fish and game afforded bountifully the means of subsistence. Toil was not absolutely indispensable for the support of life, nor did the ambition of the natives stimulate them to make any exertions to improve their rude and wretched condition. Simple existence was all they appeared to hope or care for. In the hour of danger, it is true, throwing aside habitual sloth, they fought manfully, manifesting latent capabilities of a high order. But the predominance of the better qualities was momentary only, for the innate tendency to utter degradation of life and character seemed irresistible. Yet though squalid and miserable, indolent and ignorant, they were docile in disposition, and aside from the injuries and intrigues of crafty neighbors, would probably have given no occasion for complaint. Whenever clothing came in their way, it was eagerly put on. Garments of all kinds, however, were generally considered of small importance, and the desire of appearing in cassimere or calico was not sufficiently strong to overcome constitutional idleness.

On closing the expedition against the Indians living about Clear Lake and on the Russian river, Capt. Lyon, agreeably to orders from head-quarters, continued on to the sources of Pitt river in order to bring to justice the murderers of Capt. Warner. A few hostile tribes on the way were attacked and routed. Pushing on with all practicable celerity, he reached the territory where the barbarities had been committed. But the band guilty of the murder was nowhere to be found. Having learned that troops were approaching, and foreseeing their own annihilation if they remained at their old haunts, they absconded beyond the reach of pursuit.

In the course of the skirmishes that diversified the progress of the march, Capt. Lyon met with several personal adventures of the most exciting character.

On one occasion, the Indians, after fighting vigorously till broken by severe losses, disappeared all at once from the field. The thickets that had resounded with terrific yells and whoops suddenly became as silent as the grave. Not a bush stirred, and not a sound indicated the presence of an enemy. As the character of the ground rendered flight extremely improbable if not impossible, the men began in groups to hunt for the savages. The surface abounded in patches of undergrowth, and at intervals was studded with trees of dense foliage. Some skulked among the shrubs, and some hid among the branches of the trees. In the progress of the search, Lyon having become somewhat separated from the rest, came upon a number of baskets which to all appearance had been thrown carelessly together without any ulterior object. Curiosity prompted him to raise the upper one with his sword, when a stalwart chief more than six feet in height, grasped the blade with the strength of a giant, and was preparing to spring upon his antagonist. The question of life or death to one of the parties must be decided in an instant. The greatly superior physical prowess of the Indian would have rendered the escape of an ordinary man almost hopeless. But Lyon's remarkable agility and presence of mind were more than a match for the ponderous muscle of the savage. Before he could rise from his semi-prostrate position, Lyon wrenched the sword from his hand, and as if by a single motion tore open his blanket and plunged the steel into his bosom. Self-preservation rendered the act necessary. Yet as the victor saw the purple tide streaming from the form of the chief—more manly and noble in death than in life—he had no heart to continue the work of bloodshed. The men were recalled and the Indians allowed to mourn and bury their fallen braves in peace.

From the desultory character of the warfare, the troops often became detached from each other, since it was sometimes necessary for a small force to scour a wide breadth of territory at the same time. The natives were not sufficiently formidable in fight to render close embodiment of the men, or extreme vigilance necessary. Many things were done with advantage to the service, which under other circumstances would have been unwarrantably rash.

On one occasion when no one was near enough to offer assistance, three mounted Indians made a sudden charge upon Lyon. The situation was desperate, but his resources were equal to the emergency. In this instance as in the one just narrated, celerity of movement saved him. A bullet settled the case of the foremost savage summarily. Before the smoke left the barrel of the pistol, the hand that discharged it was directing a thrust at the heart of the second. But the blow proved ineffectual, for the thick blanket of the savage was impenetrable. At this critical juncture, he caught the fold at the neck with his left hand, and making a sudden spring buried his trusty blade in the body of his antagonist. All passed so quickly that the remaining Indian had no time to interfere. Seeing the fate of the others he galloped away, making good his escape.

After searching the country about the head waters of Pitt river, and punishing such tribes as stood in need of correction, the expedition started homeward. On the way Capt. Lyon met with orders to return and seek the remains of the late Captain Warner. If obtained they were to be brought down by the detachment and forwarded to his relatives. Experienced guides were now added to the command, which began to retrace its steps toward the northern wilds. But this last mission proved fruitless. No trace could be discovered of the body of Capt. Warner. The bones of that lamented officer sleep in an unknown grave, with only the remembrance of his virtues, and the record of his public services for a monument.

This toilsome campaign of nearly five months duration, was brought to an end on the 25th of September, when the troops reached Benicia. Both officers and men were much worn by the fatigues of the long and laborious march. Lyon himself was more reduced in health and strength than ever before. But a few weeks of repose served to restore in a great measure his usual vigor.

During his brief stay at Benicia he lived in a good house—a luxury quite rare in the experience of an officer on the frontier—and amid the comforts of civilization. Respecting the even tenor of his life, he says,

"I continue in my usual and long established customs, growing old indeed but not ashamed to own it; proud perhaps but not haughty; prudent it may be in worldly affairs yet not crafty for wealth; desirous enough of fame but not infatuated with blind ambition; and in general taking the world as it comes, enjoying richly its many blessings, sympathizing with the unfortunate, and laughing with the indifference of cool philosophy at the sore disappointments with which selfishness and cupidity are ever torturing their victims."

Of the approaching congressional session, he writes:

"I foresee a great excitement this winter (1850–1) in congress on the subject of Slavery, and much deprecate the final resort threatened by the South. Yet should the crisis come, I stand ready to tender a cordial support to the measures necessary to re-establish our Union upon a basis of permanent prosperity."

The fire-eaters were lashing themselves into a frenzy of passion on account of the admission of California as a free state. To gain new acquisitions for the expansion of human slavery, they precipitated the nation into war with Mexico, and taking advantage of her necessities, appropriated a large share of her dominions. But the fruit that seemed golden in the distance, now turned to ashes on their lips. The deep-laid schemes for perpetuating the tyranny of the slave power on the Western continent, were signally overruled.

This result seems the more remarkable as the soil and climate were well suited to slave labor, while a large majority of the officers and political managers in the territory, belonged to the South. In vain, however were chicanery, threats and bribes. In high heaven was recorded the decree, "Hitherto shalt thou come, but no further." When the banners of freedom were flung to the breeze on the shores of the Pacific; when the fertile acres and treasured hills of another state—soon to become perhaps the richest and most powerful of the sisterhood—were consecrated forever to Liberty, then for the first time the remorseless giant that had long ruled with a rod of iron in the councils of the nation, grew faint with apprehensions. As the decrepit monster saw the cordon of free states closing around him like the walls of a prison, he felt that the palsy of age was near at hand. Although no one wished to meddle with the old man's legal possessions, he became more than ever before, unreasonable and suspicious. In every breath of air he heard a threat. If a stick crackled or a leaf quivered, his dimmed and disordered vision descried the dusky outlines of an assassin. Strangers passing by in the highway, called up unpleasant recollections of Guy Fawkes and the powder plot. No solace could be found for the peevishness of second childhood. Neighbors were profuse in expressions of friendly feeling and fair intentions, but soft words were petulantly spurned. Yet while his knees were shaking with the infirmities of years, his voice waxed louder and more imperious. Its shrill accents had often drowned the whisperings of conscience, and the calm utterances of argument. Although many were willing to humor his foibles, few were so cowardly as to be terrified by his ravings. During the memorable discussions that grew out of the admission of California, the vocabulary of menace was repeatedly exhausted. At length threats became threadbare. The old giant was indignant at the indifference which marked the reception of his most elaborate fulminations. Evidently the oracles of the South were falling into contempt. To such humiliation he could not submit. Attributing his own weakness to the strength of others, he foolishly imagined that he would feel better to go away by himself. The causes of the experiment are before us. What will be its fate we shall in due time discover.

Capt. Lyon was soon transferred from Benicia to San Diego, the scene of his first experiences in California. One of his duties was to keep the military post at the junction of the Gila and Colorado rivers, supplied with government stores. Fort Yuma, (the name of this station,) was one hundred and fifty miles east of San Diego. The only communication between the two places was by the over land route which presented great difficulties. Teams were compelled to take a very circuitous course to avoid the mountains and hills. Eighty miles of the traveled road lay through a desert of dry sand, destitute of herbage and affording water only at long intervals. Trains were kept in constant motion over the dreary highway. The expense of transportation was immense. Every ton of provisions carried from the coast, cost the government not less than $1000.

Lyon was not content to allow this heavy drain upon the public treasury to continue, without endeavoring at least to effect an improvement. In April, 1851, he left San Diego to make a thorough exploration of the country, and to ascertain the practicability of a more direct route. He was prevented from undertaking the hardships of the journey earlier in the season, by the periodical recurrence, during the winter, of the "chills and fever," one of the fruits of the campaign of the previous summer. The enterprise thus attempted was no holiday pastime. When fairly away from the point of departure, it was necessary to plunge into an unknown region, with no landmarks of any kind to offer their friendly guidance. No civilized man had ever penetrated the country before, and "from appearances much of it had never been traversed by the present generation of Indians." Lyon made a thorough survey of the whole region and had the satisfaction of discovering a new and direct route practicable for trains, over which supplies could be transported at great saving of cost. Still he advocated the opinion that the Colorado river ought to be used for the purpose, as a steamer of eight feet draft could ascend the stream at its highest stages, conveying at a single trip stores enough for a year.

This post (Camp Yuma) was the most important military station in southern California, commanding the land-passage into Sonora and other Mexican states on the Pacific side of the central chain of mountains; holding in check several formidable tribes of savages, and protecting the lower route of American emigration. The works, standing on the right bank of the Colorado opposite its junction with the Gila, were built on a rocky eminence eighty feet high and terminating in a kind of plateau about five hundred yards in circuit.

A presidio and mission were established here at the beginning of the second quarter of the century. Seven or eight years later, the whites having incurred the jealousy of the Indians, were attacked and overwhelmed. At the time thirty soldiers and nearly a hundred persons besides, were living within the inclosure. For three days the troops made a gallant defense, keeping at bay the horde of blood-thirsty savages. The stock of bullets having then unfortunately become exhausted, the garrison endeavored to keep up appearances by the discharge of blank cartridges. The assailants, however, quickly discovered the difference, between harmless explosions of powder. and the well-aimed fire which in the early part of the conflict, had laid low many a stalwart warrior. Venturing nearer and nearer with impunity, they were soon emboldened to rush against the defenses with clubs and other rude weapons. The barricades, too weak to resist the ponderous blows, gave way, and an entrance was effected. All the men except one were slain without mercy, and the women and children reduced to captivity.

Twenty years later when the second infantry went to occupy the site, the stone foundations and other ruins were clearly traceable.

Fort Yuma was established by three companies of the second infantry under command of Major Heintzleman, in November, 1850. In the month of June, 1851, shortly after Capt. Lyon's successful tour of observation over the mountains, the position was abandoned from want of funds to sustain it. Says Lyon, "The great expenses of California (and many of them have been entirely unnecessary) seem to have exasperated our wise ones in congress, and they have so limited the appropriations for the army, particularly the means of transportation, that we are now suffering great embarrassment. I have a debt due from this office (much of which was contracted by my predecessor) of between fifty and sixty thousand dollars, without a cent to meet it, while my current expenses are incurring additional liabilities of more than $5,000 per month. In consequence of this state of things, the post upon the Gila and Colorado rivers has been temporarily recalled till the decision of the war department shall be known upon the subject. I presume it will not be resumed till the necessary means for sustaining it shall be provided by government."

A small guard was left at Fort Yuma to take care of the public property. In the November following it was reinforced by Capt. Davidson, but a few days after was altogether abandoned in consequence of the threatening and formidable attitude of the Indians. In February, 1852, the post was again occupied by the original command and others.

Capt. Lyon's head-quarters, during the summer of 1851, continued to be at San Diego. Although at a distance from San Francisco, the political heart of California, which was then beating fiercely and tumultuously, he took the deepest interest in the civil affairs of the State. Writing in August he remarks:

"You have heard of the dread state of affairs in California, from which it appears that our attempts at organization have turned out an ignoble abortion; leaving to independent associations, self-styled 'Vigilance Committees,' 'Hounds,' &c., the control of those delicate and sacred rights which should be secured by laws and constitutions. The summary punishment by a mob, of an offender guilty of some gross outrage, you regret for its contempt of law, the palladium of civil rights, rather than for any injustice done to the individual. The 'Vigilance Committee' of San Francisco may receive our sanction so far as prudence has confined its acts to an equitable chastisement of the subjects of its charge. But that such an organization, independent of and even in defiance of law, should be made a permanent feature in the police regulations of a civilized community, presages more danger to human liberties, than all the secession murmurings or abolition insolence yet brought to light."

The proceedings of the "Vigilance Committee," as all remember, excited profound attention throughout the country. Its unparalleled usurpations of authority both astonished and alarmed order-loving, law-abiding citizens. Every one saw the step to be dangerous, and feared lest it should end in disaster. But the flagrant abuses which called the organization into existence, demanded desperate remedies. The gangrene gnawing the limbs and threatening the vitals of the body politic, was too malignant to permit delay. The ordinary forms of law might have been adequate to the correction of other evils, had not the ministers of the law stood in need of the first and severest correction. Men of the vilest character had insinuated themselves by fraud and violence into positions of the highest responsibility. Bullies in the employ of desperate political adventurers, presided at the ballot-box and counted the votes. An elaborate system of falsehood and intimidation was employed to keep the offices of state filled with the confederates of this villainous gang. If the fountains of justice were pure, its streams became sadly corrupted by the pollutions of its channels. All confidence was lost. Distrust, suspicion and anxiety tortured the minds of the community.

This disorganized and helpless condition of society gave birth to the Vigilance Committee. Although arrogating extraordinary functions, its proceedings were remarkably calm, deliberate and effective. From the history of similar associations in other lands, it was apprehended that this popular reaction against terrible wrongs would proceed with the violence of the tornado. But in escaping from Scylla, it happily avoided Charybdis also. The Committee, without intemperance or passion, having decorously finished its work, disappeared quietly from the stage.

CHAPTER VIII.

In the autumn of 1851, Capt. Lyon was transferred from San Diego to Fort Miller, where he took command of the garrison, which was composed of two companies of the second infantry. The troops were provided with "log houses, stockade defenses, and other furniture and fixtures for life in the woods." Fort Miller was located in the valley of the San Joaquin, at the base of the Sierra Nevada mountains. On one side were the mines, swarming with motley population, and on the other, numerous tribes of Indians. The principal object of maintaining a military post at this point, was to prevent the depredations of the natives, and at the same time shelter them from the outrages of evil-minded whites.

The political status of the California Indians was peculiar. Elsewhere in the territories of the United States, the Government allotted certain districts to the natives for their exclusive occupation. Within the limits assigned, they enjoyed the fullest rights of person and property. Here it was possible to establish homes and fix the affections without fear of molestation, for the time at least, from the greed of the dominant race. But in California and Oregon, the Indians held no lands by an acknowledged title, and no privileges by an express guaranty. The Senate having failed or declined to ratify the several treaties negotiated with the tribes by the government agents, every party in interest was left to decide according to the principles of his own favorite theory, whether the native proprietors still retained the ownership of all the soil or none. Equity, as usual, was lost sight of in the intoxication of power. Wherever the insolent "sovereigns" wished to enclose fields or dig the earth, they did so, regardless of any claims of the red man.

Indeed, the Indians of California were singularly incompetent to maintain their rights, either by sagacity in peace, or valor in war. Nowhere else have the pioneers of American civilization encountered tribes so debased and spiritless. All along the Atlantic coast, and thence westward to the broad basin of the Mississippi, the Aborigines exhibited many qualities to challenge the admiration of the conqueror. Shrewd, vigilant, and artful, as well as warlike and ferocious, they were no contemptible puppets to be kicked about at the caprice of the settlers, or safely subjected to injury or insolence. Though few in number and scattered in position, their terrible power was often proved on the battle-field and by the devastation of the frontier.

On the Pacific coast, however, many tribes, abject, vile and despicable, occupied the lowest place in the scale of humanity. Destitute of ingenuity and hopelessly indolent, they subsisted, like animals, on the spontaneous gifts of nature. A region so extensive, and presenting such variety of scenery and climate, would seem favorable to the development of manly and noble races. But north and south, on the plains and among the mountains, the characteristics of the aboriginal inhabitants were to a lamentable degree the same.

In the region of country supervised by the garrison at Fort Miller, the Indians did not rise above the common average. The contact of the white man served to deepen their degradation, for it added to the inherited weight of wretchedness, the vices prevalent among the lowest class of gold diggers.

They had no religion and no conception of any supernatural power, either good or evil. All ideas on abstract subjects, even the simplest and most universal, they were either unable to comprehend, or too lazy to make the effort.

Their food was coarse and disgusting. In the summer the women gathered grass seed, which was made into a kind of paste. This, with bugs and roasted grasshoppers, formed the staple articles of diet. In the autumn salmon were plentiful, but no one ever thought of providing a supply for winter. Rather than make the exertion, they preferred to live during the cold months upon a coarse flour made of acorns.

The habitations of the natives were as wretched as their diet. Huts for summer use were built of brush—protection from the sun being the only object. On the approach of the rainy season, the roofs were thatched with grass or covered with skins.

Each tribe was governed by a chief, but the degree of his authority depended mainly on the quality of the man. Marriages were affairs of temporary preference, unattended by any ceremonies, and discarded at the will of either party. Agriculture, even in the rudest form, was unknown.

The tribes of the San Joaquin valley were inferior to the Indians in some parts of the territory, for others in skirmishes with the whites not unfrequently evinced a respectable share of resolution.

Some of the government agents who traveled extensively among the natives, and enjoyed ample facilities for learning their character and capabilities, expressed the opinion that many Pacific tribes equaled in nerve and daring the best of the Atlantic Indians, attributing their imbecility to the want of experience. As war, however, in all ages and among all races, has woven its threads into the texture of tribal as well as national existence, we may well question the correctness of the conclusion.

Writing of the condition of affairs at the close of 1851, Capt. Lyon says: "We have a considerable number of Indians about Fort Miller whose peaceful disposition would indicate a period of tranquillity, did not all experience predict that intercourse between them and the whites, when in the vicinity of each other, must sooner or later terminate in a war of extermination. A number of murders on the southern border, taken in connection with the statements of friendly Indians, has led to the inference that an extensive combination exists for war upon the whites. I venture to predict that no serious alarm need be felt."

Amid the ordinary routine of duties, the winter was rapidly passing, when for Lyon its brightness was suddenly turned to gloom. A letter from Eastford, Conn., was received the 24th of January, announcing briefly and without particulars, the mental aberration of his mother. She was already far advanced in years. Time had laid upon her aged form the burden of heavy infirmities, and in the order of nature, body and mind were failing together.

With Lyon filial affection was the strongest passion. From infancy onward, he ever evinced for his parents an extraordinary degree of attachment, and after the death of the father, was unwearied in efforts to lighten the bereavement of the survivor. Whether at home or thousands of miles away, he never tired of contriving ways for her entertainment and the promotion of her happiness.

The news of her mental decay, coming without premonition, completely overwhelmed him. The thought of change in that serene countenance was agonizing. It is one of the precious gifts of affection to embalm in perpetual freshness the features of the loved. So her image, enshrined in the most sacred sanctuary of his heart, and irradiate with an aureola of golden light, seemed proof, from its heavenly essence, against the inroads of time. It was impossible to realize that the common lot of mortals was her lot also. Could it indeed be true that her smile of greeting, so gladsome and joyous, had faded forever! Was he never again to meet her eye with the assurance that it would fill with the tokens of love, or even glow with the light of recognition! He writes the next day that this is the severest shock of adversity that has yet befallen him in a life of many vicissitudes. Schooled in the philosophy that teaches fortitude in submitting to misfortune, he could have suffered with manliness any other calamity save this alone. That his mother should be bereft of the light of reason, and the consolations of religion which through life it had been her delight to enjoy and impart, penetrates him with unspeakable grief. "Mother, must the evening of thy life close in wild wanderings? O Heaven, where is thy mercy! O God! mysterious are thy providences, and thy ways past finding out."

"I have attempted to reflect upon and revolve this subject in my mind for the last twenty-four hours, but with swelling heart and maddening brain, I am lost in the absorbing thought, that Mother is wandering in clouds of mental darkness. O Mother, my dear Mother."

By the first mail Lyon applied to the commanding general for leave of absence. Thinking that his personal presence might possibly benefit his aged parent, he decided at once to incur all the hardships and losses incident to a long journey in winter, in order to fulfill this sacred mission.

We can not honor less the devotion of the son than the heroism of the soldier. It is sweet to find the flowers of affection blossoming along the roadside where the earth has often been crushed by the ponderous tramp of armies, and the atmosphere obscured by the lurid smoke of battle. Inhaling the fragrance we regard human suffering with deeper sympathy, and human destiny with livelier hope.

Neither long years of separation, nor the manifold employments which tend to obliterate early feelings by the presentation of new and engrossing objects of interest, served to weaken at all the filial love that formed perhaps the deepest and most earnest element in the character of Nathaniel Lyon. On the contrary it grew deeper as experience taught the priceless worth of maternal guidance and care. And now the strong man who could walk unmoved in the midst of carnage, is utterly overcome by the intelligence that mortal decay—the common lot of all—was taking away an aged parent whose work was done and whose reward was at hand.

So soon as leave of absence was received, Captain Lyon leaving everything behind, started for the far distant home over which the Angel of Death was hovering. Long and wearisome seemed the leagues of the never-ending journey. But he was destined never again on earth to behold the face of his mother. Already the silver cord was loosed, the golden bowl broken. On the 31st of January, one week after the news of her illness reached Fort Miller, her spirit went to the God whom she had long and faithfully served.

Mrs. Lyon was a woman worthy to be the mother of such a son. Hardly known out of the circle of relatives and beyond the limits of the small community in which she lived, her daily walk was adorned with the virtues that make life happy and death blessed. Many true heroines never figure in novels, or dress in laces. They dwell in plain houses and are busied with common duties. Their experiences are simple, their enjoyments homely, their charities noiseless. The current of life glides on so quietly that few know of its existence. Yet more heroic or noble hearts are not to be found in the halls of fashion or the retinues of queens.

> "Full many a gem of purest ray serene,
> The dark unfathomed caves of ocean bear."

Gems none the less for lacking the lustre of polish and the brilliant settings of wealth.

During the spring and summer of 1852, Capt. Lyon spent much of the time in traveling. We do not propose to follow him in his wanderings through cities and states with which all are familiar. He took great interest in the Presidential election, and being a staunch democrat advocated enthusiastically the election of General Pierce.

In the autumn he returned to California by way

of the Isthmus. On the Pacific steamer a *mass meeting* of the passengers was held the evening of November 1st to discuss the merits of the presidential candidates. Lyon having previously given his opinions frequent airing, was now uproariously called upon for a speech. Although more accustomed to fighting Indians than haranguing popular assemblages, he could not forego the privilege of bearing testimony in behalf of the "good" cause. Whether any converts were made to democracy by the arguments or eloquence of the orator, the record leaves us in doubt. The next day an election was held on board, attended by as much ceremony and excitement as if the ballot was to decide the contest for the nation. As General Pierce received a majority of forty-seven out of two hundred and sixty-nine votes, the friends of the candidate accepted the omen.

The steamer reached California the 6th of November. Lyon repaired at first to Benicia, whither his company had been ordered, to await its arrival; expecting to spend an agreeable winter in the vicinity of a large and pleasant city. But settlers in the interior being much exposed to Indian depredations, importuned the commanding general for protection. The former orders were therefore countermanded and company D directed to remain at Fort Miller for the winter. Lyon rejoined it at this post the 29th of November, after an absence of nearly ten months.

Writing almost a year subsequently to his mother's death, he speaks thus:

"A sacred and most endeared link of our family circle—the last that bound our affections to a common center—is now broken. Of our excellent parents, the last survivor, our beloved mother, is no more. The high toned purpose and unswerving resolution to pursue the pathway of duty, must needs yield to the conqueror of all. The example of her unwavering confidence in, and patient submission to, the providences of the God she so deeply loved and sincerely worshiped, is indeed lost to us, while a greater joy, we trust, remains to her. No more her deep earnest look of devoted love; no more her tears of solicitude and sympathy. Even in our loss we have much to cheer us—rich memories, affectionate precepts, bright examples of parents, of which the noblest aims in life can alone prove us worthy heirs."

Nearly three years before, the recurrence of the season when the families of New England gather around the parental hearth and board to enjoy the "thanksgiving" festivities, having recalled as usual the scenes of childhood, led him to speak of the head of the circle.—"Our good father whose cheerful countenance diffused a tranquil joy, whose anecdotes enlivened all, whose counsels, replete with wisdom, gave us an unerring guide, whose spotless integrity and purity have left us a brighter legacy than wealth can bestow. His death bereft us and our good mother of his sweet association and companionship, the recollection of which will form the richest gem of memory, bright and unfading through the vicissitudes of life and the mutations of time."

Capt. Lyon had left Fort Miller for the East the 7th of the previous February. The two weeks preceding his departure were darkened by the deepest sorrow. Every surrounding object became identified with the all-absorbing grief of the hour. Since then the mourner had traveled far, mingling freely with the world, and taking an active interest in public discussions and events. Now, on returning to this post in the wilderness, familiar places and things were all associated with the grief that had here swept over him like a flood. The wounds of a bruised heart bled afresh. The sternness of the soldier was often lost in the tenderness of the child.

But much work was to be done to render the quarters comfortable for the troops during the rainy and inclement months of winter. Lyon habitually exercised a kind of parental care for the soldiers under him, never allowing them to suffer from any cause that prudence could avert, or industry remedy. In the expectation of speedy removal to other parts of the State, the garrison at Fort Miller had taken no unnecessary pains to improve the accommodations. In the next few weeks the hammer and spade were busily plied from morning till night.

In the month of May, 1853, company D was ordered to Benicia. The officers were of course delighted at the prospect of exchanging habitations in the wilderness for the privileges and pleasures of a thriving city, yet turned regretfully from the gardens which had been planted under their oversight, and were now yielding a variety of productions "marvelous" alike for size and quality.

After a few weeks of comparative leisure at Benicia, Capt. Lyon was employed for several months in extremely laborious and fatiguing services. Indian troubles in Oregon having recently broke out afresh, company D was ordered thither to the assistance of the settlers. When it reached Rogue river, the theatre of hostilities, the difficulties were over. The savages having secured the respect of the whites by proving themselves formidable antagonists in fight, accepted the terms of peace which the citizens who had gathered for the prosecution of the war, were glad to offer. To the credit of the natives they seemed disposed to observe the conditions of the agreement. No cause of complaint occurred till several turbulent Indians shot a white man. The other members of the tribe expressed strong regret for the infraction of the treaty, and evinced their sincerity by delivering up the guilty parties.

In the month of October, urgent public business required the presence of Capt. Lyon at Benicia. Having temporarily established his company at the post on Rogue river, he started on the journey. The distance was about four hundred and fifty miles, over nearly half of which the only way was a rugged mule path.

Scarcely was this wearisome mission accomplished when the command to which Lyon belonged was unexpectedly ordered East. Having lived long amid the discomforts and privations of the frontier, and suffered many hardships in campaigns and journeyings through the almost trackless wilderness, he left California without regrets.

The record of the next few months presents no points of especial interest. After visiting New England, he spent the larger part of February and March at Washington, while Congress and the country were in a fever of excitement in consequence of the attempts of daring politicians to overthrow the Missouri compromise. In March, he repaired to St. Louis, expecting to pass the summer at Jefferson Barracks, but was soon after ordered to Fort Riley, a post in Kansas at the confluence of the Smoky Hill and Republican forks, about one hundred and twenty miles beyond the western border of Missouri. The whole region, till recently obscure and unknown, had been brought into painful notoriety by the extraordinary interference of Congress. Almost simultaneously with Capt. Lyon's arrival at Fort Riley, commenced the series of dark and bloody events which long imperiled the fate of Kansas. The din of conflict on the distant frontier soon resounded throughout the land, affecting the patriot with sadness, disquietude, and ill-defined apprehension that the struggle for supremacy between two rival and angry factions, born as it was in fraud and baptized in blood, might bring to the innocent as well as guilty, a harvest of wide-spread bitterness and woe.

Lyon, although from restraints of position a spectator rather than actor, took intense interest in the contest, espousing with all the enthusiasm of his earnest and fiery soul the cause of the "Free State" party. Uncounted were his acts of personal sacrifice and noble generosity in aid of the pioneers who had come from far distant homes to defend for Freedom the possessions of which foul hands were striving to despoil her. For the next few years the question of Liberty or Slavery in the territory engrossed his thoughts, and offered a fruitful theme for his pen.

It is not our purpose to enter at any length upon the discussion of events concerning which so much has been already written. The times are too recent, the prejudices of men too strong, and notwithstanding the multiplicity of matter, the sources of information partake too much of a partisan character, to permit cotemporaries who have shared in the fierce excitement, to view the brief history of Kansas dispassionately. The conflict inaugurated in 1854, is undoubtedly destined to mark a new era in our national development, and perhaps to affect vitally the destiny of the continent. The most stupendous act of the drama to-day claims the attention of millions of anxious people, as the several parts are slowly unfolded.

By the compromise of 1820, all the territory of the Louisiana purchase north of 36° 30′, was given forever to Freedom. For the next thirty years the country enjoyed a tolerable degree of exemption from slavery-agitation, till the controversy growing out of the organization of California aroused another tempest of excitement which was seemingly lulled by a second compromise. California gained admission as a free state, a large district of New Mexico hitherto exempt from slavery was annexed to Texas, and the remainder of the Mexican conquest subjected to a territorial government, with the stipulation that the future states to be carved from it should be allowed to determine the character of their domestic institutions without Congressional interference. A calm, brief and delusive, ensued. Permanent peace between two antagonistic systems, the one struggling savagely to maintain an impossible equilibrium, and the other sweeping onward into new regions by virtue of its own inherent and irresistible strength, was out of the question. Each side enlisted the talents of able and determined supporters; each was backed by an immense reserve of resources. The territories from time to time thrown open for settlement by the demands of emigration and trade, and offering rich prizes to be won or lost, unlocked the fountains of strife.

The slave-interest, though representing a minority of the people, had for many years exercised preponderant influence upon the policy of the government. Meanwhile the greater vitality of free institutions was noiselessly increasing the disparity of the two sections in population, wealth, and all the elements of national power, to a degree that alarmed the dominant class. The time was approaching when the South must either relinquish her lordly rule and be content to hold the balance of power between the rival parties of the North, or put everything at stake for the maintenance of the supremacy which had been enjoyed so long that it was now claimed as a right. Political leaders chose the latter alternative. Laws of commerce and nature beyond the control of legislative enactments, warned them in vain of the impolicy and hopelessness of the scheme.

The compromise of 1820, which for more than thirty years had been viewed by the good men of all sections as an inviolable compact, formed the first obstacle to the consummation of the plot. With what disregard of good faith it was overthrown, after the consideration had been paid and appropriated, is still painfully fresh in the memory of the people. Many, however, contended and no doubt from honest convictions, that the prohibition was unconstitutional, and its repeal but an act of tardy justice.

The bitter controversy was now transferred from the Halls of Congress to the soil of Kansas. Large numbers at the North, incensed at what they considered the wanton violation of a national compact, and large numbers at the South, allured by the prospect of securing extensive and unexpected acquisitions, at once began the strife for ascendency in the Territory. Under such circumstances its settlement could not fail to be forced and unnatural. The greater capacity of the free States for supplying emigrants to occupy the land, was counterbalanced by the proximity of Missouri to the scene of contention, and the facility with which hordes of resolute men could be thrown across the border, either to become legitimate citizens, or to exercise a temporary and, as they hoped, decisive control over the destinies of the future State, by violent and illegal interference at the polls. On both sides public meetings were held, societies organized, resolutions adopted, and artificial means contrived for the furtherance of their respective ends.

In November, 1854, an election was held for a delegate to Congress, and in the following March for the members of the first Territorial Legislature. On these and several subsequent occasions, the secret societies of Missouri sent bands of armed adventurers to the different precincts, who seized upon the ballot boxes, appointed new judges where those previously designated by the Governor refused to surrender themselves pliant tools to carry out the purposes of the invaders; overawed the actual settlers by numbers, threats, and the profuse display of weapons, which they were ready to use with deadly effect on the slightest pretext; and having deposited thousands of votes without a shadow of right, returned to Missouri. The Legislature, elected by non-resident partisans for the citizens of Kansas, convened in July, 1855, and having on various pretences purged itself of all obnoxious members, proceeded to enact a code of laws that bore with oppressive and unparalleled tyranny upon the free state inhabitants. Among other equally sanguinary statutes, it was made felony to maintain, by speaking or writing, that persons had not the right to hold slaves in the territory, or to print, circulate, or introduce any paper or pamphlet containing any denial of the right, and the offender was subjected to imprisonment at hard labor for not less than two years. Such are specimens of the bold and unscrupulous measures adopted to carry slavery into Kansas. Witnessing the monstrous efforts put forth to consummate a monstrous fraud, Lyon felt the bitter indignation which these glaring wrongs were fitted to awaken in an honest heart.

A little previous to the election of March, 1855, he writes: "The election of members of a Territorial Legislature is about to be held, and as this body will have power either to introduce or prohibit slavery, the election is important. The outrage committed last fall by Missourians in coming into the Territory, forcibly taking possession of the polls, keeping out free state men, and pushing in votes for a pro-slavery candidate for Congressional delegate, is again threatened. The project, if successful, will give some appearance of pro-slavery strength in Kansas. But I feel qualified to say that in not a single district are a majority of citizens in favor of slavery. Some preparations are in progress to resist the arrogant and insolent imposition of Missourians. Whether they will prove effective may be seen in the result. Indeed, it is fully apprehended that the aggressions of pro-slavery men will not be checked, till a lesson has been taught them in letters of fire and blood."

Again, a few days after this election—"The Missourians, anticipating resistance, came to the different points where their presence was most needed for the accomplishment of their purposes, in such numbers as to render effective resistance impossible, though I regret and am astonished that it was not resolutely attempted. Into our district for the *Assembly* they did not come, and we had no difficulty in electing our "free state" man; but at a distant point in our *Council* district, (Marysville,) they cast a vote of three hundred and twenty-eight, where there are not, it is said, over twenty-four legal voters. Thus was overwhelmed the majorities given everywhere else in the district for the free state party. The number of voters imported from Missouri to the different parts of the Territory is not yet known, but probably between five and ten thousand.* If the one hundred and twenty thousand militia which she has shall finally come to domineer over the people here, I suppose we must congratulate ourselves upon this display of military force, as evidence of a national greatness which should awaken the pride and inspire the hopes of every lover of our *glorious Union*."

During the summer of 1855, a strong force, under Gen. Harney, proceeded against the Sioux Indians, who had been guilty of the massacre of Lieut. Grattan and party, as well as other outrages. Lyon's company was ordered to Fort Pierre, a post on the Missouri river about six hundred miles above Fort Leavenworth, whence they expected either to join or coöperate with the main expedition. The command left Fort Leavenworth the middle of June, occupying the residue of the month in the passage up the river. On the way an enemy infinitely more dreaded than the savage, attacked the troops. For a time the *cholera* raged fearfully. As the men of his company were stricken down by the disease,

* "4908." Report of Investigating Committee.

they sent for Lyon in preference to the physician. Among other attainments, he had acquired an extensive theoretical and practical knowledge of Medicine. Always attentive to the wants and comforts of his men, he was now busy night and day at the side of the sick. They had unlimited confidence in his skill, believing that if human instrumentalities could save them, they were safe in his hands. His treatment of the disease was highly successful, for not a man died on his boat, while most of the others lost several, and one as many as ten. Having ascertained that where the cramps were checked at the outset, the patient was rescued from danger, he caused the limbs to be energetically rubbed by the attendants. Friction upon the palm of the hand and sole of the foot was found to be most efficacious. Where at least three strong men gave their attention in this way to a single sufferer, the force of the disease was generally broken in about two hours.

Fort Pierre, the destination of the company, was located in a desert of sand amid the debris of the drift period, and presented neither attractions nor comforts. The sterile earth produced neither wood, nor grass, nor vegetable. Pure air and good water were the only gifts of nature to the dwellers in this barren region.

The pressure of other duties did not permit the company to join the forces of Gen. Harney in the successful campaign against the Sioux. Early in the autumn, Lyon was summoned to Fort Leavenworth as a witness in the court-martial of Col. Montgomery. While this officer was in command at Fort Riley, Gov. Reeder selected the town of Pawnee as the capital of the Territory, and convened there the first legislative assembly of Kansas. Being anxious to secure a residence for himself near the future city, the Governor tried to purchase of the families in the neighborhood, who obstinately refused either to sell or to remove. Col. Montgomery thereupon extended the Reserve for Fort Riley so as to embrace the land in question within its limits, and forced the occupants to leave. For this transaction, and for authorizing the town-site to be established on the grounds of the Government, he was brought to trial.

Lyon writes in December, 1855:

"I have seen so much of the overbearing domination of the pro-slavery people in Kansas towards the free state men, that I am persuaded the latter have either to fight in self-defense, or submit ignobly to the demands of their aggressors. This conduct, backed as it has been in some measure by the present administration, ought to be effectually rebuked by the indignation of the North."

"The Missourians have been able to impose legislation and officers upon the people of Kansas, but find them rather unruly subjects, and are anxious to have the Government enforce their mandates. This I doubt if even President Pierce is reckless enough to attempt. If he does, it will only bring on the sectional strife more promptly, and if that must come—which the continued arrogance of the pro-slavery power will render inevitable—I am quite willing to see it now and do my share in the issue. I despair of living peaceably with our southern brethren without constantly making disgraceful concessions. But rest assured this will not always be, and in this view I foresee (or think I do) ultimate sectional strife which I do not care to delay.—Though to a superficial observer there may appear to be some fault on the part of the Lawrence people, I am well persuaded they are placed in their present attitude through the unavoidable necessities of self-defense, against unwavering and malignant persecution which seeks to drive by violence and outrage the free state citizens from the country."

Again writing in August, 1856, in reference to the employment of the army in Kansas, he says:

"Neither section of the country will be satisfied with the conduct of the army, and its employment under such circumstances is diametrically opposed to the spirit of our institutions. The move will only cause mischief, as I fear, in the end, and bring it into disfavor with the people. For should the free state party in Kansas succeed, they will have no love for it on account of its subserviency to the pro-slavery schemes of the heartless villain, (Jefferson Davis, Secretary of War,) who for nearly four years past has had control of it. Should the other side succeed they will curse the army for not allowing the hordes of Border Ruffians to kill as many of the free state men as they wanted to. In this latter view the free state men, or as they are usually termed, Abolitionists, by which are meant all opposed to the introduction of slavery into Kansas, ought to be thankful to the army for protection from the ravages which their wanton cowardice would otherwise have exposed them to."

Again,

"A portion of the army has been employed in the troubles of Kansas, and in consequence of the craven fear of Northern men in abandoning their homes and helpless families to the merciless outrages of the inexorable assassins, has done some good in restraining the barbarities which a proper manhood on the part of the friends of freedom should have met and prevented."

These strictures on the so called "cowardice" and

"imbecility" of the free state settlers, are suggestive when read by the light of subsequent events. The great body of Northern emigrants who had gone thither with their families and possessions, relied on the quiet power of the ballot-box for shaping the destinies of the State. Unfamiliar with violence either in language or manners, instinctively obedient to law, and imperceptibly taught in a thousand ways to abhor as murder the taking of human life, unless demanded as a punishment for the gravest crimes, or in self-defense, they were now thrown without intermediate preparation into the midst of savage disorder and strife. If at first they unresistingly suffered their homes to be pillaged by gangs of marauders, and hesitated to retaliate the indignities of wanton ruffians, we must not too hastily infer their deficiency in spirit or in courage. The adjustment of difficulties by the free use of deadly weapons, was a custom too strange and shocking to meet with ready acceptance. A blow for a word and a stab for a blow were precepts of a new code.

Could it be expected that men thus trained would fall at once into the habits of their antagonists? Desperadoes from the West and South-west flocked into Kansas with the determination to introduce slavery as a permanent institution. Accustomed in frontier life to bloody broils, they were prepared to resort at once to the extremest measures. "Gentlemen" of the bowie knife looked with contempt upon slow decisions through the ballot-box. Braggartism and bullying, the pistol and the dirk, were instrumentalities better suited to the genius of their institutions. It is the glory of free society that its champions in this contest, learned to use the weapons of its adversaries, only after all other means had failed, and bitter experience taught the necessity. Recklessness of life is no proof of courage. The muscular exertion required to discharge a rifle at a fellow-mortal, is easy. The only difficulty lies in the conscience and the will. If the absence of all scruples is the test of heroism, the most hardened of assassins must be considered the greatest of heroes. When at length the Northern emigrants came to realize that the coals of fire recommended by Solomon, made no impression upon the heads of their enemies, and that patient forbearance instead of conciliating good will, encouraged the commission of more daring enormities, they, too, reluctantly learned to meet violence with violence. Old scores were often settled with interest. And in the late battle at Wilson's Creek, the Kansas troops, made up in part of the men who at the outbreak of troubles in the territory, bore insults without reply and injuries without revenge, fought with the most obstinate valor. So long as homicide was tantamount to murder they scrupulously avoided bloodshed. But none were more prodigal of blood when war made homicide legal and right.

CHAPTER IX.

During the summer of 1856, Capt. Lyon seriously debated the question of resigning his commission in the army. If ordered into Kansas to aid in enforcing the laws enacted by the pro-slavery legislature which owed its election to non-resident voters, he determined to abandon the service to which he had devoted the flower of life. In regard to the troubles of Kansas, and the intervention of the administration, he took strong and perhaps extravagant grounds. A man of earnest and enthusiastic temperament, can hardly act in stirring scenes without adopting a partisan view, and giving all his sympathies to one side. Lyon considered the course of the general government selfish, partial and corrupt. He could never submit to the self-debasement and humiliation of being employed as a tool in the hands of evil rulers for the accomplishment of evil ends.

Fortunately the painful alternative was not presented. He was sent to the territory of Nebraska where no unconscientious services were imposed upon the army.

Lyon was occupied during the month of July, 1856, with the court martial of Major Howe, second dragoons, of which he was Judge Advocate.

Soon afterwards he repaired to Fort Lookout, on the Missouri river, one hundred and twenty miles by water below Fort Pierre, and two hundred miles above Sioux City, the nearest settlement. The post was just established with a view to restrain the Indians from committing depredations upon the whites, and also to preserve order among them. All the buildings were erected after the first of August, 1856. On the approach of cold weather, (and in that latitude the winters are long and severe,) the whole garrison were furnished with comfortable quarters. Lyon himself has a house "forty-five feet in length by fifteen in breadth, divided into three rooms, each fifteen feet square. One is intended for a parlor and sitting-room, one for a bed-room, and the other for a dining-room." To this he built an addition twenty-four feet by twelve, as a kitchen and for the use of servants. Between the parlor and central room was a chimney with a capacious fire-place opening into each.

Lyon draws a picture of himself on the night of Christmas, seated, as usual, before the blazing hearth. The hours are spent in reading, writing, and many of them without book or pen, in pursuing the reveries and meditations suggested by the circles of flame. On a winter's evening, as the winds moan in the tree-tops and howl around the house-corners, the old fashioned fire-place has an irresistible charm for the soldier on the lonely frontier. Its generous warmth kindles the kindliest sympathies. Bright wreaths darting up the chimney to vanish in darkness, offer an emblem of youth and age, and teach weighty lessons of wisdom and philosophy.

But even on Christmas night, pleasant reveries must give place to gloomy forebodings for the country. Even then Lyon saw on the western horizon, the gathering clouds which were destined soon to overspread the land with the deluge of civil war. He was convinced that the border strife in Kansas contained the germs of a conflict that would speedily convulse the nation from center to circumference. The disposition of the North was characterized by forbearance. But the time was approaching when her people must choose between abject humiliation and bold resistance to pro-slavery aggressions. The ambition of the radical southern party was insatiate.

It affected contempt for free society, often giving expression to its pretensions in a way that served both to wound and to exasperate. Its strength consisted mainly in the singleness of its purpose. Never was a party more united, never did a body of men move more in obedience to one will and impulse. At home, state pride had supplanted patriotism. Sentiments of regard for the common welfare and the common honor, were contemptuously rebuked as treasonable to the South. The currents of popular feeling were diverted into exclusively local channels. In a policy thus developed, retrogressive steps are impossible. Individuals may shape their course according to the exigences of interest or safety. No one of common sense will butt obstinately against the inevitable and irresistible. But communities composed of bold, united and determined men, on surrendering to the fascination of an all-engrossing passion, acquire the terrible momentum of the avalanche. That will move onward despite of obstacles, though in the final crash it be shivered into a thousand fragments.

Slavery propagandists were making a desperate attempt to secure the soil of Kansas. Success was possible either through their own superhuman exertions, or the supineness of their antagonists.

Whatever might be the issue in this particular case, no permanent deliverance from agitation could come of it. The hope of maintaining political supremacy originated the policy of the fire-eaters. Born to rule, according to the fundamental axiom of their creed, they scrupled at no means to retain the departing scepter. But at every feast appeared the mysterious handwriting upon the wall. The quiet arbitrament of time was encircling the throne of the slave-power with legions of hardy freemen. The disproportionate increase of population at the North, must in the end prove fatal to all schemes for the preservation of equality. Yet this truth, so certain and so obvious, was insufficient to teach submission to inexorable laws. Pride would not allow, passion would not suffer it. Both pride and passion were groundless, but both had been artfully stimulated to the point of madness. The North then must yield everything to a minority, contemptible in point of numbers, or a crash was unavoidable.

In the month of March, 1857, duty called Capt. Lyon to Sioux City, two hundred miles distant from Fort Lookout. It was the worst season of the year to travel. The snow, thawing under the warm rays of the sun, became too soft to support man or beast on its crust, and was at the same time so deep as to offer the most serious impediment to progress. No one accompanied him on the long, lonely, and dangerous journey. Twice, as night set in, he found his animals imprisoned in the almost impassable heaps of snow that obstructed the path. The beasts were entirely exhausted from the exertions of the day, and no one was near to render assistance. On the first of these occasions, he did not attempt to seek shelter, but slept with the canopy of heaven for a covering, and the drifts for a bed. The next morning the crust was frozen sufficiently hard to bear. The second night he left the animals behind, traveling till nearly daybreak in order to find a settlement. Obtaining aid, he returned to their relief. In this slow and toilsome manner the journey was accomplished. He says, April 7th, "I suffered very much, but was lucky in not having been overtaken by one of our terrible northwest winds which are so destructive to man and beast on these plains. We have had a very severe specimen since my return."

"Our snow is mostly gone and has raised the river very high, but there is still a fierce struggle between the winter and spring. We have scarcely had a comfortably warm day, and many deep banks of snow yet remain. I am, as I have been for the past winter, quite comfortable at my home, and have enjoyed it much in resting from the fatigues of my late trip."

Late in May, the garrison at Fort Lookout was ordered to Fort Randall, about seventy miles below.

Having obtained leave of absence, Capt. Lyon started for the East, June 23d. It was his last visit to the friends and scenes of early life.

As usual, Lyon spent a considerable portion of his time at the residence of his cousin, Capt. Miner Knowlton, U. S. A. Capt. Knowlton was Assistant Professor at West Point while Lyon was a cadet, and had great influence in moulding his character and opinions. The student looked to his relative as an elder brother, yielding ready obedience to his advice, and rèposing unlimited confidence in his judgment. In after life Lyon keenly appreciated the worth of the counsels and instructions of the Mentor of his youth.

Owing to severe and protracted mental exertion while on duty at West Point, Capt. Knowlton was attacked by disease which for several years has disabled him to engage in active service. Hoping to be benefited by travel, he visited Europe, and was for some time attached to the staff of Marshal Bugeaud, commander of the French army in Algeria, Africa. On the outbreak of the Mexican war, he joined the forces of Gen. Taylor at Corpus Christi, having meanwhile, to all appearance, recovered his health completely. A dangerous attack of camp fever now brought a recurrence of the former trouble. The nature of the malady doomed him to inaction during the brilliant campaigns which ensued, although burning with ambition to aid in fighting the battles of the Country. By the advice of physicians, he returned to the North. Expecting to live but a short time, he repaired to the quiet village of Burlington, N. J., where he has since resided. Whenever Lyon obtained a furlough, he always spent a part of the time at the home of Capt. Knowlton, enjoying the interviews with intense satisfaction.

On the expiration of his leave of absence, Capt. Lyon returned to St. Louis, arriving there the 28th of December.

During the next year or two he was quietly engaged in the duties of his calling at different posts, where there were few opportunities for the exhibition of brilliant or daring qualities. A large part of the soldier's life is spent in *waiting*. In other pursuits the diligent daily realize the rewards of industry. The skill and sagacity acquired by experience are brought into constant requisition. But a score of years may elapse before the army-officer finds an occasion for the display of the attainments which he has made during the intervals of peace. Then a day or an hour may give him immortality, rendering his name forever a part of his country's history.

Lyon passed the winter at Jefferson Barracks near St. Louis. The next August he was transferred to Fort Randall, Nebraska Territory, where he remained till the 12th of July, 1859. He then started in command of an expedition for the camp on "Prairie Dog Creek," Kansas. This stream, so named from the great numbers of little ground squirrels called the "Prairie Dog," that live upon its banks, is one of the southern tributaries of the Republican Fork. An encampment had been established near the point where the road to Pike's Peak from Leavenworth and other towns in Eastern Kansas, crosses the creek, in order to protect people going to the mines, from the Indians. From Fort Randall the expedition marched almost directly south to Fort Kearney, one hundred and eighty miles distant, arriving there the 24th of July. The country was broken up into hills and valleys corresponding to the course of the streams. The route was not difficult when the numerous rivers and creeks were so low as to be fordable, which was the case at this time. The weather was excessively hot. Several oxen died on the way from heat and exhaustion.

Leaving Fort Kearney July 28th, the company proceeded in a south-westerly direction with the view of striking the Republican Fork a little above its junction with Prairie Dog Creek. The mouth of the creek, however, proved to be nearly fifteen miles further west, than indicated on the map. Two days were lost in the discovery and correction of the mistake. The expedition reached the camp on the 3d of August. Capt. Walker, first cavalry, with his company, were at the post guarding the supplies sent out for the use of Lyon's command. Five days later Capt. Walker left for the camp on Arkansas river.

On the 11th of August, Lyon, with a small party, set out to explore a new route to Fort Kearney, by which the surplus stores might be forwarded on the breaking up of the encampment. Five days were occupied in the survey which proved highly satisfactory and useful.

The troops were ordered to Prairie Dog Creek for the protection of emigrants to the mines. But for many months not a solitary traveler had passed along the road. Indians, too, were as scarce as whites. Only one small party were seen while the command remained there, and these were met by a detachment of troops returning from Fort Kearney.

Immense herds of Buffaloes roamed through the

neighboring country. Lyon estimated the number seen in a single day, while on the march from Fort Randall, at one hundred thousand. "The air was filled with a constant din of the lowing of the bulls."

The garrison left the camp September 15th, marching to Fort Riley, a distance of two hundred miles, in ten days. This is the same post to which he was ordered five years before on returning from California. Meanwhile, many changes had occurred, and great improvements had been made. But the highest source of satisfaction, he writes soon after,

"Is the subsidence of political animosity, the return of peace and tranquillity, and that too with the ascendency of free state principles." "A handsome rebuke has in the interval been given to pro-slavery arrogance, though at a painful sacrifice of valuable life in martyrdom to the cause. Some of the effects of the strife are seen in the late fanaticism of poor old Osawattomie Brown in his attempts at Harper's Ferry to initiate a revolution to free the slaves of the South. The simpleton deserved his fate, though sympathy is natural, for so earnest, sincere and brave a character. The people of the South make fools of themselves about the matter, as they always do on the subject of slavery. This affair will probably assume other shapes in course of time."

He gives the following account of a journey performed in October. "Col. Brooks, Maj. Wessells and myself, as members of a General Court, start on the 10th, with Lt. Griffin as Judge Advocate, for Fort Kearney, where the Court-Martial is to be held on the 17th, for the trial of Capts. Clarke and Hazzard, fourth artillery, Dr. Stone, medical department, and some ten soldiers,—Court proceeded with dispatch and closed on the 28th. We were handsomely entertained by the officers at the post, and stopped with those of our regiment. Left on the 29th, and reached Fort Riley on the 2d Nov.—distance about one hundred and sixty miles—road good."

In the March following he attended another Court-Martial at Fort Leavenworth which passed off in a manner equally pleasant and satisfactory. The officers stationed at Fort Riley during the winter, with their families, constituted a numerous and quite brilliant society. Social gatherings were frequent, and characterized by great kindness and cordiality of feeling.

On the 15th of May, Maj. Sedgwick, with a strong body of troops, started from Fort Riley for a summer campaign against the Indians. Capt. Lyon was left in command of the post, which position he held till the arrival of Maj. Wessells, the 12th of the following November.

During the summer and autumn, he wrote a series of political articles, strongly advocating the election of Mr. Lincoln, which were printed in the "Western Kansas Express," a newspaper of Manhattan. These have recently been republished in New York.

November 28th, Maj. Wessells with two companies of cavalry and two of infantry, (including Capt. Lyon's,) left Fort Riley for Fort Scott in South-Eastern Kansas. Numerous atrocities had been lately committed in that vicinity by lawless gangs of marauders. So formidable was the organization that the War Department deemed it necessary to employ a strong military force to put a stop to their operations. The detachment reached Mound City, twenty-five miles north of Fort Scott, December 5th. They found affairs in a bad and unsettled state. Men had been hung by the mob not only for offenses long past, but also on mere suspicion. Several unsuccessful attempts were made by the sheriff to arrest Capt. Montgomery, the head man among the desperadoes. Lyon gives an interesting account of an interview he soon after had with Montgomery.

On the 25th of December he was conducted to the house of a Mr. Smith, where he met this notorious chief.

"I found Capt. Montgomery much such a man as

I expected. He has dark complexion, black and thick hair, heavy black beard and mustache, large mouth, thin features, and pale countenance, with a dark hazel and small eye. He has a nervous temperament, and a head not large but well proportioned,—is tall but thin in person and sinewy. He is a man of great earnestness of purpose, of quick apprehension, and great executive ability. Is much a disciple of the higher law doctrines, and feels his convictions of justice and duty to be his guide, rather than the requirements of law or the constitution. He seems conscientiously and absorbingly devoted to what he feels to be his duty, and his conduct is regulated more by what he conceives his obligations to society, than by sentiments of revenge. His capacity is due rather to activity and energy of mind, than originality and comprehensiveness. He is more fanatical than reasonable.

"He soon set to work to justify his conduct by the provocations to which he and the community had been subjected. It was observable that he generally referred to the outrages as upon the community rather than upon himself. At first he spoke slowly, not so much through caution as an apparent aversion to repeat the oft-told story of his griefs, and an apprehension that he might not have the sympathy of his listener. He soon became earnest and warm. A red glow tinged his cheeks as he went through a long and minute detail of petty annoyances and brutal outrages to which the free state people in Kansas had been subject, showing as a corollary the consequent necessity of the measures which he and his friends had adopted.

"He said he was willing to give himself up to be dealt with before the proper county courts, but was unwilling to be dragged to Fort Scott before Judge Williams, sitting in cases of offenses against the United States, wherein such power is given to the United States Marshal that he can summon jurors who would not do justice. Rather than do this, he would either keep away so as to avoid arrest, or would resist arrest at the sacrifice of life, if necessary.

"Dr. Jennison came in early at this interview, and remained and joined in much of the conversation."

On returning, Capt. Lyon found orders from Department Head-quarters, directing him to go to Kansas City with his company, in order to escort funds from that town to the Indian Agency at the Osage river. The 22d of December he went to Fort Scott to make preparations for the journey, returning the next day to Mound City. On the 24th the company started, reaching its destination the 28th.

Having taken charge of the annuities, they returned to Miami village, an Indian settlement near the southern border of Lykins County. Here the funds were paid to the natives, and the company having accomplished its mission, marched to Fort Scott, where they arrived January 7th, 1861. The trip to Kansas City was made in very cold weather and over the snow. The men suffered much from the severity of the weather.

Fort Scott was originally a post for government troops, but in the spring of 1857, was sold and evacuated. The purchasers were strong pro-slavery men, and on gaining possession put an end to the tranquillity of the neighborhood. On both sides the leaders were extreme and desperate men. Rows, riots, fights and murders followed. Capt. Montgomery's force captured the town several times. In consequence of such disturbances, troops were again ordered thither. Early in January the dragoons were withdrawn, and Lyon's company was left alone to maintain order in this notoriously turbulent district. The people were surly, evidently disliking the new commander as "unsound" on the slavery issue.

We return a little in our narrative to give extracts from the correspondence of Capt. Lyon during the earlier stages of the secession excitement.

Writing November 11th, 1860, he says in regard to the possible action of South Carolina and her confederates,

"There are periods when the dictates of reason and humanity are so totally disregarded in the pursuits of ambition or of pleasure, that nothing but the bitter fruits of folly can bring back their devotees to moderation. Such is now the state of the South, which seems bent upon a fatuous course that in its ultimate disaster and disgrace will teach her people the fatal folly of their presumption. It is a perfectly safe rule, and one which has been of service to me in my prognostications of the future, that whoever or whatever people or party set about an unworthy or unjust purpose, must sooner or later fail, and receive the disgrace due to their corrupt motives."

January 27th, 1861, he writes from Fort Scott,—"I do not consider troops necessary at all here, and should much prefer to be employed in the legitimate and appropriate service of contributing to stay the idiotic, fratricidal hands now at work to destroy our Government. I have seen Montgomery and Jennison. They say it is not the purpose of their party to commit further violence unless provoked to. They readily acknowledge the hanging of Scott and Hynes, and the shooting of two others, but insist upon the justice of their conduct, and assert a readiness to be tried before the county courts.

"This seems to be a period when the lights of experience, the plain meaning of words, and the dictates of humanity must be ignored to subserve partisan aggrandizement.

"It is no longer useful to appeal to reason but to the sword, and trifle no longer in senseless wrangling. I shall not hesitate to rejoice at the triumph of my principles, though this triumph may involve an issue in which I certainly expect to expose and very likely lose my life. I would a thousand times rather incur this, than recall the result of our Presidential election. We shall rejoice, though in martyrdom, if need be."

Capt. Lyon received orders January 31st, to go to St. Louis. Starting the next day, he reached that city the 7th of February and took quarters at the Arsenal. On arriving at the post, he asserted his right of command, as officer of highest rank in the line, against Brevet Maj. Hagner, of the Ordnance Department, who claimed it by virtue of his Brevet rank. The matter was referred to Washington and decided in favor of Maj. Hagner. Lyon writes February 14th:

"I should care nothing for the decision against

me, as I have told Maj. Hagner, if he would take proper precautions for defense. The place is in imminent danger of attack, and the Governor of Missouri will no doubt demand its surrender if the State should pass an ordinance of secession. The prospect is gloomy and forebodes an unnecessary sacrifice of life in case of hostile demonstrations. Yet I do not despair of an effective defense, and hope to administer a lasting rebuke to the traitors who have thus far had their own way."

During the winter, Lyon regarded with the utmost impatience the supineness of President Buchanan. So clear to his own mind was the path of duty and expediency, that irresolution in crushing rebellion while yet in the germ, seemed to ensue from premeditated treachery. He believed that wholesome severity at the outset would throttle in the cradle an infant which might grow in a few months to the stature and strength of a giant. At the South hundreds of thousands were devotedly attached to the Union. Large numbers, destitute of fixed principles, were ready to topple either way according to the prospects of the secession scheme. A minority only were radical and determined disruptionists. Yet the Government permitted these men to work unmolested while sapping the foundations, and planting in open day the mines which they confidently hoped would blow the noble structure to atoms. Meanwhile all classes at the South were becoming familiarized with the idea of secession. Ingenious sophisms were invented to settle the qualms of the conscientious. Mischievous men toiled with the mad energy of fiends to spread the belief that war upon the flag symbolizing all the past glories of the nation, was a holy war, undertaken in defense of wives and children, homes and property. The leniency of the United States Authorities, instead of shaming the fanatical, emboldened the timorous. Hitherto treason had seemed a crime of the deepest enormity, not to be compared with ordinary murders, but with the cold-blooded assassination of a parent. Now each one put to himself the question, can that be criminal at all which is treated so delicately, and handled so gently.

Blusterers met in secret conclave for mutual encouragement and deliberation. Brag and threats, the two weapons hitherto used with greatest success in dealings with the peace-loving North, poured in torrents from the mouths of southern orators, and through the columns of the southern press. Yet, notwithstanding the encouragement to be drawn from precedents, they were entering upon an untried path which *might* lead to the platform of a scaffold. Neither gasconade nor sophistry could dispel the vision of halters and retribution. During the interval of southern hesitation, the Government was forbearing, and her mercy was imputed to impotence. Reluctance to strike wayward children in self-defense, was mocked as helpless dotage. Owing to the prevalence of such sentiments, the era of timidity passed rapidly away. Consciousness of escaping deserved punishment, gave the courage to venture further and hazard more. And now the indulgence of the loyal States was employed with telling effect to consummate the ruthless work. Wrongs unpunished, insults unavenged, robbery of the common property tamely tolerated, were produced as the most conclusive proofs that the craven, mercenary people of the North were unworthy to be associated under the same government with the bolder and more chivalric sons of the south.

Again, a portion of the mercantile class in the principal cities from Charleston to New Orleans, looked with bewilderment and envy upon the prosperity of the commercial emporiums of the North. In the imagination of southern financiers one doctrine loomed up in magnificent and overshadowing proportions. King Cotton had built the palaces of Fifth Avenue, and lined the vaults of Wall street. King Cotton was the mysterious, omnipresent, omnipotent potentate that kept in motion the factory spindles of two continents, and clothed the world. All seas were whitened by the canvass that carried his costly bales. Yet, although so prodigal of benefits, King Cotton was the most badly used of monarchs. His servants toiled hard upon the malarial fields and beneath the burning sun of Carolina and Mississippi, only to enrich the homes of aliens. Starting with the twin propositions that the North was wealthy and cotton the cause, this class sagely inferred that the Union was an implement of extortion and robbery. Let it be broken up, and the golden streams of wealth would at once seek their natural channels. Cities would spring up on the southern coast surpassing all others on the continent in power and grandeur. Anarchy, inevitable in the "rump" of the United States when ordinances of secession had dissevered the balance wheel, would drive capital away from its haunts in old cities to find security of investment in the new.

Extravagant fancies like these met with wide acceptance as truths. The pacific policy of the national Government precluded the fear of molestation. As a consequence men of wealth, generally so apprehensive of revolution, lent a bold hand to the consummation of this one. Had they been taught by the administration that the bonds of

Union were too sacred to be rent asunder save at such cost of blood and treasure as would leave the land a desolation, they would not have countenanced the project for a moment.

After the inauguration of President Lincoln, and during the gloomy interval when it was thought to be his purpose to give up Fort Sumpter without an effort for the relief of its heroic defenders, Capt. Lyon expresses painful apprehensions for the future. Mr. Buchanan's policy had seemed the worst possible. Through his negligence, complications easily met at first, had grown to formidable proportions. And now after a month of patient waiting, Lyon fears that President Lincoln lacks the resolution to grapple with treason and put it down forever. He says:

"My hope all along has been in Mr. Lincoln, and in his ability and purpose to give such a manifestation of authority and power to our government, as to inspire every patriot with hope and courage, and every traitor with dread and apprehension. But I begin already to fear he is not the man for the hour, and that our political triumph has been vain. If matters go on we shall soon have a formidable array of hostile troops upon us. When this comes it will, I trust, arouse the supine and timid North to a patriotic resolution which shall, in spite of executive tamperings, do something to retrieve her present degradation.

"If Mr. Lincoln does one tithe of his duty, as he has promised, we must have hostilities with the South. One of the parties must back down to avoid them. The purpose of withdrawing Maj. Anderson from Fort Sumpter, when it should have been reinforced, indicates which side is to yield, till so far pushed that the people must rise in their might, and meet the issue unnecessarily aggravated by executive mismanagement.

"I have felt deeply mortified by the humiliating attitude of my country toward traitors who could easily have been put down, and can be now, under proper measures. I do not see how a war is to be avoided. Under quack management it may be long and bloody. Yet I have no apprehensions about the final triumph of almighty truth, though at the cost of many unnecessary sacrifices. But let them come. I would rather see the country lighted up with the flames of war from the center to its remotest border, than that the great rights and hopes of the human race expire before the arrogance of secessionists. Of this, however, there is no danger. They are at war with nature and the human heart, and can not succeed."

CHAPTER X.

On the accession of the present administration, Capt. Lyon took command of the St. Louis Arsenal. The position was trying in the extreme. In the city, indeed, the friends of the Union were numerous, uncompromising, and determined to remain firm in their allegiance to the Government, at any cost and at all hazards. But the garrison, consisting of a mere handful, was beset on all sides by multitudes of enemies. Spies lurked in every hiding place, to pick up information for the use of organized bands of traitors. Bitter foes hovered about in the garb of friendship, to steal advantages by mean and shameless perfidy. But Lyon was the last man to be humbugged or deceived. He thoroughly understood his position, resources, and the characters arrayed in secret arms against him. Ever on the alert, nothing escaped his knowledge. Fertile in expedients, he employed the most ingenious devices to conceal the true condition of the garrison, and embarrass the calculations of enemies. To make his little force appear the stronger, he often sent out squads of soldiers in disguise, during the hours of night while others slept, with orders to rendezvous at a distant point, and march back to the Arsenal the next morning in uniform, with drums beating and flags flying. Nothing was left undone that could be accomplished by the wisdom, foresight, and energy of the commander. Union men in the city were organized into companies, armed and carefully drilled. Every precaution was taken to insure the security of the post.

An immense amount of public property was stored at the time in the St. Louis Arsenal. Elsewhere the insurgents had commenced operations by the seizure of arms, ordnance, moneys, in short, everything belonging to the United States. Here was a rich bait to tempt the rapacity of secessionists in Missouri. Of the hostile attitude of the State authorities, there was no room for doubt. The Executive sympathized heartily with the schemes of the rebel leaders, and with a host of subordinates, labored stealthily, but energetically, for the subversion of the Federal power. The Arsenal was sure to be attacked as soon as the traitors gained sufficient strength and courage. Secretary Cameron accordingly ordered ten thousand muskets to be removed into Illinois and sent the requisition to Gov. Yates. Capt. Stokes, of Chicago, undertook the execution of the task. Hastening to St. Louis, he found the Arsenal surrounded by a tumultuous mob, and gained access to the interior with the utmost difficulty. The requisition was shown, and the resolution taken to move the arms at the earliest moment. The numbers and desperation of the secessionists who thronged about the place, required great secresy and vigilance. The following day information came through a secret agent, that Gov. Jackson had ordered down large reinforcements from the capital for the obvious purpose of capturing the stores. Capt. Stokes telegraphed to Alton to have a steamer drop down to the Arsenal landing at midnight. Meanwhile, on the inside all were busy in getting the boxes of guns ready for removal. A quantity of inferior flint-lock muskets were sent on board a boat as a blind. These were eagerly seized by the mob, which, exultant over its imaginary luck, soon dispersed. Capt. Lyon disposed of the few stragglers that remained by locking them up in the guard house. About 11 o'clock, the steamer "City of Alton" dropped alongside, when a large quantity of arms and munitions were put on board. Before daylight Friday morning,

April 26th, the boat was on her way up the river, reaching Alton at 5 o'clock, A. M. In two hours her cargo was transferred to freight cars, and on the road to Springfield, Illinois.

In a communication issued from head-quarters at Washington, April 30th, the President directed Capt. Lyon to enroll in the military service of the United States, the loyal citizens of St. Louis and vicinity, to a number not exceeding ten thousand, inclusive of those already enlisted, for the purpose of maintaining the Federal authority, and for the protection of peaceable inhabitants. The following is a copy:

ADJUTANT-GENERAL'S OFFICE,
WASHINGTON, April 30, 1861.

Capt. Nathaniel Lyon, Second Infantry, Commanding at St. Louis:

SIR:—The President of the United States directs that you enroll in the military service of the United States, the loyal citizens of St. Louis and vicinity, not exceeding with those heretofore enlisted ten thousand in number, for the purpose of maintaining the authority of the United States, and for the protection of the peaceable inhabitants of Missouri; and you will, if deemed necessary for that purpose, proclaim martial law in the city of St. Louis. The additional force hereby authorized, shall be discharged in part or in whole, if enlisted, as soon as it appears to you that there is no danger of an attempt on the part of the enemies of the Government to take military possession of the city of St. Louis, or put the city in the control of a combination against the Government of the United States; and whilst such additional force remains in the service, the same shall be governed by the rules and articles of war and such special regulations as you may prescribe, and shall, like the force heretofore directed to be enrolled, be under your command.

L. THOMAS, Adjutant-General.

On the 6th of May, the Police Commissioners of St. Louis officially demanded of Capt. Lyon the withdrawal of the Federal troops from all buildings and places outside of the Arsenal grounds. Capt. Lyon refused compliance, and the Commissioners submitted the question to the Governor and Legislature. The demand was based on the assumption that the military occupancy of grounds not owned by the Government, was in derogation of the constitution and laws of the United States. Capt. Lyon wished the Commissioners to be more specific, and designate the articles of the constitution and the laws thus violated. In reply, they claimed that originally "Missouri had sovereign and exclusive jurisdiction over her whole territory;" that she subsequently relinquished to the United States a certain interest and sovereignty in particular grounds for military uses.

How this view justified the demand does not clearly appear. At all events, Capt. Lyon had not the astuteness to see the logical connection between the premises of the Commissioners and their implied conclusion. The same principle would render it unconstitutional to march troops over the territory of a State from one post to another. Should a garrison once enter the walls of an inland fortification, it could never leave, if it pleased the sovereignty of the State so to determine, without trampling under foot the constitution in its exit. Such a conclusion presupposes the existence of a mortal antagonism between the Federal center and the constituent States, which by a kind of sufferance allow to the General Government a qualified property in isolated patches of ground. The flimsiness of the reasoning employed by the Commissioners, shows the pitiful shifts to which traitors are forced to resort for the justification of their course.

Affairs in St. Louis were approaching a crisis. Governor Jackson, though subtle, was active in preparing for hostilities. He ordered the militia in the different districts of the State to go into encampments for military discipline and drill. At ordinary times such a step would have been perfectly right and constitutional. But in this case the Governor obviously intended to use his power as Commander-in-Chief of the State forces, for the overthrow of the Federal authority. A military bill had been recently enacted by the General Assembly, which exactly suited his purposes. He only needed time to put its machinery in operation. Above all things he desired to avoid collision with the Union troops, till he could concentrate sufficient strength to drive them from the State.

In pursuance of orders from the Governor, a camp was established near St. Louis, under the command of Gen. Frost, for the instruction of the militia. Its main avenue bore the name of "Davis," and one of the principal streets was called "Beauregard." The whole concern was designated as "Camp Jackson," in compliment to the Executive. A portion of the men had been organized under the auspices of notorious secessionists, and openly wore the badge of the southern army. Quantities of arms which had been stolen from the Government arsenal at Baton Rouge, and sent up the river in boxes marked marble, had also found their way to the camp.

It was natural for the commander of troops so obviously devoted to the interests of rebellion, to apprehend trouble. Under date of May 10th, 1861, Gen. Frost sends a communication to Capt. Lyon, stating that he is in constant receipt of information that an attack on Camp Jackson is meditated. He pretends to be at a loss to comprehend why such a project should be entertained, and disclaims all hostile intention toward the United States. He professes to be engaged in the discharge of constitutional duties, and wishes to hear from Capt. Lyon personally, whether there is any truth in the rumors alluded to.

This missive Capt. Lyon refused to receive. Before the close of the day Gen. Frost was responded to in a manner admitting of no equivocation.

During the forenoon of May 10th, the extraordinary activity near the arsenal and at the various rendezvous of the Home Guards, betokened movements of importance. Several thousand troops having suddenly assembled shortly after midday, marched under command of Capt. Lyon, in the direction of Camp Jackson. The column was furnished with about twenty cannon. On coming up they immediately surrounded the encampment, planting guns upon all the commanding eminences. Files of men were stationed at short intervals on every side. Guards were placed along the line of investment with orders to prevent ingress or egress. Meanwhile the character of the enterprise having become widely known, multitudes of excited people, in all sorts of conveyances, on horseback, and on foot, were congregating in the vicinity. Crowds armed with rifles, guns, knives, clubs, or whatever weapon could be caught up in the frenzy of the moment, hurried to the scene of action in order to assist the State troops. This surging mass was kept back by the Guards. Men, women, and children swarmed in immense numbers upon the neighboring hills. At this stage of the proceedings, the following communication was sent by Capt. Lyon to Gen. Frost:

HEAD QUARTERS, UNITED STATES TROOPS.
St. Louis, (Mo.) May 10, 1861.

Gen. D. M. Frost, Commanding Camp Jackson.

Sir, Your command is regarded as evidently hostile towards the government of the United States.

It is for the most part, made up of those secessionists who have openly avowed their hostility to the General Government, and have been plotting at the seizure of its property and the overthrow of its authority. You are openly in communication with the so-called Southern Confederacy, which is now at war with the United States, and you are receiving at your camp, from the said Confederacy and under its flag, large supplies of the material of war, most of which is known to be the property of the United States. These extraordinary preparations plainly indicate none other than the well-known purpose of the Governor of this State, under whose orders you are acting, and whose purpose recently communicated to the Legislature, has just been responded to by that body in the most unparalleled legislation, having in direct view hostilities to the General Government and co-operation with its enemies.

In view of these considerations, and of your failure to disperse in obedience to the proclamation of the President, and of the eminent necessities of State policy and welfare, and the obligations imposed upon me by instructions from Washington, it is my duty to demand, and I do hereby demand of you an immediate surrender of your command, with no other conditions than that all persons surrendering under this demand shall be humanely and kindly treated. Believing myself prepared to enforce this demand, one-half hour's time, before doing so will be allowed for your compliance therewith.

Very respectfully, your obedient servant,
N. LYON, Captain
2d Infantry, Commanding Troops.

It will be seen that thirty minutes were given Gen. Frost for deliberation. Before the expiration of the time he decided to surrender on the terms imposed. Capt. Lyon offered to release the State troops, now held as prisoners of war, provided they would swear to support the Constitution of the United States, and not take up arms against the Government. Nearly the whole number declined on the ground that they had already taken the oath of allegiance, and that its renewal under existing circumstances, would be tantamount to a confession of treason.

When the details of the surrender and march had been arranged, the prisoners started, late in the afternoon, for the city. They were drawn up in a long line, and guarded on each side by a file of Union soldiers. After the column had entered the main road, it was ordered to halt. A moment after, the report of fire-arms was heard from the front. Several members of a German company, enraged at the jeers, thrusts and blows of the crowd, discharged their pieces, but without injuring any one. The soldiers thus offending were promptly arrested. About this time the mob, which pressed in great numbers upon the rear, began to throw missiles and fire occasional shots at the Arsenal troops. The spirit of riot was rising every moment to a higher point, and threatened to break out in a general attack on the lines. Hundreds of the spectators were torturing the vocabulary of abuse to find language strong enough for the expression of their bitter anger and hatred. But the raw soldiers were not very patient in submitting to blows and maledictions. Some of them, vaguely impressed with the idea that powder and ball was the most effective remedy for mobs, fired into the crowd. A number were killed and wounded, and the terror-stricken multitude hurried out of reach of danger with the same confusion and frenzy which had characterized their approach.

The subsequent night in the city of St. Louis was a season of the most extraordinary and tumultuous excitement. Hitherto the strife between contending factions had been confined to wrathful words, or occasional blows. Now the terrible image of war glared them in the eye. For many weeks the oft-reiterated predictions of carnage and conflagration, had fell unheeded as so many meaningless puffs of air. Now the baptism of blood set the seal of life upon conceptions before vague and shadowy. Reason seemed dethroned. A mighty convulsion had, as it were, obliterated all olden and familiar landmarks in a single day. Beneath a thin crust were heard the rumblings of the earthquake. A volcano might burst out at any moment to bury the land in ruin.

The multitude were too intoxicated with delirium and passion to reflect. Throngs gathered in the principal streets, filling the air with a Babel of sounds. Huzzas and imprecations, cheers and curses, discordant shouts and the long, shrill, solitary whoop, mingled indiscriminately in the Stygian concert. Restless groups hurried hither and thither, impatient for the latest news. At different points, prominent speakers addressed the people. Banners with various devices were borne through the principal thoroughfares. A mob broke into a gun store and seized a quantity of arms before the police could collect in sufficient force to arrest the proceeding. Guards were stationed at the offices of several newspapers to protect them from the populace. Squads of armed policemen stood at the principal street corners to prevent outbreaks of violence. Thus the night wore away, till at a late hour the crowds gradually dispersed to their homes.

The news of this transaction produced a deep impression throughout the country. Few understood the facts sufficiently well to pass correct judgment upon its character and bearings. Since that time public sentiment has undergone a great revolution, as the magnitude and ferocity of the rebellion have become more fully realized. To many, the action of Capt. Lyon appeared precipitate and liable to imperil, without just grounds, the tranquillity of the State. Whatever may have been the first impression at the North, all now perceive the wisdom and foresight of the measure.

Lyon well knew that the troops at Camp Jackson sympathised with the so-called Southern Confederacy, and only waited strength and opportunity to strike at the cause of the Union. Gen. Frost's professions of loyalty, and the reluctance of the prisoners to swear a second oath of allegiance for fear it might be construed as an admission of treason, go down as mere subterfuges before multiplied proofs of the fact. Lyon had no faith in warm water lotions for sores that required caustic or cautery. He had seen the rank mischief of procrastination and mistaken leniency, elsewhere. For months he had suffered humiliation and pain, as he saw the flag of the nation insulted, her citizens outraged, her property plundered by shameless miscreants, with hardly a word of feeble rebuke. At Sumpter, the Federal guns kept silent while deadly batteries rose up around it. Was forbearance to lure back revolutionary leaders to the embrace of a long suffering and forgiving Government? Experience was driving that delusion from the minds of the most cautious and hopeful. Yet Lyon did not require the lesson at Charleston harbor to teach the nature of the conflict. He foresaw it years before. The blood-stained soil of Kansas bore witness to the malignant and cruel spirit of the rebellious chiefs. They were deaf to all arguments save those of overwhelming force.

At that moment the fate of Missouri quivered in the balance. It was no time to prate about "geographical position," "soil, climate and productions," with a view to influence the minds of men to take this side or that. Such considerations offered no obstruction to the currents of popular passion. Remonstrance and reason excited the contempt of the disaffected, as indicative of irresolution and conscious weakness. The hour had arrived to *enforce* respect and fear for the Government whose habitual indulgence was now so grievously misinterpreted and abused. Every successive day, treason showed a bolder front in the State of Missouri. Both the Governor and Legislature lent the power lodged in their hands, to the behests of the conspirators. But Capt. Lyon was resolved that treason should never flaunt in the shadow of the flag which floated over him. All along, gangs of lawless men had menanced his little band. But want of troops and authority compelled him to endure the seeming ignominy in silence. Now he was prepared to strike. The opportunity came. Secessionism in St. Louis, before so boisterous and rampant, staggered and fell under the heavy blow. The dignity of the country was vindicated, and the friends of the Union took heart.

The night following the capture of Camp Jackson, Gen. Harney arrived at St. Louis and assumed command.

A few days later, Capt. Lyon was elected Brigadier-General of the first brigade of Missouri Volunteers. On the 17th of May a communication was sent to him from the War Department at Washington, officially notifying him that the President of the United States had appointed him Brigadier-General of Volunteers, to rank as such from the 17th of May, 1861.

[COPY.]

WAR DEPARTMENT, May 17, 1861.

SIR:—You are hereby informed that the President of the United States has appointed you Brigadier-General of the volunteer force raised in conformity with the President's proclamation of May 3d, 1861, in the service of the United States, to rank as such from the 17th day of May, 1861. Should the Senate, at their next session, advise and consent thereto, you will be commissioned accordingly. You will, immediately on receipt thereof, please to communicate to this Department, through the Adjutant-General's office, your acceptance or non-acceptance of said appointment.

SIMON CAMERON, Secretary of War.

Brigadier-General NATHANIEL LYON,
U. S. Volunteers, St. Louis, Mo.

Complaints having been made to Gen. Lyon of the misdeeds of the secessionists of Potosi, he determined to administer to them a little wholesome correction. Potosi, seventy miles S. S. W. of St. Louis, is widely known on account of its lead mines. Evil-minded persons were not only furnishing this commodity to the rebels, but also taking high-handed measures against the Unionists in the vicinity. Gen. Lyon wished to stop the illicit traffic, and afford protection to peaceable citizens. Accordingly, a detachment of one hundred and fifty men, under Capt. Cole, left St. Louis by a special train, at ten o'clock, P. M., May 14th, and reached Potosi at three the next morning. The troops immediately encircled the town. When day broke and citizens began to stir abroad, they found themselves prisoners. The Unionists were released without ceremony, and a large part of the others on taking the oath of allegiance. Nine, however, of the more prominent and dangerous characters, were carried to St. Louis.

The command then visited a lead manufactory, whose owner had become notorious from furnishing the article to the enemy under circumstances of aggravated enormity. Several hundred pigs of lead were secured here. Other trophies were also captured.

After partaking of the hospitable cheer provided by the Unionists, the company started for St. Louis, making a short stop at De Soto in order to attend a grand confederate flag-raising. A body of cavalry, parading here in honor of the occasion, took to their heels on sight of the Federal uniforms. From the pole raised by the secessionists, the stars and stripes were soon thrown to the breeze amid wild joy and exultation. Not wishing to leave behind the rebel flag to tempt the people into further indiscretions, Capt. Cole detached a small party to secure it if possible. They surrounded the suspected house, and made a careful but ineffectual search. At length Doct. Franklin, one of the number, noticing the uneasy attitude of the lady of the establishment, politely requested her to rise. Finding compliance unavoidable, she reluctantly moved from her seat, when a corner of the coveted booty dropped in sight from beneath her ample habiliments. The Doctor seized the fold, and with as much consideration as circumstances would permit, delivered the lady of a large secession flag. On returning with the trophy, the party were received with an enthusiasm befitting the glory of the triumph.

The company reached the Arsenal late in the afternoon and were welcomed by a large gathering of soldiers and citizens. The troops cheered Gen. Lyon and Col. Blair, closing the ceremonies by tearing into shreds the rebel banner.

May 21st, Gen. Harney, who was extremely anxious to preserve peace in Missouri, and did not seem to realize fully the implacable determination of the conspirators against the Government, entered into an agreement with Gen. Price, of the State, Militia.

The terms of peace were not very comprehensive or specific. The intention of the parties evidently pointed to the neutrality of Missouri in the impending conflict. Gen. Price pledged the power of the State to the maintenance of order among the people, and Gen. Harney promised to make no military movement.

This step was extremely obnoxious to loyal citizens and led to the speedy recall of Gen. Harney.

Writing from the St. Louis Arsenal, May 26th, Gen. Lyon speaks of the incessant labors of the past month which have left no time for attention to private or personal matters. While the arrival of Gen. Harney gave him more leisure, it seriously interfered with his projected military movements. He says of the compact between the State and Federal officers:

"All our Union people are disgusted with this treaty, and Gen. Harney gets roundly scolded; for it is regarded only a trick of the secession Governor, to gain time, get arms and prepare again for war.

"Gen. Harney arrived the evening of my 'Camp Jackson' affair, and his authority over me of course arrested other persistent and persevering measures needed to head off the villainy of secessionism. It seems to be taking comfort and consolation now under shelter of his authority. The very Government against which the secessionists have been so long and are still conspiring, is thus used to shield them from the just consequences of their own treachery. Indeed the Government seems unwilling to resist those who would cut its throat, for fear of exasperating them. Upon this pretext we have all along been betrayed. Our friends here all feel this and deep are their mutterings.

"I cannot undertake to give you an idea of the gratification and joy which loyal people in the city and surrounding country have evinced, at events here. I have the most abounding reward in the reflection that I have contributed to the relief of good citizens from the long-suffering endured under the terrorism of secession. But most richly have they deserved relief. The bold stand taken by the Union people of St. Louis, their persevering industry, patient endurance, and liberal sacrifices, make them all heroes. A grateful country can not too deeply appreciate, or abundantly reward their services. I am indebted to them for the means of doing what I have done, and could only have done with their co-operation.

"The ladies are profuse in their patriotism. They contribute much to the troops. I have been showered with numerous manifestations of gratitude from them.

"I have hardly time to advert to what remains

of our great work which seems now to have commenced in earnest, and which I trust will be pursued with energy and discretion to a successful issue. If pushed properly there can be no failure."

May 22d, the steamer J. C. Swan was, by order of Gen. Lyon, seized at Harlow's Landing, and taken to the Arsenal. The arms captured at Camp Jackson were brought from Baton Rouge on this boat.

The same day, five thousand pounds of lead intended for rebel use, were captured at Ironton. Slight resistance was offered, and several shots exchanged, but without injury on either side.

Gen. Harney having been withdrawn from the Western Department a few days after his ill-omened agreement with Gen. Price, the command of the Federal forces in Missouri devolved upon Gen. Lyon. The change carried consternation into the ranks of the secessionists, for they knew that the time for secret and subtle machinations was past. Hitherto, under the mask of neutrality, they had labored with noiseless but desperate energy, to gain time, and make thorough preparations for resistance to the General Government. A few weeks more of delay were needed for the perfection of their arrangements. But the succession of Gen. Lyon to the command of the United States troops, fell like a bomb upon the fabric of their hopes. The extraordinary activity and determination manifested by him in previous dealings with the rebellion, warned the wily plotters either to abandon their schemes, or prepare at once to sustain them by the sword.

June 4th, Gen. Price issues a proclamation to the Brigadier-Generals commanding the several military districts in Missouri. He claims that the people of the State have the right to choose their own position in the contest. He considers the agreement entered into with Gen. Harney, honorable to both parties and Governments represented. Notwithstanding the removal of that officer, he feels assured that his successor will consider himself bound in honor to carry out the agreement in good faith. He continues:

"My wish and hope is, that the people of the State of Missouri be permitted in peace and security to decide upon their future course, and so far as my abilities can effect this object, it shall be accomplished.

"The people of Missouri can not be forced, under the terrors of a military invasion, into a position not of their free choice.

"A million of such people as the citizens of Missouri were never yet subjugated, and, if attempted, let no apprehensions be entertained of the result. I enjoin upon you, gentlemen, to see that all citizens, of whatever opinions in politics or religion, be protected in their persons and property."

CHAPTER XI.

On the 11th of June, Governor Jackson, accompanied by Gen. Price, went to St. Louis to have a personal interview with Gen. Lyon, then Commander-in-chief of the Federal army in Missouri. The conference took place at the solicitation of the State Executive, Gen. Lyon neither requesting nor desiring it. The Governor proposed to visit St. Louis, provided he could secure a pass thither and back, and be protected from arrest while in the city. He was furnished with a pass exempting him from arrest till the close of the 12th.

Gov. Jackson and Gen. Price, with the private secretary of the Governor, met Gen. Lyon, Col. F. P. Blair, Jr., and Maj. Conant, acting secretary of Gen. Lyon, at the Planters' House. The Governor professed great solicitude for the public tranquillity, and presented a series of propositions for their consideration. He offered to disband the State Guard;

to disarm all companies ordered out by the State; to desist from attempts to organize the militia under the military bill; to prevent the importation of arms or munitions into the State; to guarantee the general and impartial protection of citizens in all their rights; to suppress insurrectionary movements; and finally, to prevent every attempt at invasion, from any quarter and by whomsoever made. He wished to pledge Missouri to a course of strict neutrality. These terms were offered *on condition* that the General Government would undertake to disband the Home Guard, at the time organized and armed throughout the State, and solemnly agree not to occupy with its troops any localities in the State not then occupied by them.

Gen. Lyon rejected the propositions of the Governor. He in turn demanded the disbanding of the militia, organized under the provisions of the recent military bill; the nullification of that unconstitutional and outrageous act of the Legislature; and the admission of the unqualified right of the Federal Government to march and to station its troops whenever and wherever it might be deemed necessary, either for the protection of loyal subjects, or for repelling invasion. He also refused unequivocally to disband the Home Guard or withdraw the United States troops and expressed his determination to protect the Unionists in the rural districts, who could only be secured in the enjoyment of life, property, and other rights, by the active interposition of the Federal power.

Thus the Governor wholly failed in the artful scheme contrived to entrap the United States officers. Gen. Lyon regarded the doctrine of "neutrality" in a war waged avowedly for the overthrow of the General Government, as the rankest political heresy. Was a stalwart son to remain an indifferent spectator, while assassins were struggling to plunge the dagger into the heart of a kind and over-indulgent parent? Was he to look with unconcern upon the bruised and bleeding form whose hand had lavished upon him blessings innumerable?

Even more diabolical were the purposes of Gov. Jackson and Gen. Price. Their apparent anxiety "to avert the horrors of civil war," was well known to be a hypocritical ruse to gain time and carry Missouri out of the Union by the wiles of diplomacy. These men wished to render active aid in the work of assassination.

The acceptance of the terms and conditions proposed by the Executive at the conference with Gen. Lyon, would have amounted to an acknowledgment of the complete independent sovereignty of Missouri. The doctrine of "State sovereignty," thus interpreted, would render the system of government elaborated by our fathers, one of the weakest and most contemptible contrivances of human folly. An enemy might gather armies and make formidable preparations for the invasion of the United States, just beyond her border, and the General Government not be allowed to march a soldier over a "neutral" member of the body politic to meet the danger. According to this view, the exemption of a solitary State from the presence of national troops, if such presence be obnoxious to her citizens, becomes a matter of graver moment than the preservation of national liberty. All obligations of patriotism are utterly ignored. The Federal Government is degraded to the character of general agent for the separate States, to be employed or dismissed as the caprice of the hour may determine.

The plan of Gov. Jackson for insuring tranquillity, was the one best suited to bring upon the State the desolations of civil war. Missouri contains a martial population. On each side of her, hosts were arming for the conflict. Men of human impulses and passions could never stand by with folded hands, while the noise of battle raged around them. Even if the commonwealth nominally stood neutral, her sons would flock to the camps of the belligerents. There was but one course of safety. Let the State be true to the Union, and her soil could never be defiled by the tread of a rebel soldier. The war would then be pushed further southward, to spend its fury among the people who had instigated it.

One hour after the close of the interview between the State and Federal Officers, Gov. Jackson and Gen. Price started in a special train on their return to Jefferson City. The pass furnished by Gen. Lyon protected the Governor from arrest till the close of the next day. But the loyal atmosphere of St. Louis proved extremely oppressive, and the party hastened to reach a place where they could breathe with greater freedom.

Besides, the failure to circumvent Gen. Lyon put an end to all hopes of success through double-dealing and craft. They knew that henceforth the enemies of the Government in Missouri must rely upon the sword, and from the decision and celerity previously exhibited by the Federal commander, rightly inferred that the hours for completing their preparations were few.

The next day, June 12th, Gov. Jackson fulminated a remarkable proclamation to the people of Missouri. The following extracts indicate the agitation of the Governor, and the state of mental bewilderment into which the events of the past few days had terrified him:

JEFFERSON CITY, June 12, 1861.

To the People of Missouri:

A series of unprovoked and unparalleled outrages have been inflicted on the peace and dignity of this Commonwealth, and upon the rights and liberties of its people, by wicked and unprincipled men, professing to act under the authority of the United States Government; the solemn enactments of your Legislature have been nullified, your volunteer soldiers have been taken prisoners, your commerce with your sister States has been suspended, your trade with your own fellow-citizens has been and is subjected to increasing control of an armed soldiery, peaceful citizens have been imprisoned without warrant of law, unoffending and defenceless men, women, and children, have been ruthlessly shot down and murdered, and other unbearable indignities have been heaped upon your State and yourselves. To all these outrages and indignities you have submitted with patriotic forbearance, which has only encouraged the perpetrators of these grievous wrongs to attempt still bolder and more daring usurpations.

* * * * * * * *

Fellow-citizens, all our efforts toward conciliation have failed. We can hope for nothing from the justice or moderation of the agents of the Federal Government in this State. They are energetically hastening the execution of their bloody and revolutionary schemes for the inauguration of civil war in your midst; for the military occupation of your State by armed bands of lawless invaders; for the overthrow of your State Government, and for the subversion of those liberties which the Government has always sought to protect; and they intend to exert their whole power to subjugate you, if possible, to the military despotism which has usurped the powers of the Federal Government.

Now, therefore, I, C. F. Jackson, Governor of the State of Missouri, do, in view of the foregoing facts, and by virtue of the powers vested in me by the Constitution and laws of this Commonwealth, issue this my proclamation, calling the militia of this State, to the number of 50,000, into active service of the State, for the purpose of repelling such invasion, and for the protection of the lives, liberties and property of the citizens of this State; and I earnestly exhort all good citizens of Missouri to rally to the flag of their State, for the protection of their homes and firesides, and for the defense of their most sacred rights and dearest liberties.

In issuing this proclamation, I hold it to be my most solemn duty to remind you that Missouri is still one of the United States; that the Executive Department of the State Government does not arrogate to itself the power to disturb that relation; that power has been wisely vested in the Convention, which will at the proper time express your sovereign will; and that meanwhile it is your duty to obey all constitutional requirements of the Federal Government. But it is equally my duty to advise you that your first allegiance is due to your own State, and that you are under no obligation whatever to obey the unconstitutional edicts of the military despotism which has introduced itself at Washington, nor submit to the infamous and degrading sway of its wicked minions in this State. No brave-hearted Missourian will obey the one or submit to the other. Rise, then, and drive out ignominiously the invaders who have dared to desecrate the soil which your labors have made fruitful, and which is consecrated by your homes.

CLAIBORNE F. JACKSON.

In this proclamation the Governor assumed that the Legislature could bind the people by the enactment of laws violative of the constitution; that the enrollment of volunteers under the provisions of the military bill was a legal act; and that men struggling to embarrass and destroy the General Government were peaceable citizens. The presence in the State of Federal troops is treated as an invasion, and fifty thousand militia are called into service to repel the invaders. Yet in the next sentence this "Artful Dodger" reminds the people that

Missouri is one of the United States still, innocently remarking that "the executive department of the State Government does not arrogate to itself the power to disturb that relation." He intimates that the Convention will soon release them from the odious connection with the Union. Till then, citizens are exhorted to obey all constitutional requirements of the Federal Government, but in the same breath are reminded that the Administration at Washington is a "military despotism,"—a usurpation whose edicts they are under no obligation to obey. The Governor's reasoning involved him in a maze of absurdities, and although ending in rank treason, made the most audacious assumptions to get there.

On the 13th, two days after the visit of Gov. Jackson to St. Louis, and one after the publication of his proclamation, the steamers Iatan and J. C. Swan, with fifteen hundred troops on board under command of Gen. Lyon, left for Jefferson City. The expedition was furnished with horses, wagons, camp equipage, and stores for immediate and active operations.

Gov. Jackson having been apprised of the movement, abandoned the capital and hastened to Booneville, forty miles higher up the river. The rebels took with them all the cars and locomotives that could be secured, broke down the telegraph, and destroyed the bridges behind them in their flight.

The steamers arrived at Jefferson City the afternoon of the 15th, when Gen. Lyon landed a part of his forces and occupied the town. No opposition of any kind was attempted. On the contrary, a large concourse of citizens greeted the arrival of the Union troops with enthusiastic cheers.

Gen. Lyon now issued a proclamation to the citizens of Missouri, in which he ably reviewed the events of the past few weeks. He convicts the Governor and Legislature of treasonable sympathies and treasonable acts, exposing the persistent and villainous methods adopted by them to force the people into rebellion. The proclamation recites the memorandum prepared by Gen. Harney, and read in the presence of Gen. Price, as a fundamental basis of the negotiations between those officers, and shows how grossly its terms had been disregarded by the State Authorities. It also contains the instructions of the President to the Commanding Officer of the Department of the West, and expresses the determination of Gen. Lyon to carry them out in letter and spirit.

PROCLAMATION OF BRIGADIER-GENERAL N. LYON.

To the Citizens of Missouri :—Prior to the proclamation issued by Gov. Jackson, of the date of 12th of June, inst., it was well known to you that the Governor and Legislature sympathized in the revolutionary movement now in progress in the country, and had adopted every means in their power to effect a separation of this State from the General Government. For this purpose parties of avowed secessionists have been organized into military companies throughout the State, with the full knowledge and approval of the Governor.

The establishment of encampments in the State at an unusual period of the year, and authorized for an indefinite period, could have had no other object than the concentration of a large military force, to be subjected to the provisions of the Military Bill—then in contemplation and subsequently passed—a bill so offensive to all peaceful inhabitants, and so palpably unconstitutional, that it could be accepted by those only who were willing to conform to its extraordinary provisions, for the purpose of effecting their cherished object—the disruption of the Federal Government.

That bill provides for an obligation to the State on the part of all persons enrolled under its provisions, irrespective of any obligation to the United States, when the Constitution requires all State officers to take an oath of allegiance to the United States. This of itself is a repudiation of all authority of the general Government—whose Constitution is the supreme law—on the part of the State government, its officers and such citizens as might choose to adopt the provisions of the bill, and coupled as it was, on the part of the Legislature and Governor, with declarations hostile to its authority and in sympathy with those who were arrayed in a condition of actual hostility against it—could leave no doubt of its objects.

To carry out the provisions of this extraordinary law, the Public Schools were deprived of the funds necessary to the education of your children—your asylums, even, stripped of the means of support, and an additional onerous tax imposed upon you.

This bill, regarded as it has uniformly been, by all loyal citizens of the United States, as having in direct view hostilities to the Federal Government, was so denounced by Gen. Harney, who characterized it as a secession ordinance, in his proclamation of the 14th of May last.

That proclamation doubtless gave rise to an interview between Gen. Harney and Gen. Price, that resulted in an agreement which it was hoped would lead to the restoration of tranquillity and good order in your State.

That a repudiation of the military bill, and of all efforts to organize the militia of the State under its provisions, was the basis of the agreement, is shown as well by the proclamation of Gen. Harney immediately preceding it, as by the following paper submitted to Gen. Price, containing preliminary conditions to an interview with him:

"MEMORANDUM FOR GEN. PRICE.

May 21, 1861.

General Harney is here as a citizen of Missouri, with all his interests at stake in the preservation of the peace of the State.

He earnestly wishes to do nothing to complicate matters, and will do everything in his power, consistently with instructions, to preserve peace and order.

He is, however, compelled to recognize the existence of a rebellion in a portion of the United States, and in view of it he stands upon the proclamation of the President, itself based upon the law and constitution of the United States.

The proclamation commands the dispersion of all armed bodies hostile to the supreme law of the land. Gen. Harney sees in the Missouri military bill, features which compel him to look upon such armed bodies as may be organized under its provisions, as antagonistic to the United States, within the meaning of the proclamation, and calculated to precipitate a conflict between the State and United States troops.

He laments this tendency of things, and most cordially and earnestly invites the coöperation of Gen. Price to avert it.

For this purpose, Gen. Harney respectfully asks Gen. Price to review the features of the bill in the spirit of law, warmed and elevated by that of humanity, and seek to discover some means by which its action may be suspended until some competent tribunal shall decide upon its character.

The most material features of the bill calculated to bring about a conflict, are, first, the *oath* required to be taken by the militia and "State Guards"—(an oath of allegiance to the State of Missouri, without recognizing the existence of the Government of the United

States;) and secondly, the express requirements, by which troops within the State, not organized under the provisions of the military bill, are to be disarmed by the *State Guards*.

Gen. Harney can not be expected to wait a summons to surrender his arms by the State troops.

From this statement of the case, the true question becomes immediately visible, and can not be shut out of view.

Gen. Price is earnestly requested to consider this, and Gen. Harney will be happy to confer with him on the subject whenever it may suit his convenience.

N. B.—Read to Gen. Price in the presence of Maj. H. S. Turner, on the evening of the 21st of May."

This agreement failed to define specifically the terms of the peace, or how far a suspension of the provisions of the military bill should form a part of it, though from the express declaration of Gen. Harney, at the time of the conference, as well as from the foregoing paper, a suspension of any action under the bill, until there could be a judicial determination of its character by some competent tribunal, must in good faith be regarded as the fundamental basis of the negotiation.

Nevertheless, immediately after this arrangement, and up to the time of Gov. Jackson's proclamation, innumerable complaints of attempts to execute the provisions of this bill, by which most exasperating hardships have been imposed upon peaceful and loyal citizens—coupled with persecution and proscription of those opposed to its provisions—have been made to me as commander of the United States forces here, and have been carried to the authorities at Washington, with appeals for relief from Union men in all parts of the State, who have been abused and insulted, and in some instances driven from their homes. That relief I conceive it to be the duty of a just government to use every exertion in its power to give. On this point the policy of the Government is set forth in the following communication from the department at Washington:

"ADJUTANT-GENERAL'S OFFICE,
WASHINGTON, May 27, 1861.

Brigadier-General W. S. Harney, Commanding Dep't of West, St. Louis, Mo.:

SIR:—The President observes with concern, that notwithstanding the pledge of the State authorities to coöperate in preserving peace in Missouri, that loyal citizens in great numbers continue to be driven from their homes.

It is immaterial whether those outrages continue from inactivity or indisposition on the part of the State authorities to prevent them. It is enough that they continue, to devolve on you the duty of putting a stop to them summarily by the force under your command, to be aided by such troops as you may require from Kansas, Iowa, and Illinois. The professions of loyalty to the Union by the State authorities of Missouri are not to be relied upon. They have already falsified their professions too often, and are too far committed to secession, to be submitted to your confidence, and you can only be sure of their desisting from their wicked purposes when it is out of their power to prosecute them. You will therefore be unceasingly watchful of their movements, and not permit the clamors of their partizans and opponents of the wise measures already taken, to prevent you from checking every movement against the Government, however disguised, under the pretended State authority. The authority of the United States is paramount, and whenever it is apparent that a movement, whether by color of State authority or not, is hostile, you will not hesitate to put it down.

I am, Sir, very respectfully,

Your obedient servant,

(Signed,) L. THOMAS, Adj. Gen."

It is my determination to carry out these instructions in their letter and spirit. Their justice and propriety will be appreciated by all those who take an enlightened view of the relations of the citizens of Missouri to the General Government; nor can such policy be construed as at all disparaging to the rights or dignity of the State of Missouri, or as infringing in any sense upon the individual liberty of its citizens.

The recent proclamation of Gov. Jackson, by which he has set at defiance the authorities of the United States, and urged you to make war upon them, is but the consummation of his treasonable purposes, long indicated by his acts and expressed opinions, and now made manifest. If, in suppressing these treasonable projects, carrying out the policy of the Government, and maintaining its dignity, as above indicated, hostilities should unfortunately occur, and unhappy consequences should follow, I would hope that all aggravation of those evils may be avoided, and that they may be diverted from the innocent and may fall only upon the heads of those by whom they have been provoked.

In the discharge of these plain but onerous duties, I shall look for the countenance and active co-operation of all good citizens. I shall expect them to discountenance all illegal combinations or organizations, and to support and uphold, by every lawful means, the Federal Government, upon the maintenance of which depend their liberties and the perfect enjoyment of all their rights.

N. LYON,
Brig. Gen. U. S. Vol. Commanding.

June 15, 1861

June 16th, Gen. Lyon, with a force of nearly two thousand men, left Jefferson City on the steamers A. McDowell, Iatan, and City of Louisiana, in pursuit of Gov. Jackson. Having stopped a few hours during the night, the expedition, early the next morning, came in sight of a hostile battery planted on the bluffs several miles below Booneville. The boats were turned back a short distance to an eligible place, where the troops disembarked without opposition. They immediately took the river-road for the city, a sufficient force being left behind for the protection of the steamers. On ascending the bluff a mile and a half from the place of landing, the pickets of the enemy were seen and driven in. The troops passed on up the gentle acclivity, and on gaining the summit, came in sight of the rebels. These were strongly posted about three hundred yards in advance, on the crest of a long ridge, parallel to the swell of ground now occupied by the Federals. The road which led directly over it was held by a battalion of infantry and a small body of cavalry. On the left was a brick house, and in the rear a lane extending toward the river, where the main body were stationed. The right wing of the enemy were posted in a wheat field on the opposite side of the road.

So soon as the advancing column could be prepared for action, Capt. Totten opened the engagement by throwing shell into the ranks of the rebels. They replied with a noisy discharge of musketry, and at first seemed determined to make an obstinate fight. But the terrible effectiveness of the artillery, and the steady approach of the infantry, soon threw them into a panic which ended in a disgraceful rout. Twenty minutes after the discharge of the first shot from Capt. Totten's battery, the Union troops were in possession of the whole field.

The enemy fled to their encampment a mile west of the battle-ground, and four and a half miles east of Booneville. Here they made a halt which proved to be very brief, for the rapidity of the pursuit left them little time to collect their effects. The camp equipage, provisions, ammunition, horses, and guns abandoned by the rebels, were captured.

This camp was formed the previous Friday, (the

14th.) The same day messengers were dispatched to towns near and remote, to urge the State Guards and the people generally to repair forthwith to Booneville, and to bring with them arms and ammunition. Men soon began to pour in singly and in squads, and were immediately sent forward to this position. Sunday morning a rumor reached the rebel head-quarters, that the forces of Gen. Lyon were near the city, and approaching rapidly. After a hasty consultation, the Governor and military officers came to the conclusion that the preparations for defense were not yet sufficiently complete to warrant them in giving battle. Accordingly an order was issued to the State troops to disband. Some took advantage of the license to leave, but the larger and more resolute portion preferred to remain. Gen. Price was absent, having gone home on account of indisposition. The rumor which had so alarmed the rebel leaders was soon ascertained to be false, when their courage revived. The first order was countermanded. Troops continued to arrive during the day, and by Monday morning, the time of the engagement, their number was estimated at thirty-five hundred. Only a few, however, were well armed. The weapons of six-sevenths of the force were confined to the rifles, shot-guns and knives which they brought from home. The whole mass was unorganized, undisciplined, and consequently no match for the well-trained troops of Gen. Lyon.

Gov. Jackson, with a select body guard, awaited the issue at a safe distance. When the fate of the contest became apparent, he rode to town and shortly after disappeared without indicating the place of his destination. Since then, a fugitive and a wanderer, seeking rest but finding none, he has tasted the sweets of the rebellion, to the fortunes of which he strove so earnestly and unscrupulously to commit the State of Missouri.

Capt. Cole was left in charge of the captured camp, while the main body pushed on toward Booneville. Near the town, they were met by a number of influential citizens, bearing a flag of truce. Gen. Lyon received them courteously, and gave assurances that the people need apprehend no trouble, if ready to acknowledge the laws and authority of the United States. The city was now surrendered to the Federal authorities. Loyal inhabitants hailed their deliverance from recent terrorism, oppression and tumult, with enthusiastic demonstrations of joy. Uproarious cheers welcomed the Union leaders. Ordinary business was resumed, and the blessings of peace and order quickly succeeded the brief but violent reign of treason.

Meanwhile Capt. Richardson effected a landing below the battery on the bluff, which he captured. Two cannon, twenty prisoners, several horses, and a quantity of military stores here fell into the hands of the Federals. Thus the triumph was complete.

Two of the Union soldiers were killed and eleven wounded. The loss of the State troops is not exactly known. The earliest telegraphic accounts placed it at three hundred—a wild exaggeration. Their flight was so precipitate and rapid that they were exposed to fire but a few moments, and as only five hundred of the Federal troops were *actively* engaged, the slaughter could not have been very heavy in proportion to the whole number of the secession rabble.

In the hottest of the fight, Gen. Lyon, while leading on the column, attempted to dismount, not wishing to present quite so conspicuous a target for the marksmen of the enemy. The horse at the same instant darting aside from fright, threw him upon the ground. The rumor flew along the lines that the General was shot. Till the truth was ascertained, the shouts for vengeance were loud and terrible, for no officer was ever more beloved by his soldiers.

Among other trophies, a quantity of treasonable letters and documents were seized. These contributed still further to establish the fact that the executive and other prominent officials of the State, while loud in the utterance of fair professions, were industriously plotting against the Government. Although such proofs of guilt could add no strength to the convictions of the Union leaders, they served to condemn the traitors out of their own mouths, presenting most conclusive evidence of their previous falsehood and duplicity.

Gen. Lyon issued a second proclamation, the day after the battle, to the people of Missouri. After setting forth the reasons of his expedition to Booneville, he proceeded to deal with the case of the captured prisoners. These he released on account of their immature age, and of the frauds ingeniously devised by older heads for their misguidance, on their simple promise not to bear arms against the United States. At the same time, he gave warning that the mildness of the General Government could not be expected to continue, if its clemency should still be abused as on former occasions.

He also endeavored to disabuse the minds of the people of the erroneous ideas which many of them entertained respecting the purposes of the Government, and promised amnesty for past offenses to such as would now relinquish their hostile attitude to the United States.

PROCLAMATION—TO THE PEOPLE OF MISSOURI.

Upon leaving the city of St. Louis, in consequence of the declaration of war made by the Governor of this State against the Government of the United Slates, because I would not assume, on its behalf, to relinquish its duties and abdicate its rights of protecting loyal citizens from the oppression and cruelties of secessionists in this State, I published an address to the people, in which I declared my intention to use the force under my command for no other purpose than the maintenance of the authority of the General Government, and the protection of the rights and property of all law abiding citizens.

The State authorities, in violation of an agreement with Gen. Harney, on the 21st of May last, had drawn together and organized upon a large scale the means of warfare, and having made declaration of war, they abandoned the capital, issued orders for the destruction of the railroad and telegraph lines, and proceeded to this point to put in execution their hostile purposes toward the General Government. This devolved upon me the necessity of meeting this issue to the best of my ability, and accordingly I moved to this point with a portion of the force under my command, attacked and dispersed the hostile forces gathered here by the Governor, and took possession of the camp equipage left, and a considerable number of prisoners, most of them young and of immature age, who represent that they have been misled by frauds, ingeniously devised and industriously circulated by designing leaders, who seek to devolve upon unreflecting and deluded followers the task of securing the object of their own false ambition. Out of compassion for these misguided youths, and to correct impressions created by unscrupulous calumniators, I have liberated them upon condition that they will not serve in the impending hostilities against the United States Government. I have done this in spite of the known facts that the leaders in the present rebellion, having long experienced the mildness of the General Government, still feel confident that this mildness can not be overtaxed, even by factious hostilities, having in view its overthrow; but if, as in the case of the late Camp Jackson affair, this clemency shall still be misconstrued, it is proper to give warning, that the Government can not be always expected to indulge it to the compromise of its evident welfare.

Having learned that those plotting against the Government have falsely represented that the Government troops intended a forcible and violent invasion of Missouri, for the purposes of military despotism and tyranny, I hereby give notice to the people of this State, that I shall scrupulously avoid all interference with the business, rights and property of every description, recognized by the laws of this State, and belonging to law abiding citizens; but that it is equally my duty to maintain the paramount authority of the United States with such force as I have at my command, which will be retained only so long as opposition shall make it necessary, and that it is my wish, and shall be my purpose to devolve any unavoidable rigor arising in this issue, upon those only who provoke it.

All persons who, under the misapprehensions above mentioned, have taken up arms, or who are now preparing to do so, are invited to return to their homes and relinquish their hostile attitude to the General Government, and are assured that they may do so without being molested for past occurrences.

N. LYON,
Brigadier-General U. S. Vol., Commanding.

BOONEVILLE, Mo., June 18, 1861.

When General Lyon entered Booneville many of the citizens were strongly prejudiced against him. He had been represented by the numerous calumniators of the Government, who for some time past had borne undisputed sway in the city, as cruel, vindictive and tyrannic. Popular opinion placed him at the head of an army made up of blood-thirsty and rapacious hirelings, who had enlisted in the enterprise for booty, and for the gratification of brutal instincts.

But a short experience served completely to dissipate such impressions. The bearing of Gen. Lyon, both as a soldier and gentleman, overwhelmed his enemies by the recoil of their own falsehoods, and made many converts to the Union cause. His kindness to the wounded left on the battle-field, his lenity to the prisoners, his generous and courteous demeanor toward bitter secessionists, his impartiality in punishing the men guilty of depredations upon the property of rebel-sympathizers, and the uniform beneficence with which he exercised his authority,—all stood forth in bold contrast with the illegal and desperate measures of his principal vilifiers.

A near relative and intimate personal friend of Gen. Lyon, having been often solicited by correspondents of the press and others, for information in regard to the earlier experiences of the General, requested him to make a memorandum of the most prominent events in his past life for the benefit of the public. He received the following reply:

BOONEVILLE, MO., June 28th, 1861.

DEAR COUSIN,—I have your two notes asking for points of my military service. I have not answered, because I have no time, and do not think the subject of the least importance. This great and most wicked rebellion absorbs my whole being to the exclusion of any considerations of fame or self-advancement. In this issue, if I have or shall have a conspicuous part, I would share it and the honors of it equally with every one who contributes to sustain the great cause of our country which I have so much at heart.

I have not received your notice of me in the Journal of Commerce. Most of the notices by the press are more or less erroneous. But alas the past is nothing—painfully indeed unfruitful of benefits to our race. It is with the present we are dealing, and let us all devote ourselves to it with a view to secure the future. And let that future be blank and forever oblivious rather than our cause fail before the unscrupulous villainy now at war upon it. Of the ultimate result I have no doubts, though unfavorable incidents may arise under frauds, and misrepresentations, and a heretofore demoralized sentiment at the North, so unfortunately auspicious to our enemies.

I am now deeply involved and concerned in the issues before me. My exertions and will shall not be wanting, though they may not go far to effect the result.

What is now before me in this region I hardly know. The Governor and party have gone South and may make another stand; though it is probable they intend to rendezvous in Arkansas and return with reinforcements. I have been unavoidably delayed by getting up a train, but shall pursue though I do not expect to catch the fugitives.

Yours truly,

N. LYON.

The brilliant exploits of General Lyon had excited the admiration of the country, and made him the hero of the hour. But while all eyes were turned toward him, and all were eager to do him honor, he was devoting every thought and every power of mind and body to the service of the nation, regardless of popularity or applause. He never paused to inquire how an action would affect him personally, or whether it was likely to bring favor or reproach. If a particular course was obviously demanded by the public good, that alone was a sufficient warrant to attempt it. No man less selfish, or more patriotic, ever lived.

CHAPTER XII.

Two weeks were busily occupied at Booneville in collecting a train and making other preparations for a march. Owing to the vigorous policy of Gen. Lyon and his associates, the principal towns on the Missouri river, and indeed throughout the State, were now under the control of the Federal authorities. The presence of loyal bayonets proved to be the weightiest of arguments for turning secessionists from the error of their ways. Remarkable conversions everywhere rewarded the labors of the Union armies. Villages before wholly given over apparently to blindness of vision and hardness of heart, repented when National troops proclaimed in their midst the terrors of a broken law. Men of evil intentions had no time to organize formidable movements in opposition to the General Government. As a consequence the disaffected rapidly returned to their first love, and the loyal sentiment of the people grew stronger every day.

Meanwhile the whereabouts of Governor Jackson attracted no small degree of curiosity and comment. Rumor placed him at numerous and widely distant localities, surrounding him with a great diversity of retinues. Repudiated by the people whom he had striven to betray, and almost encircled by the gleaming bayonets of the Federal power, his position at best seemed full of peril. Kansas on the West remembered the cruel efforts put forth by Claiborne F. Jackson a few years before, to trample under foot the rights and liberties of her people. Having just entered the constellation of States, she testified her gratitude for freedom, by arming a large proportion of her sons in defense of the institutions which had already cost her no small share of suffering and blood. Escape in that direction was impossible. General Lyon was preparing to sweep southward from Booneville, and it was certain that the fugitive Governor would take good care to avoid another "interview." General Sweeny and Col. Siegel held the country about Springfield and the line toward St. Louis.

It was necessary to procure a train at Booneville before starting for Southwestern Missouri. Notice was sent into the surrounding country that teams *must* be had, and that a fair price would be paid for such as were brought in voluntarily. Three army officers and two citizens were appointed to make a selection from the property offered for sale, and to arrange the terms.

The patriotism of the people was wonderfully stimulated by the prospect of ready money, and every owner of a dilapidated wagon or spavined horse, hastened to Booneville to place it at the service of the Government. From the motley and ludicrous collection of animals and vehicles, the commissioners succeeded in making up a train which proved much more useful than showy.

Heavy rains delayed the departure of troops several days. At length the sky became more propitious, and on the 3d of July, Gen. Lyon's army, numbering twenty-seven hundred men, with four pieces of artillery and a long baggage-train, started for Springfield. The day, like many following, was intensely hot. At one o'clock, P. M., the troops encamped on the banks of a small stream sixteen miles from Booneville.

At three o'clock on the morning of July Fourth, the roll of drums aroused the weary men to resume the march. But on this national holiday the army paused not for parade or merriment. Through stifling dust and fiery heat, this column of earnest warriors celebrated the birth-day of the Nation by hurrying bravely forward to strike the Nation's foe.

The line of march was as follows:

A company of regulars, armed with rifled muskets, led the way.

Next followed one hundred pioneers, with Sharps' rifles slung across their shoulders, and with axes and shovels in their hands.

Then came Capt. Totten's battery, each gun drawn by four powerful horses, and attended by a body of cannoneers ready for instant service.

The artillery was succeeded by Bates' Iowa regiment and Blair's St. Louis regiment.

A baggage-train two miles in length, followed by a drove of cattle and a company of soldiers, brought up the rear.

Gen. Lyon, mounted on an iron-grey horse, and accompanied by his body-guard, galloped up and down the line, encouraging the men, and keeping a watchful eye on everything.

This body-guard was composed of ten German butchers from St. Louis, conspicuous for their stalwart forms and fearless horsemanship. Mounted on powerful chargers, and armed with revolvers and massive cavalry swords, they rode by the General's side wherever his duties called him.

The fifth of July, the army, while marching across a broad, open prairie, was overtaken by a terrific thunder storm. The men were all drenched in the torrents which fell upon their unsheltered heads. Toward night the clouds passed away, and the troops, encamping in a field of tall, dank grass, partially dried their clothing in the rays of the setting sun.

The sixth, the army marched more than twenty miles before noon, when they encamped upon the prairie. At night Gen. Lyon dispatched two companies under Capt. Cole, to secure the ferry at Grand River, eighteen miles distant. This detachment, having marched forty miles in twenty-four hours, was entirely successful in the object of its mission. At this ferry (in Henry county,) Gen. Lyon was joined the next day by three thousand troops from Kansas, under command of Maj. Sturgis. A small scow, capable of accommodating but forty men, afforded the only means at hand for crossing the stream. This was kept in constant motion during the night, and by ten o'clock the next morning the troops and the long baggage-train were all on the opposite bank. Two cavalry companies crossed first, the evening of the 7th, and immediately pushed forward under cover of night, to gain the ferry on the Osage, twenty-two miles ahead. Reaching the river shortly after day-break, they discovered the ferry-boat tied to the opposite shore. A few of the men swam over and secured it.

The main army reached the Osage on the afternoon of the 9th, striking the stream in the heart of a dense forest, ten or twelve miles west of Osceola. Here they first heard of Col. Siegel's fight at Carthage, and of his retreat toward Springfield. Rumor magnified the peril of his situation, and the necessity of immediate aid. The news produced the most intense excitement. Different commanders implored Gen. Lyon to allow them to cross first with their detachments, promising to march the whole distance (eighty miles) to Springfield in thirty-six hours. Gen. Lyon decided, however, that the troops should cross the stream in regular order, and then hurry forward by forced marches. He also changed the direction of his march, which had hitherto been directed toward a point considerably west of Springfield.

Shortly after sunrise on the 11th, the army started from the south bank of the Osage. Most of the night had been occupied in transporting the men and teams over the stream. But the prospect of soon meeting the enemy seemed to render the troops insensible to fatigue. All were eager for battle, and under the stimulus of the recent news pressed on, unmindful of the scorching heat. At three P. M., the army halted for dinner, twenty-seven miles from the Osage ferry.

At sundown the line of march was again formed. The road soon struck a heavy forest, where the dense foliage of the overhanging limbs shut out the glimmer of the stars, leaving the men to grope their way through almost total darkness. The road was little traveled, and extremely rough. Steep hills, deep gorges, swift streams, miry sloughs, gullies washed out by the rains, rocks scattered about everywhere, stumps and fallen timber, were among the obstacles which had to be encountered in the darkness. Many were the bruised limbs and broken vehicles. For thirty-six hours most of the men had hardly closed their eyes, and now insupportable drowsiness overpowered them. If the line came to a momentary halt, scores fell asleep in their tracks. Arousing as the column moved on, the men struggled bravely against fatigue till three o'clock in the morning, when Gen. Lyon ordered a halt. Scarcely was the order issued, before nine-tenths of the army were buried in slumber. Few waited to unroll their blankets, or seek a sheltered spot for a couch. Wherever they stood, they dropped upon the ground—officers and privates indiscriminately—with the earth for a bed and the sky for a covering.

Within twenty-four hours, the army had marched nearly fifty miles, over a horrible road—and that, too, when worn down by previous hardships and the loss of rest.

The next morning, a messenger announced the safety of Col. Siegel. The remainder of the route was leisurely finished the two following days, the army encamping in the vicinity of Springfield on the 13th.

The entire distance of nearly two hundred miles, including the passage across two rivers with very inadequate means of transportation, was accomplished in eleven days. Such celerity of movement, in the face of such obstacles, tells its own story and needs no comment.

By means of incredible exertions, Gen. Lyon had forced the armed enemies of the Government into the South-Western corner of the State. Barely a month before, the rebel leaders menanced St. Louis, and confidently predicted the speedy extinction of all Federal authority in Missouri. But the vigor of Gen. Lyon happily thwarted their nefarious plans. Within the short period of five weeks he had driven Gov. Jackson and Gen. Price from Jefferson City, from Booneville, and now to the very borders of Arkansas.

In the terrible struggle which ensued, every advantage was with the enemy. Many of the troops who had captured Camp Jackson, seized the State

Capital, and won the victory at Booneville, had now served through the period of enlistment, and were about to return to their homes. On the other hand, the numerous rebels of Missouri who had gathered in this vicinity under command of Gen. Price, were here reinforced from all of the South-Western States. Gen. McCulloch, the Confederate commander, had at his disposal an overwhelming army, and was prepared to enter upon offensive and aggressive movements. The force of Gen. Lyon grew weaker every day. He called repeatedly for reinforcements, but no reinforcements were sent. Yet he was determined to hold the position at all hazards. The strategic importance of the country, the great value of the Granby lead mines which he hoped to wrest from the enemy, and the protection of Unionists, induced him to remain notwithstanding the great numerical superiority and other advantages of the rebel army.

Information having reached Springfield that the rebels were preparing to move upon the town in two divisions, Gen. Lyon decided to make a forced march and fight them separately. Late in the afternoon, on the first of August, his entire army, with the exception of a small force left behind to guard the city, set out on the expedition. At ten o'clock they reached the place of rendezvous on Crane Creek, and encamped for the night. The next morning the troops were in motion at an early hour. The hardships of that and the several subsequent days, were excessive. Most of the streams and wells were dry, the air was filled with clouds of fine dust stirred up by the tramp of men and animals, the sun shone with tropical fervor upon the parched fields, and few trees were found along the way to shelter the troops from its overpowering rays. The road, in many places, was lined with forests of scrubby oaks and other stunted growths, which afforded little shade, yet rendered the march much more slow and laborious on account of the precautions necessary to avoid possible ambuscades and masked batteries.

In the afternoon the army arrived at Dug Springs, nineteen miles South-west of Springfield. On entering the valley, clouds of dust moving hither and thither at the opposite extremity, announced the presence of the enemy. The column advanced cautiously in order of battle, ready and eager for immediate action. Capt. Steele's company of regular infantry, supported by a company of cavalry, held the advance position on the left. A strong body of the enemy now hurried forward from their cover in the woods, for the obvious purpose of cutting them off from the main body, which was some distance in the rear. The cavalry, numbering about one hundred and fifty, under command of Capt. Stanley, prepared to receive them. Several volleys had been exchanged, when a small squad of twenty-seven horsemen, under Lieut. Kelley, made a plunge into the ranks of the rebel infantry, as brilliant in results as rash in conception. Panic-stricken and appalled at the unexpected charge, many of the enemy were cut down, and the rest prudently withdrew to make room for the remainder of Capt. Stanley's company, now galloping down to the support of their comrades.

Capt. Totten, of the artillery, having planted a couple of guns upon a commanding eminence, soon had an opportunity to show his skill upon a body of mounted rebels which had just emerged from the wood and was forming for an advance. Shell after shell was sent with unerring certainty into their midst. Saddles were emptied by the explosions, the horses became unmanageable, and the gay cavalcade, with characteristic discretion, galloped enthusiastically out of the range of Capt. Totten's missiles.

This skirmishing seemed the fitting preliminary to a great and important battle. The Union army had patiently endured the heat, the thirst, and the dust, in the hope of meeting and routing the enemy.

But the desperation of the cavalry charge, and the fatal accuracy of the Federal gunners, led the Southrons to beat a precipitate and inglorious retreat.

Upwards of forty rebels were killed and many more wounded. Lyon's loss was about one-fourth as great.

The morning of the third, the troops were quietly aroused, and by four o'clock were again on the road. Advancing cautiously over the hills for six or eight miles, the column came upon a body of the enemy at "McCulloch Spring." To try their strength and mettle, Capt. Totten sent a few shot into their midst, and Lieut. Dubois gave them a shell which struck the chimney of the house where the officers were preparing to breakfast. At this point the discretion of the rebels got the better of their valor, and they hastily fled, leaving behind a large quantity of provisions, as well as blankets, muskets, and other trophies, to fall into the hands of the Federals.

A little later, Gen. Lyon and his staff rode up to the deserted premises, and in doing so met with one of those narrow escapes which sometimes occur in the fortunes of war. At this place the highway winds through a narrow valley bounded on each side by steep and wooded hills. The house, which seemingly formed the head-quarters of the rebel officers, and the granary connected with it, stood on opposite sides of the road, while near by McCulloch Spring gushed copiously from the earth. Gen. Lyon and his attendants were now in advance, but erroneously supposed that two companies of cavalry were ahead, and that two regiments were flanking the right and left. Having dismounted and led the horses into the inclosure of the granary, the party stood in the shade waiting for the forces to come up. Soon a dozen of the Federal skirmishers descended from the hill and Gen. Lyon inquired, "What has become of the first Missouri? I thought they were just behind us." Hardly was the question asked, when the regiment appeared in sight, around a bend in the road, a quarter of a mile in the rear. Beside them came a squad of cavalry who approached unconcernedly, as if fully satisfied with their present situation and future prospects. Advancing at a lively walk, they reached the place where Gen. Lyon was standing. He inquired, "What men are you?" but received no reply. At the same time Maj. Shepard stepping up to one of the horsemen in the center of the column, asked, "What company is this?" The fellow kept silent, and the question was repeated. The horseman now turned deadly pale and stammeringly referred the Major to the Captain of the squad. Maj. Shepard saw at once that they were rebels, and turning to the first Missouri who were now a little behind, shouted, "Forward, double quick." Without waiting for further invitation, the rebels spurred their horses into a furious gallop, and plunged into the woods. The skirmishers standing by the fence gave them a parting volley. Numerous blood-stains were found along the way, and several horses were disabled.

The rebel cavalry were armed with rifles and might easily have cut off Gen. Lyon and his staff. But their fright totally unmanned them, and not one offered to discharge his piece.

A number of prisoners and deserters were brought in who gave conflicting accounts of the position and strength of the rebel forces. It seemed impossible to overtake and engage them. Provisions were becoming scarce, and the prospect of procuring further supplies from Springfield over a road menaced by a strong and vagrant enemy, was not very encouraging. At this juncture General Lyon called a council of the principal officers which decided in favor of returning to Springfield. On the fourth of August the army began to retrace its steps, and marched half the distance before encamping for the night. The column then moved leisurely back to the town, where the troops were joyfully welcomed by the people, who for several days had apprehended an attack.

Tuesday, August 6th, the Federal army was stationed in the city and upon the roads emerging from it. Major Sturgis, with two thousand men, held a position five miles distant on the Fayetteville road. General Lyon had determined to make a night attack upon the enemy, and accordingly kept this strong force in advance, ready to move at a moment's notice. At nightfall, Tuesday, every preparation was made for a forward movement. Soon after dark, an incessant stream of visitors and messengers poured into the head-quarters of General Lyon, to communicate information, receive orders and transact other business with the Commander-in-chief. Amid the pressure of duties time slipped unconsciously by, and the hour of twelve arrived before he left his apartments. He now proceeded to Camp Hunter to direct the forward movements of the column. Here, on consulting his watch for the first time, he found that it was three o'clock A. M.,—two hours later than he supposed. The night was too far gone to justify any hope of taking the enemy by surprise. He therefore called a council of officers and acting upon their advice ordered the whole army to fall back to Springfield. Daylight broke before the troops reached the city.

Wednesday, General Lyon remarked to a friend, "I begin to believe our term of soldiering is about completed. I have tried earnestly to discharge my whole duty to the Government, and appealed to them for reinforcements and supplies; but, alas, they do not come, and the enemy is getting advantage of us."

A week before (July 31st) he wrote to the same effect:

"We are deeply grieved over the retreat of our forces at Manassas. If our people shall learn from this a little more moderation, and substitute a little resolution for the overweening confidence they have too much indulged, this defeat will have its benefits.

"I have been compelled to remain quiet here for want of supplies to move, and I fear the enemy may become emboldened by our want of activity. I have constant rumors of a very large force below, and of threats to attack us with overwhelming numbers. I should have a much larger force than I have, and be much better supplied."

The same day, August 7th, a council of war was held. The officers with great unanimity favored the evacuation of Springfield. Some proposed to withdraw in the direction of Kansas, and others to retreat to Rolla. General Sweeney, however, strenuously opposed the measure, pointing out the intolerable hardships that would befall the Union men, and the ruin that would overwhelm the Union cause in that part of the State, if abandoned to the enemy. He also urged that the southern invaders, flushed with bloodless triumph, would impute the step to cowardice, and make great capital of the assumption. He thought the army should strike so soon as opportunity offered, and maintain its ground till absolutely forced to leave. The views of Gen. Sweeney coincided with those of the Commander-in-chief. The next day, on being asked when Springfield was to be evacuated, General Lyon replied, "Not before we are whipped."

Thursday morning the rumor came that the enemy were marching upon the town. Preparations were quickly made for defense. Troops were drawn up for action, incumbrances removed, and the baggage-train sent to a secure place near the center of the city. In this posture of affairs the hours wore away without any appearance of the rebels. As a part of the Kansas troops were much exhausted from services the night before, the project of surprising the enemy was again deferred, and all the men except those on guard were ordered to retire to rest.

Let us now return a little in our narrative to review the previous movements of the enemy. In the month of July, General Price, commander of the Missouri State Guard, collected a large force in McDonald county, near the extreme south-western corner of the State. His experience during the early part of the season had inspired him with a wholesome dread of General Lyon. A more venturesome leader could hardly have remained contentedly amid the seclusion of those wild and unfrequented prairie lands, while an antagonist at the head of a comparatively small force was dealing out constant and heavy blows at the party in rebellion. Although General Price might believe in the prevalent theory that one "true southerner" was equal to two or three Unionists, he manifested no impatience to make a trial of strength on any terms. But at length the rebel force became so numerous in South-western Missouri, that further inaction could not fail to demoralize the hordes who had assembled from near and far in the hope of easy and brilliant victories. Four southern armies were stationed at different points along the border, under Generals Price, McCulloch, Pearce and McBride. Arrangements were made to unite all these forces late in July, and Cassville was selected as the place of rendezvous. On the 29th of the month the junction was effected.

The combined army left Cassville in three divisions on the 1st and 2d of August. After pursuing a somewhat circuitous course, it reached Wilson's Creek on the 6th. It was the advance guard of this force under General Rains, that sustained the repulse at Dug Springs. But the main body showed no disposition to come to a general engagement at that time, although it would have been easy to throw forward strong reinforcements.

At Wilson's Creek, ten or twelve miles south-west of Springfield, twenty-three thousand men now encamped.

Gen. Lyon's effective force numbered but little over five thousand. He felt keenly the embarrassments and dangers of his situation. Weary days and sleepless nights he had waited for a response to his numerous appeals for aid, but waited, alas, in vain. Even to his sanguine and hopeful spirit, to advance seemed extremely perilous, and to retreat hardly less so. But he resolved to make one desperate effort to retain the advantages which hard fighting, long marches, and months of ceaseless toil had given him. Even in this hour of gloom he was cheered by the proud consciousness of having accomplished all that it was possible to accomplish. It was no fault of his that after a series of brilliant achievements in the service of his country, he was now left with a small body of troops, in a region of doubtful loyalty, to cope with the legions which all of the South-western States had deliberately armed and sent forth for the subjugation of

Missouri. As perils thickened around the heroic band, the genius of their leader rose to meet the terrible exigency of the hour.

Springfield could not be made defensible against a superior force, as the town was built upon a broad plain without natural bulwarks. To remain quietly while the enemy blocked up every avenue of exit with overwhelming numbers, would end in the sacrifice of the whole command. Gen. Lyon now conceived the bold design of marching forth by night and surprising the rebel camp. By striking a sudden and effective blow, he hoped to inflict so deep a wound as to paralyze the enemy till he could either be relieved by reinforcements, or, if none came, retreat in safety to Rolla. The execution of the plan had been postponed twice already. Friday, August 9th, preparations for an attack the following night were perfected.

He divided his little army into two columns, with a view to attack the Southern camp in two places. The main column, under his own immediate command, consisted of three brigades.

The first brigade, under Maj. Sturgis, was composed of one battalion regular infantry, under Capt. Plummer; companies B, C, and D, first infantry, Captains Gilbert, Plummer and Huston, with one company of rifle recruits, under Lieut.

Wood; Maj. Osterhaus' battalion, second Missouri Volunteers, two companies; Capt. Totten's light battery, six pieces; Capt. Wood's mounted company, second Kansas Volunteers; and Lieut. Canfield's company of regular cavalry.

The second brigade, commanded by Lieut. Col. Andrews, of the first Missouri Volunteers, consisted of Capt. Steele's battalion of regulars, two companies, second infantry; one company of recruits, under Lieut. Lathrop, fourth artillery; one company of recruits, under Sergt. Morine; Lieut. Dubois' light battery, consisting of four pieces; and the first Missouri Volunteers.

The third brigade consisted of the first and second Kansas Volunteers, Cols. Deitzler and Mitchell; the first Iowa Volunteers, and about two hundred Home Guards, (mounted.) These three brigades made up the column led by Gen. Lyon in person.

The second column, under Col. Siegel, was composed of two regiments Missouri Volunteers, the third and fifth; Capt. Carr's company of cavalry; one company of dragoons, Lieut. Farrand; and one light battery, six guns. Col. Siegel was ordered to advance by the Fayetteville road, so as to fall upon the right and rear of the encampment.

Gen. Lyon's column left Springfield at five o'clock P. M. on the 9th of August, and moving cautiously forward, came in sight of the guard-fires of the enemy at one o'clock the next morning. The men now halted, sleeping on their arms till daybreak, when the march was resumed. Capt. Gilbert's company still continued in advance as before.

By a singular coincidence, Gen. McCulloch had made arrangements to precipitate his forces upon Springfield the same night. Friday afternoon, orders were issued to the rebel army to be in readiness to start at nine o'clock. They were to proceed in four separate columns, so as to surround the city, and make a simultaneous attack at the dawn of day. Owing, however, to the threatening appearance of the clouds, he countermanded the order just before the time of departure, directing the men to rest on their arms and be prepared to move at the shortest notice. In consequence of the projected operations against Springfield, McCullock withdrew his advanced pickets on the 9th, and as nothing was further from his apprehensions than a visit from Lyon's small force, he had not taken the precaution to throw them out again. Consequently the advancing column had only to drive in the camp-pickets, and were thus enabled to effect a complete surprise.

Gen. Lyon directed his course so as to strike the extreme northern point of the rebel encampment.

Soon an outpost on the right was alarmed, and hurried away to communicate the news. But the Federal center and left had already partially cut them off, and they probably failed to join the main body in time to render their information at all valuable. Gen. Lyon's advance was within gun-shot of the Southern camp, before the rebel officers were aware of their approach.

Gen. Price, in his official report of the battle, says: "About six o'clock, I received a messenger from Gen. Rains, that the enemy were advancing in great force from the direction of Springfield, and were already within two or three hundred yards of the position where he was encamped."—"A second messenger came immediately afterward from Gen. Rains, to announce that the main body of the enemy was upon him."—"Gen. McCulloch was with me when these messengers came, and left at once for his own head-quarters, to make the necessary disposition of our forces."

Wilson's Creek here flows through a narrow valley, inclosed on each side by gently sloping hills. The grounds were covered with patches of low trees, which served very much to hide the movements of the enemy. The tents extended for a long distance on both banks of the stream. Portions of the valley and the hill-sides had been cleared, and converted into corn and wheat-fields.

When the camp pickets were driven in, Gen. Lyon directed the mounted Home Guard and Capt. Plummer's battalion to cross Wilson's creek, and move forward on the opposite side, on a line with the advance of the main body, for the purpose of thwarting any attempts of the enemy to turn his left flank. The principal column now traversed a ravine, and on ascending a steep ridge, came in sight of a strong force of southern infantry. Maj. Osterhaus' battalion was deployed to the right, and two companies of the first Missouri Volunteers to the left, to act as skirmishers. The left section of Capt. Totten's battery, under Lieut. Sokalski, now opened upon the enemy in the woods, and a few minutes later the remaining four pieces were planted on a commanding eminence to the right, and further forward. A well directed fire from the artillery, assisted the infantry in speedily clearing the ground in front, and driving back the enemy to the tops of the hills overhanging their own camp.

The first Missouri and the first Kansas, with Totten's battery and the first Iowa, hurried forward to occupy the crest of the ridge. As the line was now formed, Maj. Osterhaus' battalion occupied the extreme right, his own right resting on the edge of an abrupt ravine. The first Missouri was posted in front, upon the summit of a slight elevation; the first Kansas sixty yards to the left, on the opposite side of a ravine; and the first Iowa still further to the left. Capt. Totten's battery was planted in the rear of the interspace between the first Missouri and first Kansas. Dubois' battery was stationed to the left and rear of Totten's position in order to play upon a battery posted on the crest of the ridge, on the opposite side of the creek, in such a way as to sweep the whole field where the Federal troops were drawn up.

The camp of Gen. Rains lay directly in front and under Capt. Totten's guns, and was wholly deserted. On the left bank of the stream was a masked battery to which he gave his first attention, the gunners aiming at the flash and smoke which alone betrayed the situation of the cannon. Meanwhile, in the thick underwood on the right, the first Missouri were fighting with great gallantry against vastly superior numbers. Having an advantage in the quality of fire-arms, their frequent and well directed volleys made terrible havoc. But when one of the enemy fell, two fresh men were ready to take his place. The encampment seemed to vomit forth regiment after regiment, as if the supply were inexhaustible. In the unequal contest, many of the

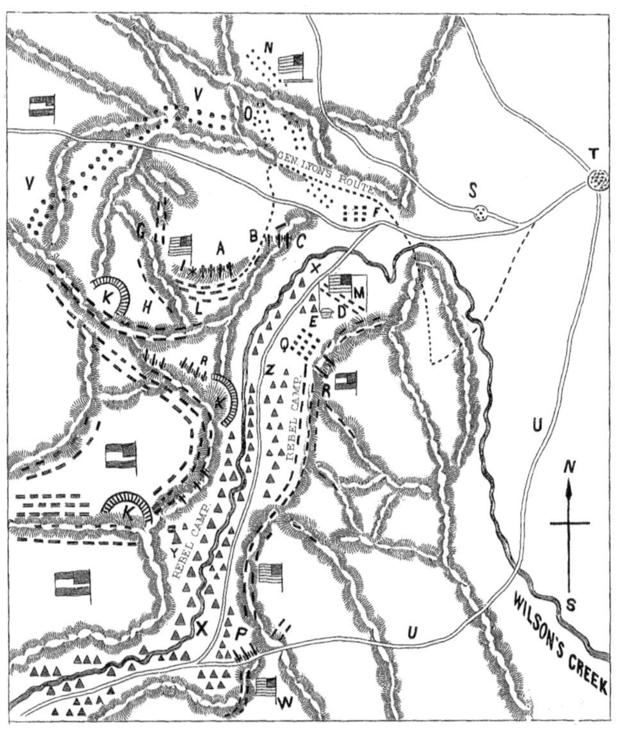

PLAN OF THE BATTLE OF WILSON'S CREEK MO.

EXPLANATION OF DIAGRAM.

*A*_Capt. Totten's Battery.
*B*_Section of Capt. Totten's Battery.
*C*_Capt. Dubois's Battery.
*D*_Corn-field-hotly contested.
*E*_Log house-hotly contested.
*F*_Ambulances for Sick.
*G*_Second Missouri Volunteers.
*H*_Second Kansas Volunteers.
*I*_* Spot where Gen. Lyon fell.
*K*_Masked rebel batteries.
*L*_First Kansas, First Missouri, First Iowa Capt. Steele's Battalion.
*M*_Capt. Plummers Battalion.
*N*_Home Guards-mounted.
*O*_Kansas Rangers-mounted.
*P*_Col. Siegel's position.
*Q*_Train of rebel's_part.
*R*_Concealed battery-rebel.
*S*_Town of Little York.
*T*_Springfield.
*U*_Fayetteville road-the road by which Col. Siegel advanced upon the rebel camp.
*V*_Rebel cavalry-1,200 strong.
*W*_Siegel's Brigade-Third and Fifth Missouri.
*X*_Road through rebel camp.
*Y*_McCullough's head-qua.
*Z*_Rains's head quarters.

brave Missouri first had fallen in death, and many more were disabled by wounds.

Gen. Lyon now ordered Capt. Totten to move a section of his battery forward to their support. This manœuvre he executed in person, bringing several guns into position in front of the right wing of the regiment. At a distance of less than two hundred yards, a body of southern troops were drawn up in order of battle, with the stars and stripes flying side by side with the rebel banner. By this base and cowardly trick, they hoped to reach a point near the Federal lines in safety, and then to capture the guns by a sudden dash and turn them upon the Union columns. At first, Capt. Totten hesitated to fire, but discovering the deception he received them with repeated rounds of canister which laid many upon the earth, and sent the rest in confusion from the field.

Meanwhile, Capt. Plummer's battalion in moving toward the encampment on the opposite side of the creek, encountered a large body of infantry in a cornfield. Being thoroughly acquainted with the ground, and partially sheltered from view by the dense growth of stalks and weeds, the enemy delivered their fire with great effect. The regulars fought manfully till two or three thousand men, in a dense mass, came pouring into the field from the woods beyond, threatening the small handful of Union troops with instant annihilation. While they were retiring in good order before the overwhelming flood, Dubois' battery, on an eminence opposite, began to throw shell into the ranks of the pursuers. The missiles were directed with fearful certainty into the thickest groups, where they scattered death on every side. Several burst at the instant of reaching the ground. The enemy fell by scores and soon fled precipitately. This was their last attempt during the day to turn the left flank of the Federal army.

Till now the roar of artillery had been incessant. Peal followed peal in such rapid succession that the sounds commingled in one continuous and awful volume. At intervals the continuity, interrupted for a few seconds, would be broken by the report of a single gun, which formed the prelude to another chorus like the last. The boom of heavy ordnance, the whirr of missiles, the bursting of shell, and the ring of fire-arms, blended undistinguishably in this concert of mortal wrath.

At length there was a brief lull along the whole line, except on the extreme right. The silence seemed more terrible than the deafening din of battle. The hostile armies stood like two grim giants, breathing a moment after a desperate encounter to gain strength for a final and fatal grapple. But the stillnes was brief, leaving little time for indulgence in reflections or apprehensions. The first Missouri, on the right of the line, having repeatedly driven back the enemy, were in imminent peril from the hordes of fresh troops now hastening to attack their decimated ranks. Side by side with the first Missouri, the first Kansas and first Iowa fought with obstinate valor. Gen. Lyon, at this critical juncture ordered the second Kansas to their support. It came up in time to save the shattered columns, and hold in check the enemy. Gen. Lyon riding up and perceiving the desperate character of the conflict in that part of the field, sent an order to Capt. Totten to support the regiments on the right. He at once dispatched Lieut. Sokalski with a section of his battery, to their relief, which he effected in admirable style, managing his guns with great skill and effect.

Soon after, a body of eight hundred cavalry, which had formed in line beyond a ridge on the right of the battle-ground, suddenly appeared, moving toward the rear of the Federal army, where two or three companies of Kansas troops were guarding the ambulances for the wounded. They obviously expected to trample all opposition under foot. As the troop advanced, several companies of infantry fired upon them without checking their approach. When they had come within two hundred yards of Totten's battery, he unexpectedly turned several guns in that direction. Each shot plowed a diagonal furrow through the column, tumbling horses and riders into heaps. In a moment the charge became a rout. Valiant men spurred their steeds to the shelter of the hills, while the unhorsed made vigorous use of their nether limbs. This was the only demonstration made by the Southern cavalry during the day, and was in every respect weak and contemptible.

During this time, Capt. Steele's battalion of regular infantry was transferred from the support of Dubois' battery, to Totten's battery. Scarcely was the line of battle reformed, when an immense force of the enemy, emerging from behind the wooded hills, moved down upon the entire Federal front, and against each flank. All at once the previous silence was broken by the roar of cannon and the crash of musketry. The Southern regiments, often advancing within a few yards of our guns, swayed back and forth as their repeated charges upon Totten's battery were repulsed. Some were standing, some kneeling, and others lying down. Exasperated at the disgrace of allowing so small a handful to hold them in check, they fought with the frenzy of madmen. All of Gen. Lyon's available troops were now engaged, and the fighting became incredibly fierce. Along the whole line the storm of leaden hail whistled through the air, leaving hardly a square foot of ground unsearched. Each side made prodigious but unsuccessful efforts to gain some decisive advantage. The fate of the day trembled in the balance. Both armies by daring and vigorous charges repeatedly won a little ground, and then fell back to rally for a fresh attack. With obstinate bravery the shattered regiments closed up the gaping chasms in their ranks, and returned to the fight.

Gen. Lyon moved along the lines in the thickest of the fight, encouraging the men by his example and his words. His horse was shot, and he himself received three wounds, one near the ancle, one in the thigh, and still another which cut the scalp to the bone, while striving to bring up his disordered troops. Anxiety for the issue, however, banished every personal thought and care. Upon the fate of the battle depended the safety of thousands of peaceful homes whose inmates looked to him for protection from pillage and ruin. Before the sun could reach the meridian, the fierce trial of arms would decide whether the flag of the Union was thenceforth to spread its sheltering folds over the people of South-western Missouri, or whether the banners of treason were to float in insolent triumph over the towns and hamlets which the patriot-army had come forth to save. The roar of battle was not to perish among the hills and valleys around the scene of carnage, but to reverberate in never-dying echoes through the country and through time. Gen. Lyon, unconscious of pain or danger, heeded not the wounds from which blood and strength were fast oozing. Walking a little to the rear, he remarked despondingly, "I fear the day is lost." Friends urged him to withdraw to a place of safety, and have his wounds attended to. But to such importunities he turned a deaf ear. Mounting another horse, he rode back to the front, in order to rally the thinned and bleeding, but not disheartened lines for a fresh attack. He now directed the fragments of one or two regiments to charge the enemy with the bayonet. Many of their officers were disabled, and they called for a leader. The situation of the army was extremely perilous, and deeds of desperate daring could alone save it from total overthrow. With countenance blanched from the loss of blood, and haggard from anxiety, Gen. Lyon threw himself to the head of the column, and with hat waving, cheered it onward. Inspired with almost superhuman energy by the heroism of their chief, the men rushed forward, scattering the enemy like chaff. But in that charge the brave Lyon fell. Our country, in the crisis of her darkest peril, lost that hour one of her clearest heads and stoutest hearts. He placed no value upon repose, comfort, or even life, when the land that he loved with all the devotion of his generous soul, demanded their sacrifice.

Gen. Lyon was amply endowed with those rare and precious qualities which enter essentially into the composition of the hero and martyr. Noble, magnanimous, self-sacrificing, he had taken his country for a bride, and never was marriage-union consecrated by a holier or more absorbing love. Ever may the American people revere and cherish the name of Nathaniel Lyon, as his devoted patriotism and signal services deserve.

The fatal ball entered his left side, and passing near the heart, escaped on the right. His faithful body-servant, Albert Lehman, received him in his arms. The General remarked, "Lehman, I am going," and in a few seconds expired. His death was without a struggle—calm and peaceful.

Gen. Lyon fell about nine o'clock, A. M. Maj. Sturgis, in his official report, alludes to the event in language as eloquent as it is truthful. "Thus gloriously fell as brave a soldier as ever drew a sword,—a man whose honesty of purpose was proverbial,—a noble patriot, and one who held his life as nothing when his country demanded it of him."

Immediately after the death of Gen. Lyon, and the repulse of the enemy along the whole length of the lines, there was another interval of almost total silence for the space of twenty minutes. The command now devolved upon Maj. Sturgis, and he called together the principal officers for consultation. To understand the subsequent events of the day, we must revert briefly to the doings of the column under Col. Siegel. He was ordered to advance by the Fayetteville road, which led circuitously to the left, and would bring him out near the right wing and rear of the Southern encampment. Each column was to reach its respective point of attack by daylight on the 10th, and open fire simultaneously.

Col. Siegel left his position south of Springfield, between six and seven o'clock P. M., the 9th, and at the dawn of day the following morning, was within a mile of the enemy's camp. While cautiously advancing, he cut off several squads of men in such a way that no news of his approach was conveyed to the main body of the rebels. He gained the position designated without incurring any mishap of any kind, and with his excellent battery began in beautiful style to shell the tents spread out before him. The enemy were completely surprised, and fled from their quarters in dismay. At the same time the heavy roar of Lyon's artillery was heard in the northern part of the field. Thinking that the victory was won, a portion of Siegel's infantry broke ranks and made an indiscriminate rush for plünder. While the men were thus basely occupied, the Southerners rallied, and making a vigorous charge, captured the whole battery, took a large number of prisoners, and put the rest to flight. Siegel afterwards succeeded in retaking a single gun.

Thus, early in the engagement, were twelve hundred of Lyon's little army lost to him. But this was not all. The part assigned to Siegel's command, was to turn the right wing of the enemy and gain the rear so as to enfilade the ravine, or failing in that, to form a junction with the main body near the northern line of battle. At the proper time for the appearance of Siegel's column, a body of infantry, wearing a dress much resembling that of Siegel's brigade, and carrying the American flag, were seen to advance from the direction whence his guns had been heard at the commencement of the fight. This was a few minutes after the death of Gen. Lyon, and while Maj. Sturgis was deliberating with the other officers. The consultation was brought to a hasty close, and a line formed for the purpose of moving forward and effecting a junction. From the belief that they were friends, they were allowed to approach quite near, when a battery was unexpectedly planted on the hill in front, and their true character revealed. Simultaneously with the first demonstration of hostility, the treacherous foe began to pour shrapnell and canister into the Federal ranks. They had not only counterfeited the appearance of Siegel's brigade, but were actually using his guns and ammunition for the destruction of our brave troops, as was evident from the fact that these varieties of shot had been furnished to Siegel's artillery, and were now fired by the enemy for the first time during the engagement.

Then the enemy run up the secession flag, and the bloody conflict was renewed along the whole line. Dubois' battery on the left, supported by Osterhaus' battalion and the remnants of the Missouri first, speedily silenced the guns on the hill in front, and drove back the right wing of the enemy. Totten's battery, occupying with the Iowas and regulars the center of the line, was the special object of attack. The contending armies were within a few feet of each other, the smoke of their guns commingling and rising in one dark, dense volume from the field. Before overwhelming numbers the Union troops stood perfectly firm at every point. Any wavering now could hardly have failed to inaugurate a ruinous rout. Not a man, however, faltered. At this critical juncture, Capt. Granger hurriedly brought up from the rear the supports of Dubois' battery, consisting of six or seven companies belonging to the first Kansas, first Missouri and first Iowa regiments, which overwhelmed the right wing of the enemy with a volley that swept the earth for the space of sixty yards. The entire rebel front now rolled back in confused and broken masses. With the exception of a feeble attack on the right flank, which was gallantly repulsed by Steele's battalion of regulars, the Southerners made no further demonstrations of hostility, but fled precipitately to the shelter of the woods and hills.

Meanwhile, the rebel wagon train was discovered to be on fire. Heavy volumes of smoke, rising in the distance, plainly indicated that the enemy had commenced the work of destruction, from fear that the day was lost. Repulsed several times already, they were obviously on the point of giving up in despair.

But the Federal troops were in no condition to take advantage of their repeated successes. A very large proportion of the little army of heroes which had stood so long and so immovably against the legions of the enemy, were either killed or disabled. Many had not only exhausted their own cartridges, but all that could be found on the persons of the dead. After a fatiguing night march, the men had fought for six hours without water. The day was hot, and the sufferings of the soldiers, from weariness and thirst, began to be intense. Accordingly, at half past eleven o'clock, during the pause which succeeded the final repulse of the Southern forces, the order for retreat was given. Dubois' battery, with its supports, had been previously sent to occupy a hill in the rear, in order to protect the movement. While Capt. Steele was engaging and driving back the enemy on the right flank, the main body retired slowly and in good order to the open prairie, two miles from the scene of conflict. In the mean time the ambulances went back and forth, bringing away the wounded.

After a brief halt, the column resumed its march to Springfield, meeting at the Little York road Lieut. Ferrand with his company of dragoons, and a part of Col. Siegel's command, with the cannon which they had succeeded in saving.

The battle at Wilson's Creek is one of the severest ever fought upon the Western Continent. Never, in modern warfare, have men moved to conflict against greater odds, or held their ground with more obstinate valor. Gen. Lyon's disposable force at Springfield consisted of five thousand two hundred men. About one-fourth of the number were sent under command of Col. Siegel to attack the enemy on the flank and rear. Gen. Lyon, at the head of less than four thousand troops, attacked more than twenty thousand rebels in the stronghold which they had deliberately selected and fortified. The enemy, though outnumbering their assailants five to one, were repulsed time after time, and in the last repulse so completely routed that they were compelled to suffer our little handful of troops to retreat without molestation. Had Col. Siegel's detachment executed the part assigned to it equally well, or could two or three fresh regiments have come to the reinforcement of the main body, the rebel army in South-western Missouri would certainly have been crushed; Springfield would have been saved; the invading hordes driven back into the swamps of Arkansas; and all the subsequent loss of blood, treasure and prestige, avoided. As it is, the battle of Wilson's Creek, in the glorious achievements of time, will rank with Thermopylæ and Leuctra. Coming generations will find parallels to the heroic self-sacrifice of Gen. Lyon, in the death of Leonidas, and the fall of him who closed his brilliant and useful life on the bloody field of Mantinea.

Before the engagement many officers questioned the wisdom of General Lyon's decision to give battle on the ground of the enemy, rather than retreat to Rolla without making any hostile demonstration. No one proposed to await an attack within the confines of Springfield, for the town was obviously indefensible against the armies from all of the southwestern States, which were rapidly concentrating in the neighborhood. But the result showed the extraordinary sagacity and foresight of the commanding officer. An inglorious retreat, giving to the rebels a bloodless triumph, would have emboldened beyond measure an enemy peculiarly prone to magnify his own exploits and boast of invincibility. The hope of plunder would have drawn large accessions of force to the swollen ranks of the pursuers. It was a week's march to Rolla. A government-train five miles in length and valued at $1,500,000, was either to be lost or defended along the whole length of that wearisome and perilous route. It is too much to expect that even the highest order of generalship could have conducted a retreat safely and successfully for the distance of one hundred and twenty miles. An army of twenty-three thousand men abundantly provided with artillery and cavalry, by making a vigorous pursuit could hardly have failed either to capture, disperse, or annihilate the Union forces. Under the circumstances, General Lyon's night attack, desperate as it may seem, was the only course which contained any promise of success.

And here we may remark that the measures of General Lyon in Missouri, were so bold, sudden, anticipatory and far-sighted, that they generally appeared at first premature and rash. But in every instance the issue of events proved the accuracy of his judgment, and the wide scope of his calm, clear forecast. In this case the rebels were so terribly cut up and crippled that they were forced to allow the remnant of the Federal army to retire in perfect security both from the battle ground and from Springfield.

The official reports of the engagement show the following Union losses:

	Killed.	Wounded.	Missing.
Capt. Plummer's battalion,	19	52	9
Capt. Elliot's Co. D, first cavalry,		1	3
Capt. Dubois battery,		2	1
First Missouri volunteers,	76	208	11
Capt. Steele's battery,	15	44	2
Capt. Carr's Co. I, first cavalry,			4
First Kansas volunteers,	77	187	20

Second Kansas volunteers,	5	59	6
Capt. Totten's Co. F, 2d artillery,	4	7	
Col. Siegel's brigade,	15	20	231
Capt. Wood's Co. Kansas Rangers,		1	
Capt. Clark Wright's Co. H, Guard,		2	
First Iowa Volunteers,	12	138	4
Total,	223	721	292

Whole number killed, wounded and missing, 1236.

The rebel loss was much greater, but the exact figures will probably never be known. They acknowledged over five hundred killed, to say nothing of the wounded and missing.

It is aside from our purpose to mention individually the men who distinguished themselves on that bloody but glorious field. Where all behaved so nobly, the voice of a grateful country will pronounce all to be heroes.

General Lyon's body was placed in an ambulance to be conveyed from the field, but being temporarily removed to make room for the wounded, was subsequently left behind in the hurry of retreat. After the return of the army to Springfield, a flag of truce was sent back to the battle-ground for the remains, which were given up by the enemy. Doct. Franklin, with the aid of other surgeons, endeavored to preserve the body by the injection of arsenic, but were frustrated in the attempt.

In the confusion of abandoning Springfield the remains of Gen. Lyon were again left behind. The day after the battle, Mrs. Phelps, wife of Col. Phelps, member of Congress for the south-western district of Missouri, and a staunch Unionist, learning that the body was still lying in town, asked and obtained the privilege of interring it. She caused it to be placed in a wooden coffin, and the whole to be inclosed in a case of zinc, which was then hermetically sealed. At first Mrs. Phelps placed the coffin in an out-door cellar on her farm, and covered it over with a pile of straw four or five feet deep, but afterwards apprehending, though without any just grounds for suspicion, that it might be molested by the soldiers of Gen. Parson's brigade, which was then encamped on the place, she had it quietly removed and buried in the night time.

Maj. Sturgis, who assumed command of the Union army after the first day of the retreat, for the reason that Col. Siegel had not at the time received his commission as general, supposed that the remains were with the army till he was twenty-five miles from Springfield. It was then too late to secure them.

The Federal army left Springfield at three o'clock in the morning, the day after the battle. It reached Rolla in safety, having brought off the baggage train and a large amount of public and private property.

On the 25th of the month, Gen. Fremont issued the following general order:

"HEAD-QUARTERS WESTERN DEPARTMENT,
ST. LOUIS, MO., August 25.

I. The official reports of the commanding officers of the forces engaged in the battle near Springfield, Mo., having been received, the Major-General commanding announces to the troops embraced in his command, with pride and the highest commendation, the extraordinary services to their country and flag rendered by the division of the brave and lamented General Lyon.

For thus nobly battling for the honor of their flag, he now publicly desires to express to the officers and soldiers his cordial thanks, and commends their conduct as an example to their comrades whenever engaged against the enemies of the Union.

Opposed by overwhelming masses of the enemy in a numerical superiority of upwards of twenty thousand against four thousand three hundred, or nearly five to one, the successes of our troops were nevertheless suffieiently marked to give to their exploits the moral effect of a vietory.

II. The General commanding laments, in sympathy with the country, the loss of the indomitable General Nathaniel Lyon. His fame can not be better eulogized than in these words from the official report of his gallant successor, Major Sturgis, United States cavalry: 'Thus gallantly fell as true a soldier as ever drew a sword; a man whose honesty of purpose was proverbial; a noble patriot, and one who held his life as nothing where his country demanded it of him.' Let all emulate his prowess and undying devotion to his duty.

III. The regiments and corps engaged in this battle will be permitted to have 'Springfield' emblazoned on their colors, as a distinguished memorial of their services to the nation.

IV. The names of the officers and soldiers mentioned in the official reports as most distinguished for important services and marked gallantry, will be communicated to the War Department for the consideration of the Government.

This order will be read at the head of every company in this department.

By order of Major-General Fremont.

J. C. KELTON, Assistant Adjutant-General."

CHAPTER XIII.

Wednesday, August 14th, Gen. Lyon's death became known throughout the country, and produced a universal feeling of gloom. Danford Knowlton, Esq., of New York city, cousin of the deceased, immediately telegraphed to Gen. Fremont, requesting him to have the remains secured in a sealed coffin. He also sent dispatches to several members of the family. On the 15th, John B. Hasler, Esq., of Webster, Mass., brother-in-law of Gen. Lyon, joined Mr. Knowlton in New York, and at eight o'clock P. M. of the same day, they started westward for the purpose of bringing to its native home the body of their lamented relative. Traveling day and night, without detention except from the loss of bridges on one or two of the railroad lines, they reached St. Louis Sunday morning, the 18th. Here they were disappointed in finding that the remains had not yet been brought forward. They at once determined to proceed in person to Springfield for the prosecution of their mission. Letters from the General commanding the Western Department seemed to be essential to insure their admission into the lines of the enemy and their protection on the route. Notwithstanding the urgency of their business, and their efforts to obtain the requisite papers, they were unable to gain access to Gen. Fremont during the day. At a late hour the following night, however, the letters were sent to them.

The party left for Rolla by the early train, Monday. Arriving at that town in the afternoon, they were courteously received by Col. Wyman, who furnished them with his best ambulance, four excellent mules, and a good driver, besides making other provisions for their comfort on the way. He had already sent a wagon to Springfield in charge of Mr. Lynch, an undertaker of St. Louis, for the purpose of accomplishing the same object. Monday afternoon the party drove to Maj. Sturgis' camp, three miles from Rolla, where they spent the night. Here they met Capt. Emmet McDonald, of the Confederate army, who had come to effect an exchange of prisoners. As this gentleman was about to return to the head-quarters of the Southern forces in Missouri, he kindly volunteered his services, and subsequently rendered valuable assistance to the relatives of Gen. Lyon in the accomplishment of their mission.

The road thence to Springfield is one of the worst conceivable—rough and rocky, stretching for more than a hundred miles over a barren, monotonous and dreary country. Extensive growths of "black jacks" and other stunted forest trees, bear gloomy witness to the poverty of the soil.

Driving as rapidly as the character of the road would permit, they encountered the Confederate out-posts on the 21st, at Lebanon, eighty miles from Rolla. The Southerners surrounded them at first with curious and inquisitive looks, but on learning the object of their journey, behaved with the utmost politeness. The same day they hurried forward fifteen miles further through a heavy rain, and spent the night at a way-side inn.

On the afternoon of Thursday, the 22d, the company drove into Springfield, without interruption from pickets, or questionings of any kind, and repaired immediately to the head-quarters of Gen. Price, to whom they made known their business and presented their credentials. The communication of Gen. Fremont was directed, "To Whom it May Concern." Gen. Price, glancing at the address, threw the paper contemptuously aside with the remark that he could read no document thus directed. At the same time he offered to grant them every facility for procuring the remains of Gen. Lyon.

Repairing to the farm of Col. Phelps, they disinterred the body, and placed it in a metallic coffin weighing three hundred pounds. Gen. Parsons, whose brigade was encamped on the place, introduced himself and extended numerous civilities to the company. Among other attentions, he tendered a guard for the body and team over night, which was accepted.

Col. Phelps was absent from home, having remained in St. Louis after the adjournment of Congress. Mrs. Phelps, a devoted and self-sacrificing friend of the Union, who had shown the spirit becoming an American Matron in the watchful and holy guardianship that she had exercised over the remains of one of the bravest defenders of American Liberty, now extended to the relatives of the lamented Lyon the generous hospitalities of her home. The name of this noble woman, openly true to her country in the midst of defection, perfidy and treason, will ever be honored by the children of our Republic.

Friday morning the party visited the hospital to obtain a list of the wounded and their condition. They left Springfield the same day, and reached Rolla Sunday night, August 25th. Everywhere within the lines of the enemy, the secessionists treated them with distinguished kindness, attention and courtesy, even tendering a military escort for the body from Springfield, which was declined. The rebels feared the fallen hero in life, and honored him in death.

They reached St. Louis Monday evening, the 26th, and at the solicitation of Gen. Fremont, remained over Tuesday, in order to give time for a suitable demonstration. The whole city seemed buried in the profoundest grief. Everywhere the insignia of mourning met the eye and touched the heart. Dwelling-houses, stores and other buildings were hung with crape. But the sadness stamped upon the features of thousands, bore more expressive witness than could any outward symbols, to the depth and sincerity of the sorrow felt for the fate of the mighty chieftain who had passed forever from their midst.

Wednesday afternoon, the remains were attended from the head-quarters of Gen. Fremont to the depot of the Ohio and Mississippi railroad, where they were delivered to Adams' Express Company to be conveyed East, under an escort of officers.

This company generously offered to carry the remains and the escort, free of charge, from St Louis to the place of burial. The offer was accepted, and separate cars were provided on all the routes for their exclusive use. Washington King, Esq., president of the company, although in feeble health, went to St. Louis contrary to the advice of his physician, to make the tender and perfect the arrangements for carrying it into effect. Having but just accomplished the object of his mission he was stricken down by death,—prematurely it was thought, from the fatigues and excitement of the occasion.

The escort consisted of

Major H. A. Conant, U. S. A., aid-de-camp of General Lyon—commanding the escort.

Captain J. B. Plummer, U. S. A., classmate of General Lyon—wounded at Wilson's Creek.

Captain Edgar, of General Fremont's staff.

Doctor G. G. Lyon, brigade surgeon,—distant relative of the General.

Lieut. E. J. Clark; Sergeant J. P. Taylor; Corporal F. H. Kearsum and six privates in uniform.

Danford Knowlton, Esq., and J. B. Hasler, Esq.,—relatives. M. McQuillan and J. Brown, reporters for the press.

On the whole route from St. Louis to the place of sepulture, people gathered in throngs at every city and village to honor the memory of the dead. Nor did the stately processions and imposing solemnities of the larger towns, afford the only or strongest evidence of the love and devotion which the heroism of Gen. Lyon had awakened in the hearts of the people. At different stations where the cars made but a brief stop, maidens and matrons reverently and tearfully placed upon the coffin wreaths of fresh flowers. Silently they came and went, for such sorrow had no need for words. Old men dropped upon the crape many a tear, weeping as if a son and not a stranger had fallen. The crowds assembled at the depots of rural villages were hushed and noiseless, as if it were sacrilege even to breathe audibly in such a presence. Many eyes were moistened, and some gave way to bitter lamentation. Little children begged to be lifted up so that they might see the coffin, and from that one eager gaze learned, we may trust, lessons of patriotism never to be forgotten. Some asked for the withered flowers that had gathered sanctity by resting on the pall, and pressed them to their lips with tears and kisses.

The funeral cortege reached Cincinnati a little before seven o'clock on the morning of the 29th. The military of the city were waiting at the depot to receive it. The colors of the various companies were shrouded in crape, and officers wore upon their arms the sombre scarfs of mourning. Here the coffin, wrapped in the United States flag, was transferred from the cars to the hearse and borne in solemn procession to Smith and Nixon's Hall, where the body lay in state during the day, and was visited by thousands.

On the 29th, at ten o'clock P. M. the escort left Cincinnati, proceeding by way of Columbus and Pittsburgh to Philadelphia, where they arrived Saturday morning, the 31st. The remains were placed in a hearse, elaborately adorned for the occasion, and were followed through the city by the police in full uniform; several military companies; and the Mayor, Common Council and escort in carriages, to the depot of the Camden and Amboy railroad.

On the 31st of August the cortege reached our great commercial metropolis, where the most distinguished honors were shown to the memory of General Lyon. For three days the corpse lay in state at the Governor's room, which had been fitted up for its reception. The apartment was draped in mourning within and without. Flags at half-mast were placed on all the public buildings throughout the city, and a portion of the shipping in the harbor. Notwithstanding the notice in the papers that no visitors would be admitted on Sunday, a large crowd thronged around the City Hall during the entire day, anxious to catch even a glimpse of the coffin.

On Monday the doors were thrown open from nine o'clock A. M. till one P. M. A body of policemen guarded the entrance to the room, while two soldiers stood at the head and two at the foot of the coffin. A constant stream of people numbering more than fifteen thousand in all, walked slowly and reverently, with uncovered heads, around the remains, making their exit through another door at the further end of the apartment. Some one, evidently a lady, had pinned the following inscription to the flag thrown over the burial-urn:

"To the Lion-hearted Gen. Nathaniel Lyon.

Thy name is immortal;
Thy battles are o'er;—
Sleep, sleep, calmly sleep,
On thy dear native shore.

New York, Sept. 2, 1861."

At four o'clock in the afternoon, the remains were borne from the Governor's room to the hearse, and were escorted by an imposing military and civic procession through the saddened city to the depot of the New Haven railroad.

Tuesday afternoon the funeral cortege reached Hartford, where, notwithstanding the inclemency of the weather, a similar ovation had been prepared in honor of the dead. As the body was carried from the cars to its temporary resting-place in the Senate Chamber of the State House, minute guns were fired from the park, the bell of the State

House was tolled, and the band gave forth a solemn dirge.

At Hartford, several military companies and a large number of citizens joined the escort. On Wednesday a special train conveyed the remains to Willimantic. Although this is a quiet, inland village, and no public demonstration was expected, thousands had assembled from the surrounding country, to receive back the lifeless form of him who had gone forth from among them to fight the battles of Liberty. Here, too, the outward insignia of mourning were everywhere displayed.

As this was the terminus of railroad communication, the party prepared to finish the remainder of the journey to Eastford in carriages. The people had considerately provided a large number of vehicles of multiform style and capacity, for the conveyance of the guests called by this sad occasion to their homes. After considerable delay, the procession at length started, and reached the village of Eastford, sixteen miles distant, shortly after nightfall. The corpse was deposited in the Congregational Church, in charge of the City Guard of Hartford, while the concourse of strangers found entertainment in the hospitable homes of the inhabitants.

Thursday, September 5th, the last funeral rites

were performed over the body of Gen. Lyon. The day was singularly beautiful, even among the lovely autumnal days of New England.

Ten o'clock had been appointed for the commencement of the services. But hours earlier, people began to pour into the village in continuous streams. For miles around, the principal roads were filled with long and nearly unbroken lines of conveyances,—all moving toward the common center. Numerous fields in the neighborhood were thrown open to make room for horses and vehicles. By ten o'clock, fifteen thousand people had assembled within the circumference of the village. This immense concourse seems doubly great when we remember that Eastford is an inland town, remote from railroads.

In front of the pulpit of the Congregational Church, the remains of Gen. Lyon lay in state. Upon the coffin were placed the hat which he waved aloft when rallying his brave but shattered ranks to smite the rebel host on the field of Wilson's Creek, and the sword which had become scarred and weather-beaten from sharing in the long, hard service of its owner. The worn hilt and battered sheath of that trusty blade told the spectator, silently though eloquently, that the life of him who bore it had been spent in no holiday parades or showy pageants, but in facing storms and hardships and perils. Flowers were strewn upon the lid, and the banner which he had followed so devotedly, and upheld so gloriously, threw its graceful fold over the head of the sleeping warrior.

The multitude gathered in front of the church, pressing eagerly toward the entrance to gain a view of the burial-case containing relics so precious. The lid was not lifted, nor were the features disclosed. Yet as the long procession, comprising representatives of every age and condition in life, passed slowly around the chancel with noiseless and reverent step, many learned to appreciate as never before the value and cost of National Liberty. Numerous were the tears of sincere affection, for the princely devotion of the dead to the welfare of their common country, made him the common brother of all his countrymen. They knew that in the hollow box before them lay one of the strongest pillars of the Nation—now, alas, prematurely broken. The scenes in which Gen. Lyon had recently been the foremost actor,—the events of his brief but brilliant career in Missouri, thrilled the hearts of the people as they gazed upon the bier. Less than a month before, that lifeless form was breasting upon the battle-field the murderous storm. The tongue now hushed forever, was heard amid the clash of bayonets and the roar of musketry, as it uttered in clarion tones, words of command and lofty cheer. The arm now stiff and cold, was pointing that battered sword defiantly at the foe. But that teeming brain had finished its earthly work. The soul, adorned with the qualities that are noblest in man, had gone to its God. The ruined temple alone remained.

In front of the church, on the slope of the hill, a temporary platform had been erected for the accommodation of speakers and invited guests. At the foot of the platform were placed several rows of benches, for the use of the relatives, the escort, and the military in attendance. The gentle declivity between the platform and the church was occupied by an immense auditory.

About eleven o'clock, EX-GOVERNOR CLEVELAND, President of the day, called the assembly to order, and in a few appropriate remarks directed their attention to the exercises of the occasion. The choir then sung the hymn commencing—

"Hark! from the tomb a mournful sound,"—

after which a touching and impressive prayer was offered by Rev. Mr. WILLIAMS, formerly pastor of the Congregational Church in Eastford.

The President then introduced Hon. ELISHA CAR-

PENTER, Judge of the Superior Court of Connecticut, who delivered an elaborate historical address on the life and character of Gen. Lyon, tracing his career from childhood to the final scene at Wilson's Creek.

Judge Carpenter was followed by the HON. GALUSHA A. GROW, of Pennsylvania, Speaker of the National House of Representatives, in a lengthy oration, which eloquently enforced the lessons of the hour.

Both of the orators were born on the soil of Eastford. It was a happy thought to invite them back to their native heath to pay these final tributes to the name and virtues of their departed townsman.

After brief speeches from GOVERNOR BUCKINGHAM, of Connecticut, GOVERNOR SPRAGUE, of Rhode Island, SENATOR FOSTER, MAYOR DEMING, and others, the public exercises in the village of Eastford were brought to a close. The people now dispersed for refreshments. After a suitable interval the body was borne from the church to the cemetery at Phœnixville, two and a half miles distant.

This cemetery, containing two or three acres of ground, forms of itself a perfect amphitheatre—the small and comparatively level plat around the entrance, being inclosed on three sides by the inner slope of a semicircular hill. In front, on the opposite side of the highway, lies a placid pond, formed

15*

by damming the stream which winds through the valley. Further on, the eye rests upon the western declivity of a long range of hills.

About one-half of the cemetery is covered more or less thickly with graves, but the outer portion is yet unoccupied. The lot of the Lyon family, a little south of the center, is inclosed by stone posts and chains which General Lyon himself placed around it several years ago.

Hours before the arrival of the funeral cortege, spectators began to gather by thousands in and around these grounds. About four o'clock P. M. the regular report of minute guns announced that the procession was approaching. As it drew nearer the notes of the unearthly and solemn dirge fell upon the ear. At length the head of the long procession arrived at the gate; the hearse drawn by four magnificent black horses entered the portal; the military formed around the open grave; the mourners took a farewell look of the coffin; and the mortal remains of General Nathaniel Lyon were lowered to their last resting place. Rev. C. C. Adams read the Methodist Episcopal services; Maj. Conant and Capt. Edgar, of the St. Louis escort, partially filled the pit; and the City Guard of Hartford fired three volleys over the grave, while the band performed a dirge.

J. J. SAWYER.

† Grave of Gen. Lyon.

Thus ended the funeral ceremonies. That vast concourse, drawn hither to pay the final tribute to the remains of the dead, began to separate for their homes—homes that lie scattered over many States, from the rugged shores of the Atlantic to the broad prairies beyond the waters of the Mississippi.

It was General Lyon's desire that whenever and wherever he might die, his body should be interred by the side of his honored parents. He sleeps his last sleep in the chosen spot of his own selection, in the valley and among the hills which he trod in boyhood, and whither it was his delight to return in riper years.

APPENDIX.

[A.]

PATERNAL LINEAGE OF GEN. NATHANIEL LYON.

THE family of Gen. Nathaniel Lyon descends, it is believed, in direct male line from Hon. Sir Thomas Lyon,* Knt., of Auldbar, Forfarshire, North Britain, who was designated Master of Glamis, brother of John, 8th Lord Glamis. Sir Thomas was one of the principal agents in the seizure of King James VI. at the Raid of Ruthren, Aug. 23, 1582. Was banished to England. Returned again to Scotland, and with the Earls of Angus and Mar, seized Sterling Castle. Again fled to England. Returned, 1585, received again by

* Our New England Lyons are unquestionably descended from the noble family of that name in North Britain, of which mention is so fully make by Burke, in his Landed Gentry, I., 779.

Family records and traditions point in that direction. Besides, there are striking traits of character, common to those bearing the name in this country and to their trans-Atlantic ancestors.

the King to favor. Appointed Captain of the Guards, High Treasurer of Scotland, and Extraordinary Lord of Sessions. Knighted, 1590. Married, 1st, Agnes, daughter of Patrick, 5th Lord Grey, relict of Sir Robert Logan of Restalrig, and of Alexander, 5th Lord Howe. Married, 2d, Euphemia, 4th daughter of Wm. Douglas, Earl of Moreton.

Issue: John, married a daughter of George Gladstone, Archbishop of St. Andrews.

ARMS.—Arg. a lion, rampant, az. armed and langued, within a double tressure, flowered and counter-flowered, gu. *crest.* A lady holding in her right hand the Royal thistle, &c., in allusion to the alliance with the daughter of the King.

MOTTO.—In te, Domine, speravi.

Political and civil troubles forced several members of this family to emigrate to New England in the 17th century. Thomas and Ephraim Lyon, who were brothers, came in company. Gen. Nathaniel descended from Ephraim, three of whose ancestors successively bore that name.

3d EPHRAIM LYON, born 1737. Settled in Ashford, Conn., where he died May 25th, 1798. See page 18. He married Esther Bennett. Issue:

(4) I. NATHAN,[4] b. April 29, 1763, m. Latimer Badger, 1788.
(5) II. ESTHER,[4] b. March 1, 1765, m. Nathan Burnham, 1781.
(6) III. EPHRAIM,[4] b. March 15, 1767.

(7) IV. Zerviah,[4] b. March 3, 1769.

(8) V. Amasa,[4] b. Nov. 19, 1771, m. Keziah Knowlton, Jan. 3, 1805. See page 20.

(9) VI. Lucy,[4] b. Dec. 24, 1773.

(10) VII. Betsey,[4] b. June 25, 1776.

(11) VIII. Lois,[4] b. March 18, 1780.

(12) IX. James,[4] b. May 11, 1784, m. Polly Trowbridge, 1808.

Amasa (5) and Keziah[7] had issue as follows:

(13) I. Amasa Knowlton,[5 8] b. July 4, 1806, d. Aug. 28, 1822.

(14) II. Marcus,[5 8] b. July 3, 1809, d. April 29, 1810.

(15) III. Delotia,[5 8] b. Oct. 15, 1811, m. April 10, 1837, Jno. W. Trowbridge.

(16) IV. Sophronia,[5 8] b. Jan. 4, 1813, m. Jno. W. Hasler.

(17) V. Lorenzo,[5 8] b. Feb. 9, 1815; resides in Eastford.

(18) VI. Elizabeth Ann,[5 8] b. Nov. 8, 1816, m. Ebn. Knowlton.

(19) VII. NATHANIEL,[5 8] b. July 14, 1818.

(20) VIII. Daniel,[5 8] b. Nov. 14, 1819; resides in Eastford.

(21) IX. Lyman,[5 8] b. March 30, 1822; lumberman, resides in Leverett, Mass.

Amasa Lyon died April 11, 1843.

Mrs. Keziah Lyon died Jan. 31, 1852.

MATERNAL LINEAGE OF GEN. NATHANIEL LYON.

WERE you to make inquiries among the people of New England generally concerning their ancestry, in nine cases out of ten they would tell you that they were descended from one of three brothers who came over from Old England *about* the year 16—; and in nine times out of ten they would be wrong. But it so happens in the Knowlton family that three brothers did actually come to New England and settle in Ipswich; John,[1] William,[1] and Dea. Thomas;[1] for both John[1] and Thomas[1] call William[1] their brother; evidence of the most satisfactory character.

The second brother, WILLIAM[1] KNOWLTON, was a bricklayer. He married Elizabeth ———. He died in 1654 or 5. The inventory of his estate taken July 17, 1655, was £37 2*s*. 1*d*. His debts were £27 14*s*. 1*d*. We have his descendants for several generations, but it is not our present purpose to include his branch of the family in this brief sketch.

The third brother, Dea. THOMAS[1] KNOWLTON, was born in 1622. He m. first, Susanna ———. His second wife was Mary Kimball, to whom he was m. May 17, 1682. It does not appear that he had children.

On the 19th of Nov., 1678, Dea. Thomas thus writes: "I gave a coat to brother William, and his two boys I keept to scool from the age of 5 to 8 years, and a girl from the age of one & a half years till she was married." He died April 3, 1692, aged 70 years.

(1) JOHN,[1] though the last to be noticed, was the eldest of the three brothers. He took the freeman's oath in 1641, was in Ipswich in 1641, perhaps earlier. He made his will Nov. 29, 1653. He married Margery ——, and had John,[2] Abraham,[2] and Elizabeth.[2]

(2) John[2] m. Sarah ——. He took the freeman's oath in 1680, and died Oct. 8, 1684. His children were—

(3) I. WILLIAM,[3] b. ——. Lived in Wenham and had wife Lydia.

(4) II. JOSEPH,[3] b. 1651; married Aug. 14, 1677, Mary Wilson.

(5) III. SAMUEL,[3] b. ——; married April, 1669, Mary Wilt or Witt.

(6) IV. NATHANIEL,[3] Dea. b. June 29, 1658. He m. May 8, 1682, Deborah Jewett.

Dea. Nathaniel[3] (6) and Deborah had—

(7) I. NATHANIEL,[4] b. May 3, 1683; m. Feb., 1702–1703, Mary Bennett.

(8) II. JOHN,[4] b. Dec., 1685.

(9) III. JOSEPH,[4] b. April, 168–.

(10) IV. Abraham,[4] b. Feb. 27, 1688–9.

(11) V. Elizabeth,[4] b. Sept. 18, 1692.

(12) VI. Thomas,[4] b. Nov. 8, 1702.

(13) VII. David,[4] b. May, 1707; m. Feb., 1731-2, Esther Howard. David,[5] son of David,[4] died Dec. 10, 1732.

Nathaniel[4] (7) and Mary had:

(14) I. Mary,[5] b. June 3, 1704.

(15) II. William,[5] b. Feb. 8, 1705-6; m. Martha, of Boxford, to whom he was published, Feb. 13, 1728. He removed to Ashford, Conn., about 1740. His estate was distributed in March, 1757.

(16) III. Nathaniel,[5] b. June 30, 1708.

(17) IV. Jeremiah,[5] b. July 13, 1712, and d. young.

(18) V. 2d Jeremiah,[5] b. Aug. 2, 1713.

William[5] (15) and Martha had:

(19) I. Lucy,[6] baptized Feb. 20, 1736.

(20) II. William,[6] baptized.

(21) III. DANIEL,[6] baptized Dec. 31, 1738; m. 1st, Nov. 3, 1763, Elizabeth Farnham, of Ashford, Conn.; m. 2d, April 24, 1788, Rebecca Fenton, of Willington. He served through the French war and that of the Revolution. During the last he was commissioned as Lieut. He died May 31st, 1825. See page 23.

(22) IV. THOMAS,[6] baptized Nov. 30, 1740; m. April 5, 1759, Anna Keyes, of Ashford. Col. Thomas Knowlton was slain in battle at Harlem Heights, Sept. 16, 1776. Anna, wife of Col. Knowlton, d. May 22, 1808. See page 21.

(23) V. Nathaniel,[6] baptized March 9, 1745.

(24) VI. Mary,[6] baptized; m. March 9, 1748-9, Ezekiel Tiffany, of Ashford.

(25) VII. Sarah,[6] baptized; m. —— Kendall, of Ashford.

(26) VIII. Lucy,[6] baptized; m. Abijah Brooks, of Ashford.

(27) IX. Priscilla,[6] baptized.

Lieut. Daniel[6] (21) and Elizabeth had:

(28) I. Daniel[7], b. Dec. 7, 1765; m. Betsey Burchard. He died Feb., 1834. He had 7 children, the fourth of whom, son, Phineas, died a soldier in the army.

(29) II. Elizabeth[7], b. March 24, 1768; m. Frederick Chaffee, of Ashford.

(30) III. Nathaniel[7], b. Dec. 24, 1770; m. Hannah Farnham.

(31) IV. Ephraim[7], b. Oct. 3, 1773.

(32) V. Martha,[7] b. Feb. 24, 1777, m. Charles Brandon of Ashford.

(33) VI. Keziah,[7] b. Feb. 9, 1781, m. Jan. 3, 1805, Amasa Lyon, Esq., of Ashford.—Lineage of husband and children already given. See page 351.

(34) VII. Hannah,[7] b. April 19, 1783, m. Daniel Knowlton, Esq., and had sons, Miner,[8] Danford,[8] Edwin,[8] and daughters, Amanda,[8] Miriam,[8] and Elvira.[8] Their eldest son, Miner, was educated at West Point; was subsequently Assistant Professor in that institution, and now holds a commission in the army of the United States. See page 225.

By wife Rebecca, had:

(35) VIII. Erastus Fenton,[7] b. Jan. 29, 1790, m. Waite Windsor of Gloucester, R. I.

(36) IX. Marvin,[7] b. Sept. 3, 1794, m. Calista Leonard of Stafford, Conn.

Col. Thomas (22) and Anna had:

(37) I. Frederick,[7] b. Dec. 4, 1760, d. Oct. 9, 1841. He served in the campaign of 1776, and was with his father in the battle at Harlem Heights.

(38) II. Sally,[7] b. Nov. 23, 1763.

(39) III. Thomas,[7] b. July 13, 1765.

(40) IV. Polly,[7] b. Jan. 11, 1767.
(41) V. Abigail,[7] b. June 20, 1768.
(42) VI. Samson,[7] b. Feb. 8, 1770, d. Sept. 10, 1777.
(43) VII. Anna,[7] b. March 19, 1773.
(44) VIII. Lucinda,[7] b. Nov. 10, 1776, d. Feb. 16, 1805.

[B.]

ACTION OF THE GENERAL ASSEMBLY OF CONNECTICUT, OCTOBER, 1861.

GOVERNOR BUCKINGHAM, in his message to the General Assembly of Connecticut, convened in Special Session October 9th, 1861, says: "General Nathaniel Lyon, a native of this State, was entrusted by Government with the command of a Division of Union forces in Missouri, and on the 10th day of August last, was killed at Wilson's Creek, while leading his column against a force of rebels, in number three times his superior. He possessed the confidence of his command and was highly distinguished for his modesty, energy and undaunted courage. His remains were brought by a military escort to this State, honored with a public reception, and buried in Eastford, his native town, by the side of his fathers. The expenses incident to the ceremonies will be cheerfully met by those who appreciate the services of the gallant soldier, unless the State shall claim that privilege. His family relatives have presented the sword and belt worn by him at the time of his death, as well as his chapeau, to the State, which are at your disposal."

Report of the Joint Select Committee to whom this section of the Governor's Message was referred.

"GENERAL ASSEMBLY, Special Session, October, 1861.

Resolved, That the State of Connecticut accepts the gift of the sword, belt and chapeau of the late General Nathaniel Lyon, presented by the relatives of that gallant officer, and while she mourns the sudden death of a beloved son, who bore so distinguished a part in defense of the Constitution and the suppression of rebellion, and who offered his life, and all* that he possessed, on his country's altar, she will cherish the sad mementoes with fondest pride, and as she places the sword of *Lyon*, by that of *Putnam*, would bid her surviving children, emulate their deeds and share with them a nation's gratitude.

That the State of Connecticut shares in the bereavement of the afflicted relatives of the lamented deceased, and tenders them her warmest sympathies.

That the sword, belt and chapeau, as the property of the State, be deposited, for safe keeping, with the Connecticut Historical Society, and that the Secretary of State be authorized to procure a suitable case for the same."

Resolution passed.

---

* The *newspaper* statement that Gen. Lyon gave his property by will to the Government, is erroneous.

[C.]

OBITUARY ADDRESSES

ON THE DEATH OF GEN. LYON; DELIVERED IN THE SENATE OF THE UNITED STATES, DECEMBER 20, 1861.

Resolved by the Senate and House of Representatives of the United States of America in Congress assembled, That Congress deems it just and proper to enter upon its records a recognition of the eminent and patriotic services of the late Brigadier General Nathaniel Lyon. The country to whose service he devoted his life will guard and preserve his fame as a part of its own glory. Second. That the thanks of Congress are hereby given to the brave officers and soldiers who, under the command of the late General Lyon, sustained the honor of the flag, and achieved victory against overwhelming numbers at the battle of Springfield, in Missouri; and that in order to commemorate an event so honorable to the country and to themselves, it is ordered that each regiment engaged shall be authorized to bear upon its colors the word "Springfield," embroidered in letters of gold. And the President of the United States is hereby requested to cause these resolutions to be read at the head of every regiment in the Army of the United States.

Mr. POMEROY. Mr. President, the resolutions which have just been read to the Senate, were introduced to the House of Representatives by the distinguished member from St. Louis, and passed the House very unanimously. I trust they will in like manner pass the Senate; but to me there is one reason why they should receive at least a passing notice. The State of Kansas was largely interested in that battle at Wilson's Creek, near Springfield. And the country and mankind have a large interest in the fame of the immortal Lyon, who fell in that battle. Such a man and such a general is not often found, and very rarely combined in one person. Perhaps I may be pardoned here for saying that I had the pleasure of a personal acquaintance with Gen. Lyon for years; and it was an acquaintance formed and matured under the most impressive circumstances. The early struggles for the freedom of our own State were not unlike in their nature the present struggles of the nation. The same questions to a great extent entered into the one that now convulse the other. The same interests, passions, and barbarity, so disgraceful to our age and humanity, entered as largely into that struggle as in the present.

Gen. Lyon, whose deeds and fame now belong to the whole country, was then Capt. Lyon, of the regular army, stationed at Fort Riley, in Kansas. He had for ten years served the country in that capacity, and without promotion. He was as true a soldier as ever stood in the line of battle; a sagacious officer, strict in habit and discipline, and an honest man.

His attention to me on an occasion of great personal fatigue and exposure—taking me to his quarters, welcoming me to all his comforts, and then loaning me his own horse fresh and strong, and taking in charge mine, exhausted and worn—were acts of generosity and kindness that I will never forget. The elements of a friendship cemented by a unity of sentiment and principle, in an hour of great extremity, are the most enduring attachments of this life.

* * * * * * * *

But the hero of that battle [Wilson's Creek] sleeps beside other graves, in his dear native valley. He has been literally "gathered to his fathers." There need be no monument of marble or granite for him. All the way from St. Louis to Connecticut, his remains were honored by tributes of respect from a grateful people. I had the melancholy pleasure of seeing the almost spontaneous gathering of his old friends at Hartford. They honored suitably the noble dead. In that they honored themselves. From Hartford to Eastford, where he now sleeps, the way was all marked by tokens that were becoming to a returning conqueror. The dear old people at home have garnered up his memory; it shall be to them as endearing as liberty and life.

Mr. Dixon. Mr. President, the language of eulogy is so often heard in this Chamber, that its value may be impaired by its frequency; but there were certain qualities in the character of Gen. Lyon, so peculiar and so admirable, that it seems eminently proper to invite the attention of the Senate, and of the country, for a few moments longer to their consideration, while this resolution is before the Senate. It is not my design to dwell on the circumstances of his death. The country knows by heart the story of that brilliant charge in which his life was sacrificed. I shall not linger upon it now, nor enlarge upon that undaunted courage which was one of the least of his noble qualities. I propose to say a single word upon certain other qualities of a higher order, which Gen. Lyon possessed to a degree so distinguished as to render him remarkable among those heroic characters whose lives and services have illustrated our history.

A high sense of official duty—devotion to the public service—these were the peculiar and striking points of Gen. Lyon's character. Other men equaled and surpassed him in originality, in fertility of expedients, in ingenuity, perhaps in power of combination; but I think it would be difficult to find one in our list of public men, since the days of Washington, civil or military, who, in this utter, downright, unshrinking, uncalculating devotion to duty, excelled or even equaled him. He was remarkable for his regard for his friends; but he looked upon their claims upon him as nothing in comparison with the duty he owed the public. This had always seemed to be his governing principle; and when he was called to lead our forces in the West, it was strikingly manifested. Then it was seen how this high devotion to duty could inspire the heart with the noblest courage, and elevate the mind into that exalted condition where it seems to be moved by the inspiration of genius. Thus inspired, he entered upon that brilliant career of victory which was closed only by his death on the field of battle. How great was the loss to his country when he fell, it is impossible now accurately to measure; but this I may safely presume to say, that had he lived, his career, as it began, would have continued victorious.

I will not reflect upon others. I know well the difficulties which delay and obstruct the progress of our armies; and I will not add to the perplexities of our military leaders by my own unskilled criticism of plans which I do not understand, or by comments upon purposes of which I am uninformed; but thus much I may say in behalf of the dead hero who now sleeps within the bosom of his native State, near the grave of Putnam, that, had Lyon lived and led our forces in Missouri, the mistakes and disasters which, since his death, we have there had occasion to deplore, would not have occurred, and to-day we should not have been disputing the possession of that State with rebels in arms.

In him, as the people hoped and believed, the hero of the war was found; in him—such was the wondrous will of Heaven—the hero of the war was lost as soon as found.

> "This man, the glorious vision of a day,
> Was only shown on earth, and snatched away."

Mr. Foster. Mr. President, I must be pardoned a word as a tribute to the memory of a departed friend. It is not necessary that I should remark upon the character or services of the deceased, and I shall not; they are familiarly known to the country, and will make a bright page in that country's history. I rose only to say that I mourn the loss of Gen. Lyon from personal as well as from national considerations. He was among my most valued friends; I was in correspondence with him to the last days of his life, and some of the last letters he ever wrote were written to me. In common with a vast assemblage of the citizens of Connecticut, and other States, I attended his funeral on a calm, bright day in the early autumn; and there, on the quiet hillside where his fathers slept, near a retired country village which was his birthplace, I assisted in bearing his mortal remains to an honored grave. Brave men shed tears over him; Connecticut mourns him as a trur and gallant son; the nation deplores the loss of a patriot and a hero.

[The joint resolution was reported to the Senate without amendment, and ordered to a third reading. It was read the third time, and passed.]

www.ingramcontent.com/pod-product-compliance
Lightning Source LLC
LaVergne TN
LVHW010135110826
845151LV00002B/360

* 9 7 8 1 4 2 5 5 4 0 2 6 5 *